What Is Symbolism?

BOOKS BY HENRI PEYRE
PUBLISHED BY THE UNIVERSITY OF ALABAMA PRESS

---

*The French Literary Imagination and Dostoevsky
and Other Essays* (1975)

What Is Romanticism? (1977)

What Is Symbolism? (1980)

Victor Hugo: Philosophy and Poetry (1980)

HENRI PEYRE

What Is Symbolism?

TRANSLATED BY EMMETT PARKER

THE UNIVERSITY OF ALABAMA PRESS
UNIVERSITY, ALABAMA

Library of Congress Cataloging in Publication Data

Peyre, Henri, 1901-
  What is symbolism?

  Translation of Qu'est-ce que le symbolisme?
  Bibliography: p.
  Includes index.
  1. French poetry—19th century—History and criticism.
  2. Symbolism in literature.   I. Title.
  PQ439.P413   841'.8'0915   79-4686
  ISBN 0-8173-7004-8

CONTENTS

What Is Symbolism?

INTRODUCTION

Literary and artistic criticism would have long since been reduced to silence if the terms that designate movements, periods, tendencies, or various styles were all so precise that their meaning could be agreed upon once and for all time. Productive misunderstandings would be avoided and a dull uniformity would reign over the comparative history of the arts and letters if the ambitious and misleading terms by which a given language (often, in modern Europe, that of France, the country most endowed with literary legislators and manufacturers of literary catch-phrases) designates the Rennaissance, mannerism, classicism, existentialism, were placidly accepted by intellectuals and professors in other countries. Interchangeable labels would be applied to products that one might believe to be of one and the same kind.

Such, as we know, is not at all the case. From the Alexandrian, Roman, and medieval rhetoricians to Taine, to Emile Hennequin (who died young in 1888), the author of a book on *La Critique scientifique* published in the very middle of the period that we call symbolist, to the linguists and structuralists closer to us, the attempts to fix critical judgment on a firm scientific foundation and to endow it with objectivity have given more proof of stubborn daring than happy results.

Of all these terms, born in the heat of polemics, *symbolism* is without doubt the one most often subject to confusion. Its use was time-honored in mythology, theology, anthropology, and psychology; but the most influential of French philosophers of the early years of the twentieth century, Henri Bergson, clothes it with a meaning exactly opposite that given it by the poets. The symbolists of 1888–95 were in agreement, even in their disputes, on many points other than the use of symbols. One of the difficulties of the word *symbol* lay precisely in its being both too restrictive and too vague. In the poetics and the poetry of those years of innovative intellectual ferment, there is also literary impressionism (barely related at all to the impressionism of the painters), hermeticism, the cultivation of the bizarre, decadence, or the showy pretense of decadence, decorative graciousness, exasperated romantic subjectivism, the desire to renew versification and language. One or the other of these aspects of Parisian and Belgian symbolism was to radiate its prestige abroad. For the first time perhaps, it was in the form of expression (prose style, liberated verse form, the musicality of words) of the new French literature that foreigners were to seek models or encouragement. The French Renaissance, following the Italian, had laid little claim to innovation. La Fontaine's versification, Racine's, or even Hugo's had exercised less attraction outside France than—alas!—Boileau's. The Parnassians' example had been much more appealing, doubtless because it filled a need at the time for the Germans, the Russians, the poets of the Americas. For we shall have occasion to note that in France alone and in a few manifestoes and declarations, symbolism had to set itself in clear opposition to its immediate predecessors in order to define itself. Everywhere else, even the most well-informed poets did not separate Gautier from Baudelaire, Banville from Mallarmé, Heredia from Régnier.

Neither the Pléiade nor the French romantic poets, nor even the prose-writers or dramatists of the midseventeenth century claimed to follow any reigning philosophy. It takes quite a lot of artifice and very little respect for chronology to attribute to Descartes a profound influence on Corneille, Madame de Sévigné, Molière, or La Fontaine. Neither Diderot nor Hegel nor Schelling contribute much toward explaining the foundations of the French romantic poets' thought. Vico or Swedenborg contribute only a little more in the case of Michelet, Nerval, or Balzac. To reproach Gautier or Leconte de Lisle with Comtian positivism is to force matters even further when the attraction of a distant past, Hellenic or Hindu, was much stronger than that of a despised present. The symbolist movement of the 1880s and after sometimes quoted Schopenhauer, Hegel, more often Carlyle, but rarely invoked French thinkers. If a kind of Bergsonism (before the actual movement itself) might have been, as is somewhat too easily said, "in the air," neither the works of Bergson nor those of Nietzsche, as well, were read—and for good reason—before the very last years of the century or even before the publication of *Le Rire* (1900). Even so, symbolism, more than preceding literary movements, liked to make use of a philosophical language, and usually a pretentious and confusing one. It took to task the turn of mind that it considered to have molded its elders and the literate bourgeoisie of the second half of the century: rationalism, the scientific and positivistic mind, the refusal to go beyond what is reasonable and real. Nearly all artistic and literary creation for two hundred years had challenged the form of intellect that might claim to dominate or even to understand life. It proclaimed the right of the imagination to replace the analytical intellect or to surpass it. Symbolism, in this respect the continuator of romanticism, constituted in France the most conscious form of revolt against the claims of reason. Its manifestoes and statements never had the logical and dogmatic firmness of surrealist and existentialist proclamations. The influential criticism of the time, evincing an obstinate incomprehension that was nearly as odious and abstruse as the musical criticism of the period (and as that of the academies of painting, too) mocked heavy-handedly while thinking itself witty. There was no literary critic, not even Rémy de Gourmont whose "masques" are only very oversimplified outlines, to serve as interpreter of symbolism to the movement itself or to win for it followers among the public. No literary review acquired or long maintained the necessary authority to speak in the name of the symbolists. No poet or theoretician of the time brandished his stick as Breton later did, or defined, like Sartre would do, his position as a committed existentialist humanist or as a phenomenologist. There is no reason to deplore the fact. Symbolism, thanks to that absence of clearly formulated doctrine, retained in fact the variety and independence of each individual talent. It never became officially sanctioned and long held a place as a rebellious movement, and thus it was dear to nonconformist youth. It was not until Thibaudet's book on Mallarmé (that is, until 1912) that the one who could figure as the master among the symbolists finally received a kind of official recognition.

Another difficulty should put us on guard against any excessive retrospective oversimplification of French symbolism. It had its precursors—every movement uncovers certain of them: the preclassicists, the preromantics, Blake, Poe, or Lautréamont for the surrealists. But these precursors or forerunners include, ahead of all others, Baudelaire the poet who, in the eyes of many, passes for the symbolist par excellence, the decipherer of correspondences and hieroglyphs, and even for the theoretician of synesthesia. He died fifteen years before symbolism thought of linking itself to him or, even longer before, since the first official recognition of his role as forerunner came only with the collective work published in 1896 as his "Tomb" in the review *La Plume*. Moreover, the person who initiated this homage was a Russian prince. Rimbaud, the second inspired precursor, was dead so far as literature was concerned when *La Vogue* published his *Illuminations* in 1886, and he knew nothing (or wanted to know nothing) about those who might have taken his work as a justification for their own—and these were very few among the poets of the years 1885–92! It is doubtful that Mallarmé himself read closely the prose works of this "considerable passerby," and the brief sketch that Gourmont gave of Rimbaud in his *Livre des masques* certainly did not enlarge the reputation for lucidity of this "dislocator of ideas." Symbolism's precursors date still further back, and one unhesitatingly places in the first rank of the manipulators of lyrical alchemy Aloysius Bertrand and Gérard de Nerval, who had died in 1841 and 1855, respectively. Only the place occupied by those who in fact spoke of the symbol and thought of themselves as effecting a philosophical and literary revolution around 1890, is of very limited consequence. None among these—Mallarmé and perhaps Laforgue excepted— can sustain comparison with those great precursors, and none appears today to have been an authentic symbolist.

Our perspective is still more clouded by the assertions, frequent since 1940, according to which the truest symbolists are writers who had scarcely attained their thirtieth year when the nineteenth century was dying and who, outside of a few appearances at Mallarmé's Tuesdays, frequented no offical salon or even set their own independent course (Gide, Claudel, Ségalen) in order to flee the oppressive atmosphere of Parisian literary circles. Guy Michaud sees in Claudel's drama the final culmination of symbolism. Fiser hails it in Proust. Others celebrate Valéry as the only poet worthy of being placed beside Mallarmé, and the academic and social triumph of the author of *La Jeune Parque* as the brilliant and very belated victory of symbolism in official France. There were in fact, as we shall see, several waves of symbolism as there were several waves of romanticism, and it is by distinguishing between the spirit, the ambitions, and finally the contributions of these successive generations that one best understands symbolism in its development.

Nothing in history is so harmonious and clear as posterity (in retrospect and

thanks to much careful retouching) makes it appear to be. All things coexist, and
it is only because of the subsequently recognized fecundity of certain ideas,
certain works, that the contribution of an artistic group or an esthetic doctrine
seems to us important. It is permissible, and moreover necessary, to cut a slice
from within the internal history of the years 1860–1900, and to label it symbolist.
But it is no less necessary to recall that at the same time there lived, prospered,
and wrote, survivors of romanticism: Hugo, whom the symbolists attacked only
rarely; Gautier, whose *Tombeau* in 1872 was the most sumptuous to have been
composed for a French poet since Ronsard; and even Lamartine, whose vagueness, obscurity, and musicality were praised by many in the little reviews at the
time of Moréas's and Samain's poetic debuts. Symbolism and Parnassianism are
clearly set apart only in the literary manuals and in certain declarations (rare in
any case) such as the one that Mallarmé made to Jules Huret. The poets of these
two esthetic viewpoints were rarely enemies. It was through Banville, Mérat,
Leconte de Lisle himself that Rimbaud, Verlaine, Mallarmé had first discovered
poetry and dreamed of a new poetic language. The misfortune of Parnassianism
(and of the two or three series of *Le Parnasse contemporain* of 1871 and 1876)
was in counting in its ranks too many very mediocre poets. (This is the weakness
as well of every anthology of symbolist poets that does not limit itself to five or six
names revered today.) But Parnassian doctrines and the ambition of achieving a
carefully crafted, self-aware form of poetry that was impersonal or indirect in its
lyricism have been and have remained, ever since the Pléiade, constants of
French poetry. *L'Hérodiade*, Valéry's sonnet "Hélène," and even his "Dor-
meuse," numerous poems by Régnier, and those of other symbolists once their
inspiration wanes, derive from some aspect of Parnassianism. It is equally naïve
to imagine the poets of the symbolist cenacles at war before Banville or Heredia
as to think of Mallarmé as fiercely hostile to Zola (whom he appreciated and
praised) or to Huysmans at the outset of his naturalist period, or to see naturalism
as hermetically closed off to poetry. It was the Théâtre Libre, realistic as it may
have wished to be, that first played Ibsen's plays, soon to be judged as symbolist
in the Nordic manner. And it is Huysmans, one of the collaborators in the
Soirées de Médan in 1880, who, with *A Rebours* (1884), was to assure Mallarmé's
success with a wider public.

The difficulty with following step by step the controversies, the proclamations,
sometimes the stammerings of the symbolists or the decadents around 1890 is
that one diminishes what symbolism became for posterity when seen through
Valéry in France, Arthur Symons and Yeats in Great Britain, various Russians a
little later, and finally through Edmund Wilson, who placed it so high in his
Axel's Castle. The poets of the little reviews frequently revealed themselves to be
quarrelsome, exaggerated the importance of minute questions of metrics, and
sometimes cultivated a pretentious and abstruse style. Moreover, their impulses
toward revolutionary innovations, in the case of Moréas, Vielé-Griffin, Henri de
Régnier, were ephemeral, and they quickly passed on to other more traditional
and more backward-looking allegiances; however, one cannot entirely disregard

them and admit only two or three giant precursors—Baudelaire, Mallarmé, Rimbaud (perhaps), and Verlaine, the latter with some condescension—as alone worthy of being called symbolists. For it was thanks to that unmethodical youth of 1888–92, to its combative fervor, to that plethora of small heretical sects that a new conception of poetry and music was finally to be imposed. For years yet to come, and right up to World War I, it was through Verhaeren or Claudel that many young people were directed towards Rimbaud; it was through *Tel qu'en songe* or *Les Poèmes anciens et romanesques* that they were attracted to the deciphering of Mallarmé's differently powerful but differently difficult verse. Those who reached their fiftieth year around 1915 or 1920 still recalled with a shiver the poetic discovery provided by the collection *Les Poètes d'aujourd'hui, 1880–1890* of Van Bever and Léautaud. However, neither the truly original work of Mallarmé nor the better and more disturbing work of Verlaine was represented therein. And it included not a single prose work by Rimbaud or even the most profound of his poems composed in Alexandrine verse, "Mémoire."

Valéry had smiled, not without a certain secret satisfaction and while savoring the victory of the enthusiasts and friends of his youth over the incomprehension of Anatole France and other critics, when the Third Republic celebrated the fiftieth anniversary of symbolism (1936). Let us be willing to wager that the celebration of its centennial will bring together still more poets, professors, and officials assembled from twenty different countries and will display even more piety than the two hundredth anniversary of 1789, which will follow on its heels. It will be commemorated, in keeping with current custom, in enormous volumes of learned colloquies. Enough documents are available to us today, enough volumes of recollections have appeared, so that one can set forth here, subsequent to several others, a synthesis of what French symbolism thought itself to be, was, and appears to us today to have been. And we are not yet so far removed from that era of the cult of the beautiful and the rare that we may not be tempted to venerate too punctiliously all its esoteric oddities and the exhilaration of its apparently philosphical vocabulary. "The clear mind," Valéry maliciously suggested, "makes understood what it does not understand." It ought to be possible to be reasonably clear without too much schematizing and to generalize without pinning to very divergent individuals, often anarchical in their esthetic individualism, labels that are too misleading.

1

THE WORD AND ITS ANTECEDENTS

No one word generated from designations for other literary or artistic movements —except perhaps *structuralism* (which, however, includes scarcely any imaginative creations)—enjoys a prestige equal to that of *symbol*. Even the amphigoric mannerisms of the manifestoes from symbolism's feverish years or the puerile scribblings that certain versifiers took for mysterious poetic expressions do not succeed in tarnishing the brilliance with which this word shines. Young readers and others who refuse to admit after years of study or of teaching that they like what the popular imagination likes, and for the same reasons that it likes them, will always feel their intellect stimulated by the process of deciphering a more secret meaning hidden beneath the surface. The very vagueness of the word, which has frequently been used in conjunction with others hardly less vague (*myth, emblem, analogy, allegory*) has done much to invest it with majesty. It could be wished—in vain—that some international congress of critics might one day propose two or three precise meanings for the word *symbol*, according to which it would henceforth be used in the several Western languages. Of course, nothing of the kind will ever happen. In each of the European languages, the word already carries the ballast of a past it cannot jettison. The word *symbolism* is even more heavily weighted, serving as it does to designate both the eternal symbolism common to many religions and the literary symbolism of the Parisian and Belgian groups of the end of the nineteenth century, as well as similar movements (similar at first sight, at least) that took place in Germany, Italy, Russia, and Latin America.

Etymology can be a fascinating science, but the accretion of meanings or of associations that a word acquires through the centuries and in the passage from one language to another transfigures willy-nilly the unadorned, primitive value of concrete terms raised to the abstract. In the case of *symbol*, etymology provides us with little information. In Greek the term meant a portion of an object (a piece of pottery, for example) broken in two; it was a gesture of hospitality on the part of a host to offer to a guest one of two such fragments as a sign of trust and as a promise of protection in the future from the host's family or tribe, whose members would welcome the outsider at the sight of this "symbol." The substantive form is derived, of course, from the verb that also produced *parable, hyperbole*, and *ballistics* and that means "to throw together," that is, to unite in an immediate fusion the concrete or external sign and the thing it signifies.

Briefly, the word was given a generalized usage in mythology and religion where it was not always distinguished from *emblem*. In 1924 an art historian, Vladimir Déonna, wrote in the *Revue de l'histoire des religions* an article entitled "Quelques réflexions sur le symbolisme, en particulier dans l'art préhistorique." He states therein: "Symbolism occurs when the idea, the object itself, is translated by means of an appearance that is not its immediate copy, but that serves to evoke that object in an oblique way, more often by analogy or by some other mental process." He shows how replete with symbolism prehistoric art is. Medieval philosophy is no less so, as Etienne Gilson has explained. The same may be said for the religious art of the Middle Ages whose system of analogies has in fact been interpreted by Emile Mâle and others. J. K. Huysmans, in his strange descriptive and mystical novel *La Cathédrale*, shows his hero, Durtal, listening, absorbed, to a priest who explains to him, in accordance with Hugues de Saint-Victor, that "the symbol is the allegorical representation of a Christian principle by way of a palpable form." The symbol, the novelist goes on to maintain, is found in all religions, and in Christianity from Genesis through the Book of the Apocalypse. He adds: "The symbol comes to us, then, from a divine source . . . this form of expression responds to one of the least questioned needs of the human mind, which takes a certain pleasure in giving proof of intelligence, in solving the enigma submitted to it and, also, in preserving the solution reduced to a visible formula and a lasting configuration." In this sense, Mallarmé is, Durtal-Huysmans notes, very near to Saint Augustine.

The word *symbol* (and occasionally "the symbolic" used in French as a feminine substantive) occurs after the Middle Ages; later it is used in a less religious sense, often applied to pagan mythology that was being rediscovered and relived at the time by a few poets or sculptors. It was applied as well to Egyptian hieroglyphics and even to various emblems. An Australian critic, Lloyd Austin, who has added much to our understanding of Baudelaire and Mallarmé, has set forth a quick sketch of various uses of these words in the works of Rabelais, Henri Estienne, and, finally, in those of Diderot and his most zealous collaborator on the *Encyclopédie*, Louis de Jaucourt. Austin has especially emphasized certain curious usages given the word along with an extraordinary interest in the symbolic in the treatise of an early seventeenth-century Jesuit, Le Père Caussin. This work, *La Sagesse symbolique des Egyptiens* (1618), is in Latin and was apparently quite widely read. To be sure, Egyptian writing was known at that time only through the writings of ancient religious authors, and Father Caussin took hieroglyphics for symbols. It is possible that Friedrich Creuzer may have borrowed something from this treatise, or rather from this collection of ancient treatises. Therein, Austin tells us, nature was proclaimed "as a collection of symbols that manifest God." But it is doubtful that the German romantics and the French symbolists—not so much scholars as poets—may have borrowed anything whatever from that work. Someone probably should take up the entire question of the use of the word *symbol* before the symbolists or up to Baudelaire and the meanings in which the word's content may be understood; the efforts of a thorough and systematic research project on the subject would most likely be rewarded.

It is doubtful, however, whether such a project would shed much light on French symbolism from 1885 through the years following. Neither artists nor poets are scholarly researchers and, for them, as for the great majority of us, many abstruse books from the past are as if they were never written.

That such should be true is not at all surprising if what has been asserted by

Goethe, who was nonetheless an inquisitive reader who led a tranquil existence, is true: that to know a great deal or too much is harmful to creativeness. What is more, the allusions to symbolism that one encounters before what we call the symbolist period, the sometimes penetrating insights that may strike us in Coleridge, Hölderlin, Nerval, and Hugo are imbued with all the meaning they do have and, one might say, with their originality, only because symbolism came after them and reinterpreted the past. All the questions that fascinate scholars—romanticism before the romantic movement, primitivism before Diderot or Rousseau, surrealism before 1920—are based in fact on a begging of the question. Precursors' different flashes of insight, often fortuitous and set down in passing, later seem to us inspired only because others coming after have read them and, unlike their precursors and perhaps, it is said, because the time was ripe for it, have perceived their true import and what follows therefrom. The searching out of sources for esthetic theories and for ideas, as for those of poems and works of art, too much cultivated out of the erudition of learned scholars, must be seen for what it is in fact: a sometimes fascinating pastime, but one that risks putting the accent on the nonessential.

The word *symbol* was to keep from its origins and the still unsure uses that had been made of it before the second half of the nineteenth century a few connotations that, succinctly enumerated, seem to be these: It is a sign that as such demands deciphering, an interpretation by whoever is exposed to it or is struck by it and who wishes to understand it and savor its mystery. This sign represents or evokes in a concrete manner what is innate within it, the thing signified and more or less hidden. The two meanings, one concrete and the other ulterior and perhaps profound, are fused into a single entity in the symbol. The meaning hidden beneath appearances is not necessarily a single one; the symbol is not a riddle within which human ingeniousness (that of an artist, a priest, a legislator, or a prophet) or a god's careful doing has been pleased to enclose a certain meaning that would otherwise be too clear, too pedestrian, too lacking in inspiration, had it simply been stated as a moral precept or mathematical theorem. Within the symbol there is therefore a polyvalence, a multiplicity of meanings, certain ones addressed to all, others to the initiated alone. But these signs, these formulas or images, are not merely convenient mnemotechnical or iconographic instruments like some object recalling such and such a saint or martyr, some beast designating one of the evangelists, the five Greek letters meaning "fish," because these form the first letters of the phrase "Jesus Christ, Son of God, Savior," or whatever detail associated with Hercules or Vulcan. Each person, on beholding a sign or symbol, may according to his turn of mind (concrete, esthetic, oniric, metaphysical, artistic) extract from it the meaning that is most enriching for him or her. This person supplements, feels, or thinks anew what he believes he perceives in the symbol. In this process there is, then, as with the fragment of pottery or other object offered as a sign of hospitality to a visitor, something shared, a duality. For the *fin de siècle* French poets this was to turn into a necessity to avoid an art intended for all and to obtain active collaboration from the reader, the listener, the viewer of a picture or a statue. It must be the task of the public that wants to penetrate the mystery and pierce the silence to go at least halfway along the path to meet the creator. Insofar as the press, textbooks, and oral means of diffusion vulgarize art more and more, since everyone who knows how to read thinks himself capable of judging a work of art, especially insofar as criticism continues so grossly to mistake its way and to renounce (out of facility or superficialness) interpreting for the public original forms of expression, nonconventional techniques, and new sensibilities, the creator will believe he has the right to refuse every concession to the *vulgum pecus*. Often the artist, while refusing to explain his intentions and weaving his ideas around a work of music, sculpture, or poetry that does not necessarily carry any ideas of its own, will call for a new watchword: to suggest, and by so doing to touch the imagination, the sensitivity, the associations of images, even the subconscious of those in whom he hopes to re-create a state analogous to the one that enabled him to create.

The consequences of that new esthetic were to be numerous and far-reaching. "All things that are sacred and that wish to remain so swathe themselves in mystery," in art as well as in religion, Mallarmé observed in *L'Art pour tous* (1862), at the age of twenty. Whatever seeks to be of value to all is of little value. Prose and genius must, in their very language and in their images, be approached with a certain "esthetic distance" and a kind of reverence. The particular language that renders the author's vision and that strives to communicate while evoking that vision, especially that of the poet, must be a language that, if it is not necessarily out of the ordinary, is at least purified. The essence of poetry, as Valéry was to repeat in the wake of Poe and Baudelaire, must be chemically or alchemically isolated. We find a return to a poetic diction that the romantics had claimed to banish but that will be something quite different from the tired, worn-out, colorless diction of the eighteenth century, with its descriptive, didactic, gnomic poetry, stripped of its power of evocation and its musicality.

The visible, the carnal, the sensual, will not necessarily disappear from this symbolistic art. But poets and even painters (Paul Klee was later to say it in a now famous remark) today have the ambition of rendering the invisible visible. They assume, then, and will affirm, in the footsteps of various theologians, estheticians, and mystics, that there is between the visible and the invisible an often secret correspondence. To these vertical correspondences, poets (and especially musicians), harking back to a few works of romantic virtuosi (like Théophile Gautier) and borrowing certain theoretical views from Wagner, were to join lateral or horizontal correspondences. They came to speak of the "correspondence of the arts," of forms of synesthesia as E. T. A. Hoffmann had already done. The arts, addressing themselves to our various senses are parallel translations of a vast and profound secret that lies within them and that transcends them.

Such ambitions could not attempt realization except through a recasting of the means of expression, whether they be musical, pictorial, or, especially, linguistic and literary, that is, through a renovation of vocabulary, syntax, of both verse and stanza forms, and by breaking with constricting rules. In France especially, and to some extent in Germany, this revolution in what is called form is what clashed most with the reading public's ingrained habits or with its intellectual comfort. That revolution is what caused the greatest uproar, but it was not to have the most lasting effect. It is doubtless regrettable that neither Mallarmé nor Valéry should have conferred upon free verse—or verse freed of constraints—the homage of their genius and that Claudel should have preferred instead the biblical verse form, that Jules Laforgue should have died too soon, and that Gustave Kahn should have had more critical and creative intelligence than musical gifts. The boldness of the liberators of verse, all the more timorous to our contemporary eyes, gave way very quickly to a return to forms of expression closer to traditional ones. At least a considerable step forward had been made, and to the symbolist movement falls the honor of having finally rendered French verse more supple and of having permitted a multitude of new experiments.

It would be contrived and obstinate to rely on chronology alone and seek to restrict the use of the term *symbolists* to those writers who openly laid claim to it around 1885, for they were very far from rejecting everything from the past. Only on rare occasions did they rise up against the Parnassian poets, there having been more marked differences of esthetics and intentions between the symbolists and the naturalist prose writers. They treated nearly all the romantics, Alfred de Musset sometimes being an exception, with deference and knew full well that they were pursuing in their own way and in a completely different intellectual climate the romantics' revolution. They say relatively little of Baudelaire, and it was not the symbolists of 1885–90 but the literary historians of the midtwentieth century who called attention to the sonnet "Correspondences" and the critical articles collected in *L'Art romantique* and in *Curiosités esthétiques*. In so doing, these historians and critics doubtless went too far in isolating Baudelaire, to the exclusion of his precursors and contemporaries, and in seeing in him the departure point for all modern poetry and an innovator who broke with all that had preceded him. Yet our perspective need not coincide with that of readers of 1857–68, none of whom saw, as we think we do, the originality of this or that remark tossed out in *Les Paradis artificiels* or in the *Salons*. We cannot deal with symbolism today without devoting a few pages to what Baudelaire might have meant in those texts, no matter how uncertain may be his use of the term. His originality, moreover, is apparent only if one recalls certain uses of the word *symbol*, certain affirmations before the appearance of *Les Fleurs du Mal*, of the correspondences between heaven and earth, between the concrete and the idea. This is in no way a question of sources, for Baudelaire had not read, and did not have available to read, what had been written in the first half of the century by little-known French thinkers or by illustrious Germans whose works were rarely translated. But it would falsify the image of this period, which corresponds to the flowering of romanticism, to ignore all that it involves of speculations around the deeper meaning of art and of foreshadowings of the future for which it was preparing the way.

Lloyd Austin in his work on Baudelaire, Pierre Moreau in an essay on "Le Symbolisme de Baudelaire," and still others like Jean Pommier, in analyzing the origins of the Baudelairian mystique, have all cited certain interesting texts from the beginning of the nineteenth century. It is possible to go back even further: a hundred statements on the multiplicity of meanings inherent in fables may be found in the hermeneutics of the Stoics who devoted themselves to the analysis of myths, in those of interpreters of mythology at the beginning of the Renaissance (Boccaccio, for example), and in the subtleties of Christian theologians. We know the Greek word that designated those works evolved into the word *myth*. Jean Cocteau cites as an epigraph to his *Le Sang d'un poète* a passage from Montaigne that expresses what had already been suggested by the earliest mythographers of Italy and France:

> Most of Aesop's fables have several meanings and understandings. Those who explicate them choose from them certain aspects which sum up the fables quite well. But, usually, this is only the immediate and superficial aspect; there are others that are sharper, deeper and more to the point, which they have not succeeded in penetrating. (II, x, *Des Livres*)

Madame de Staël, with more precision and doubtless echoing thinking already current among German metaphysicians, went even further; the entire universe was for her a symbolic image of the human soul. In the tenth chapter of the second part of her *De L'Allemagne* (1810 and 1813) she declared:

> In order to conceive of the true grandeur of lyric poetry, one must wander, through the imagination, in the ethereal regions, forgetting the tumult of the earth while listening to the celestial harmonies and considering the entire universe as a symbol of the soul's emotions.

She paid the Germans the honor of judging them more than any other nation capable of the contemplative self-communion and boldness of thought necessary for the composition of this superior form of lyric poetry.

It is not easy to determine exactly what borrowings from the other side of the Rhine were made by French philosophers or professors of philosophy under the Empire and the Restoration. None of them knew the German thinkers as well as did Coleridge, who incorporated in his speculative writings views and entire passages "borrowed" from Schelling, Schiller, or Hegel. Pierre-Simon Ballanche, in his *Orphée* (1829), reveals an intuitive conception of a kind of symbolic poetry, that is, one that translates the divine word on the human plane. Following Le Père Castel and Diderot, he had perceived the theory of synesthesia or of the horizontal correspondences between parallel sensations, the concrete mark of a higher harmony. Two of his most interesting texts, the second of which is drawn from *La Ville des Expiations* (1832), have been cited by Herbert J. Hunt in his erudite and penetrating work of 1941, *The Epic in Nineteenth-Century France*:

> Our poetry is a symbol, and that is what all true poetry must be, for the word of
> God, when it is transformed into the word of man, must render itself accessible to
> our senses, to our faculties, become incarnate in us, become ourselves. It is in-
> vested with an obscure coloration because it is reflected by obscure organs.

And again:

> All the senses awaken one another reciprocally. There could be, in a way, an
> onomotopoeia of colors so much in harmony is everything in man and in the
> universe.

Victor Cousin, less original and less mystical than Ballanche, but more adroit
at publicizing himself and in asserting his own authority, was nonetheless an
influential disseminator of ideas, an eloquent and often ingenious master. He
oriented many young people of the time toward Plato and Alexandrian philosophy and others toward German thought. In his course, given in 1818, which
created a sensation at the time but was not published until 1836 (by his disciple
Adolphe Garnier), "Du Vrai, du Beau et du Bien" (lesson eight), Cousin made
use of several grandiloquent but felicitous phrases:

> The true, the good, and the beautiful are only forms of the infinite. . . . Love of
> the infinite substance is hidden in the love of its forms. . . . Art is a reproduction of
> the infinite by the finite.

He returned to a theme similar to that expressed above in lesson twenty-three
while trying to characterize the imagination, and in lesson twenty-six where he
said again that art is "symbolic" and, also, "sympathetic." Théodore Jouffroy,
more given to reflection than his master, Cousin, and one of the best estheticians
of nineteenth-century France—which counted few great ones—in 1822 taught a
Cours d'esthétique that was only published in 1843 by Jean-Philibert Damiron.
After various considerations on the beautiful, distinguished from the useful and
the new, as a marriage of variety and unity, he devoted the eighteenth lesson to
the symbol. He stated without reservation:

> Every object, every idea, is to a certain point a symbol. . . . All that we perceive is
> symbolic since it excites in us the idea of some other thing that we do not per-
> ceive. . . . The romantic prefers precise symbols. . . . He tends to spiritualize mate-
> rial nature. . . . Poetry is only a series of symbols present to the mind in order for it
> to conceive the invisible.

Concerning the French romantic poets themselves, the poet's claim to the
privilege of seeing everything symbolically had been set forth in *La Muse française* by Alexandre Guiraud in terms first cited by Pierre Moreau: "All is symbolic
in the eyes of the poet. . . . " and afterward by Guy Michaud: "The role of the
poet is in effect to rediscover the traces of a primitive language revealed to man by

God." A little later, an inquiring mind, Pierre Leroux, who had directed *Le Globe* for a short while, who had later founded *La Revue encyclopédique* that for a time attracted the attention of George Sand, and who had, while the two men were in exile, undertaken to win Hugo over to socially oriented poetry, gave an interesting and prophetic article to his own *Revue encyclopédique* in November 1831. "On the Poetry of our Time," was its ambitious title. Leroux assigned to poets the eminent role of legislators and prophets, the absolute interpreters of their times. For, he claims, poets see their epoch as it truly is beneath the surface, and they glimpse as well the approaching epoch or prepare the way for it: "Poets are men of desire and it is their thought that is seminal. True poets are always prophets." An earlier article by Leroux in *Le Globe* of April 8, 1829, and yet another on Jean-Paul Richter, on March 26 that same year, had shown how much Leroux was fascinated by the notion of the symbol. In *La Revue encyclopédique* of November 1831 he came back to the subject:

> The fact is that the entire world, including that of art, which is a part of the world in the same way as natural monuments, which art supplements, becomes symbolic. The symbol: here we touch upon the very principle of art. . . . The principle of art is the symbol.

Charles de Sainte-Beuve in 1830, addressed precisely to this same Pierre Leroux, whom the young poet and critic considered at the time with respect, one of the pieces from his *Consolations* wherein the symbolic mission of poetry is affirmed. Of poets, Sainte-Beuve in fact writes:

> They understand the waves, they listen to the stars
> Know the names of the flowers; for them the universe
> Is but one idea sown in symbols diverse.

For the first time in verse a Frenchman defined the role of the poet as decipherer of analogies and translator of the unheard of, as Rimbaud was to say, the interpretation of which is given to him alone. In prose, in *Joseph Delorme*, the same Sainte-Beuve had already proclaimed no less affirmatively: "The artist received at birth the key to symbols and the understanding of forms" (*Pensée* XVIII).

If among these scattered texts, of which Baudelaire could have known only two or three (those of Sainte-Beuve and perhaps of Leroux), there are any points in common, they seem surely to be these: the poet is not content to accept the superficial appearance of things; it is not in the reality that stands before his eyes that he may find his ideal of beauty. For him everything is mysterious, and he deciphers and translates the spiritual truth toward which the material world tends. Thereby he seizes upon the unity behind multiplicity and it is through his imagination that he forms his model of a form of beauty of which the things of this world can be only a pale approximation. The latent symbolism of the romantics, then, is a form of Platonism. It expresses the aspiration of poets to a higher world: the world of ideas and the world of beauty that overwhelms the soul. Among French poets, it was not toward Alfred de Vigny that Baudelaire looked, despite his respect for the poet of "La Maison du Berger," which he sometimes recalled. Nor did the symbolists of the late nineteenth century. The wolf dying in silence, the house on wheels, "the poor little Bottle," to use Vigny's own expression in one of his letters, serve to translate certain ethical ideas in a convenient, sometimes striking way. The critic who has most astutely commented on Vigny's symbols, Pierre Moreau, declares that in *Les Destinées* "the symbol and the idea, instead of fusing into one, get in the way of one another." Nor did Baudelaire and the symbolists look to the awkwardly "symbolistic" poems of the early Hugo, before his exile ("La Vache," for example). Only later, after having formulated his own ideas, did Baudelaire speak of his admiration for Hugo's genius as a decipherer of hieroglyphs. They were rather to look to Alphonse de Lamartine, the only French romantic with a Platonic sensibility, in search of a spiritual country beyond this ephemeral and perishable world. The Parnassians had, not without reason, been severe with regard to the flaccid and vague form of the *Méditations*, although Leconte de Lisle had highly praised the grandiose philosophical epic contained within *La Chute d'un Ange*; but the symbolists of 1885–90, answering the numerous queries about their tastes in poetry in the little reviews of the period, were far from despising this poet whose imagination was "diffluent" rather than plastic, to use the distinction of the psychologist Théodule Ribot. Henri de Régnier reports in a statement cited by Henri Mondor in his life of Mallarmé, that the poet spoke of Lamartine with his customary kindness. An account of the fortune of Lamartine's poetic production has yet to be written and would be instructive. If anything might redeem Jules Lemaître's obstinate incomprehension of the young poets of his time, it would indeed be his long article on Lamartine (1893), collected in the sixth volume of *Les Contemporains*. With very keen insights, he salutes him as a "demigod" who was, for the subjective, impressionist critic that Lemaître was, "up to now, the greatest of poets."

Vigny, Musset, Baudelaire, Verlaine, Mallarmé, Valéry himself, and, later, Claudel had a less imperfect knowledge of English letters than of German literature; they felt the strongest affinities with the romantic poetry of Great Britain. Without doubt much of what is found in the author of "Correspondences" and *Les Paradis artificiels*, afterward in Verlaine's "Art poétique," and even a certain pre-Raphaelite estheticism in Mallarmé, are prefigured in English poetry between 1770 and 1870. William Blake, however, never became known to the French, and one must be satisfied with imagining what Gérard de Nerval would have found in his work, had he ever opened it. Certain of Coleridge's views were transmitted to France by way of the borrowings Poe made from him. Sainte-Beuve sought from those poets, whom he called "the Lakists," models for personal and intimate poetry. He seems not to have been very profoundly struck by the boldness of William Wordsworth's theories in certain of his prefaces or by the quest for a nearly mystical ecstasy in the greatest of Wordsworth's poems, "Tintern Abbey" and "The Simplon Pass." He knew nothing of Wordsworth's *Prelude* (for good reason, since the poet, feeling himself misunderstood, refused to publish the poem during his lifetime and did not die until 1850), that autobiography in verse in which the poet says what it was that as a child he had sought in nature: transcendence beyond the concrete and appearances toward "the light which never shines on the sea or on the earth," the aspiration toward some communion with the divine. The brilliance of Lord Byron's elegant and tempestuous verse so dazzled the eyes of French and other continental readers that they did not see the profound symbolism they might have discovered, around 1820–30, in Keats and especially in Shelley. Yeats, at the end of the nineteenth century, his imagination set afire by the French symbolists made known to him by his friend Arthur Symons, was to write the first enthusiastic article on what he then called "Shelley's symbolism." I have tried to describe in another earlier work how and why Shelley came only slowly to be known to the French and what role he played in reaffirming the poets of 1885–95 in their symbolist quest. Shelley, at a time when Victor Hugo had not yet attained his twentieth year, had prefigured symbolist formulas and beliefs, not only in his poems such as "Hymn to Intellectual Beauty," "Mont Blanc," and "Epipsychidion," but also in a theoretical piece, his *Defense of Poetry*, which gave to the poet the role of tearing away the veils that hide the invisible from us. The term *symbol* was used rarely, and the English did not take the trouble to define it with precision. They often preferred the term *allegory*, which Keats uses in a letter to his brother on February 18, 1819; he decries superficial people who take everything at face value when, he says, the life of a man of some value, the life of Shakespeare, for example, is "a continual allegory, and there are so very few eyes that know how to see the mystery of such an existence which is 'figurative' in the way the Scriptures are." Baudelaire does not seem to have known more than a very few of Shelley's works, and these are not among the most profound. Hugo apparently resisted the instances of Pierre Leroux who, during their months of closeness in exile, tried to preach to him the example of the English poet who was no less visionary than he and perhaps purer for having served the cause of oppressed peoples.

In another English-speaking country beyond the Atlantic, there flourished, however, a form of symbolism whose formulas might have attracted and assisted the French theoreticians of symbolism in the last third of the century. But the prestige of Edgar Allan Poe, praised and translated by Baudelaire, shut off the French almost entirely from the esthetic and philosophical theories, the novels and the poetics of the American Transcendentalists. Thomas Carlyle, who had been their precursor in certain respects, was cited in several symbolist reviews. Ralph Waldo Emerson is mentioned less often and rather for his sermons on morality and for his elevated viewpoint. Emerson, however, in a very fine chapter, "Poetry and Imagination," in his posthumous book *Letters and Social Aims* (1875), comes quite close to the symbolist process by which the mind projects thought and the sensibility that gives it form beyond itself. Great men express themselves entirely naturally in a symbolic or metaphorical manner; Emerson does not distinguish between the two terms and gives as examples Pythagoras, Jesus, and Napoleon. He adds:

> A happy symbol is a sort of evidence that your thought is just. . . . There is no more welcome gift to men than a new symbol . . . the higher use of the material world is to furnish us types or pictures to express the thoughts of the mind. . . . Poetry is the perpetual endeavor to express the spirit of the thing, to pass the brute body and search the life and reason which causes it to exist. . . . The invisible and imponderable is the sole fact. . . . A symbol always stimulates the intellect; therefore is poetry ever the best reading.

Emerson, the philosopher of the New England group of Transcendentalists, had, one can see, read Emanuel Swedenborg and had read him more closely than had Nerval and Baudelaire. Moreover, he states in the same work that man's life, to the extent that it is more closely wedded to the truth, directs his thought so that it becomes parallel to natural laws and finds expression through symbols and in a poetic or "ecstatic" language. His friend Nathaniel Hawthorne, echoing these Swedenborgian accents, wrote: "Everything, you know, has spiritual meaning, which to the literal meaning is what the soul is to the body." Melville, in Ahab's monologue on the skull of the whale in *Moby Dick*, has his strange character cry out:

> O nature, O soul of man! how far beyond all utterance are your linked analogies! Not the smallest atom stirs or lives in matter, but has its cunning duplicate in mind.

The most recent interpreters of American literature during those productive years of 1850–65, "The American Renaissance"—to use the expression of D. H. Lawrence, who was the first to point out the somber strangeness of these American writings, in their own way as pessimistic and metaphysical as those of Victorian England—turn to the word *symbolism* to characterize its spirit. Following in the path of F. O. Matthiessen, Harry Levin has shown how little of realism there is in this completely transcendental and symbolic area of the American novel, shot through with allegories of biblical origin, or at least derived from John Bunyan. Charles Feidelson, maintaining that these American writers are infinitely closer to symbolism than to romanticism, states that symbolism, in this sense, is even a typically American phenomenon. It is, he says, "the coloration taken on by the American literary mind under the pressure of American literary history." He adds to the list of these symbolist theoreticians and novelists the name of Henry David Thoreau whose statement he cites: "My thought is a part of the meaning of the world, and hence I use a part of the world as a symbol to express my thought."

Unfortunately, the poetry of Emerson, that of Melville, or the more troubling work of the great recluse Emily Dickinson is often gauche, moralistic, and gnomic, and does not attain the freshness of imagination and the suggestive and musical power of the best of the English romantics. Perhaps that conscious and more stubborn reflection on the meaning of symbolism to which the Transcendentalists lent themselves marred the musical and evocative qualities of their verse. Thus the American poets who were to follow, the imagists Ezra Pound, T. S. Eliot, and Wallace Stevens, were to be more than generous in paying homage to the French symbolists. Robert Lowell and Richard Wilbur, among those who were still writing after 1960, have made emulative translations of Baudelaire's poems, and Stanley Burnshaw has pondered over Mallarmé. The English of 1800–30, without so great a fondness for theories, had designated the power of suggestion—often heightened by musical fluidity—as the essence of poetry and saw in the symbol one of the elements of that magic. An eminent French specialist in English literature, Louis Cazamian, has said as much and has reinforced his remarks through his excellent translations of the English poets who were "symbolists" before the fact, and in various articles and a book published during World War II.

French emigrants to the German states, a few Germans who came to reside in France for political reasons or by simple affinity—or attracted by the possibilities offered by the Paris of Louis-Philippe and Napoleon III in music, criticism, or the study of religious mysticism—transposed into French the plays and poetry from the other side of the Rhine. The German lieder particularly attracted many Frenchmen besides Nerval and, later, Edouard Schuré, who wanted to introduce into their own language a lyrical form that would be more musical, more haunting, in its visionary evocativeness. About 1885–95, this process of introduction was to become one of the ways in which symbolist poetry would take hold with the greatest originality and the least disappointing results. But France devoted much less attention to the theoretical reflections, very often cryptic and too philosophical in tone to be transposed, that various Germans had made concerning the symbol.

To be sure, there have been nearly as many definitions of the symbol or declarations concerning it from Leibniz or Herder and Friedrich Hebbel, Theodor Storm and, lastly, Stefan George, as there have been theoreticians in the German language. Moreover, the same thinker, depending upon the occasion that led him to express himself on the subject, might contradict himself or emphasize different aspects of his esthetics of the symbol. Goethe, especially, often changed his mind during his long life, according to whether he was more or less open to scientific thought or whether he was impatient with poorly comprehending listeners. Even a very summary overview of the Germans' successive formulations of the symbolic (or of symbolism as related to poetry) would require a specialized competence in things Germanic that we do not have, and would probably need more than an entire volume. In any case, these ideas from across the Rhine scarcely touched French symbolism from 1885 to 1892 or, before that, Baudelaire. The peculiar aspect of symbolism that pertains to correspondences between the arts (those between color and the auditory sensation, for example) impressed Baudelaire more, but he found this not in the German philosophers but in the storyteller E. T. Amadeus Hoffman. One or two symbolists around 1890 (Jean Thorel especially in his *Entretiens politiques et littéraires* of 1891) were to become aware that the movement whose triumph they were trying to ensure in France had had its precursors among the German romantics. Some, pointed in that direction by Maurice Maeterlinck, read Novalis. They knew Friedrich Hölderlin scarcely better than they had known Blake. As for Goethe, France long remained content with knowing *Werther*, *Faust*, and a few short lyrical love poems or ballads. It is true that Goethe's declarations concerning the symbol are to be found scattered in minor occasional pieces or in conversations recorded by admirers of the grand old man.

It is risky to generalize about "German romanticism" for it arrived in several waves spaced by what is called the "classicism" of Weimar, and because Schiller and Goethe, once the *Sturm und Drang* had quieted down, excluded themselves from the romantic movement or disdained it. Nevertheless, among the theoreticians, whether they be erudite thinkers or poets—Goethe included—there is discernible in them, to a certain degree, the same reaction against what is static, rigid perhaps, bound by defined contours. As opposed to French literary theory or the idea the Germans had of it (Goethe took care to except Diderot), they lay claim to the privilege of pursuing the fluid, the yet-to-be, and of plunging directly to the center of things and beings. "The artist is he who finds his center in himself," declared Friedrich Schlegel around 1800. Wilhelm Wackenroder and Novalis similarly affirm such descent into the depths of oneself, even if one slips vertiginously into his own internal chaos, as a prelude to the sensitive understanding of others. In like manner, all these German romantics became apostles of intuitive knowledge. It is to such knowledge that Immanuel Kant lends the name *symbolic* in his *Critique of Judgment*. The romantics often repudiate cerebral knowledge. The young Wilhelm Meister, for instance, speaking to Jarno, evokes heatedly "this splendid epoch when what is comprehensible seems to be vulgar foolishness." The French, Cartesians by long tradition, had in their dualistic fashion separated the physical world from the spiritual or moral world. This tendency had led them toward the allegory that seeks determinedly, awkwardly, to envelop an already clear meaning in a concrete wrapping. In their revolt against this kind of dualism, the romantics struck down the barriers that separated true reality—that of the limitless spirit—and the finite and more material reality of the world of appearances. They rejected allegory and praised symbolism as a means toward the immediate fusion between these two worlds. The profound truth enclosed within the concrete object or in the image that gives it life becomes one with its artistic or poetic expression.

Hegel, in the first volume of his *Esthetics*, defined the *symbol* as "an exterior manifestation present to the powers of perception but which must be understood not immediately and for itself alone, but in a broader and more general sense." Expression is thus sacrificed to the most intimate meaning. For all that, such a view established a too conscious and calculated separation between the two elements of the symbol. Much earlier, in 1774, Herder had declared: "The body is the symbol, the phenomenon [the real manifestation] of the soul in contact with the universe." In the same year, 1774, the young Goethe (who in 1770 had met Herder at Strasbourg) wrote *Werther*, in which artistic creation (Werther draws and paints) is the mirror of the soul and the soul is the mirror of the infinite God.

The clearest of Goethe's declarations on the subject are found in his "Maxims on Art" (*Sprüche über Kunst*, nos. 1112–13), many years later. Allegory, he writes, changes a phenomenon into a concept and the concept into an image. But the concept remains as though independent, limited, retaining its identity. By contrast, "symbolism" (which can also be translated as "the symbolic") "transfigures the phenomenon into an idea, the idea into an image in such a way that the idea remains always infinitely efficacious within the image and beyond reach; even expressed in every language it still remains inexpressible." Elsewhere, in a piece entitled "On Art and Antiquity," Goethe has stated even more strongly:

> True symbolism is that in which the particular represents the general, not in the way a dream or a shadow does, but as the living and instantaneous revelation of the impenetrable.

In another "supplementary" piece "On the Paintings of Philostratus," Goethe defined the *symbol* thus:

> It is the thing without being the thing, and yet it is the thing: an image caught in a spiritual mirror and yet identical to the object.

Hence to his eyes every dramatic work, for example, is symbolic that bears in each moment of the action its meaning in itself and that nevertheless directs us toward something still more important that lies behind it. *Tartuffe*, which Goethe so admired, is in this respect a great example; so proclaimed the poet in one of his *Conversations*. On May 2, 1824, he admitted to Eckermann to not having regretted his activities as a socially popular theatrical director, which had consumed time he could have devoted to his work:

> I have always looked upon my actions and my accomplishments as purely symbolic, and, in the end, it is all the same to me whether I made jugs or porridge bowls.

However, the most striking—because the most enigmatic—and the most concise of Goethe's declarations is practically the only one known until the end of the nineteenth century by readers not especially versed in German literature: the next to last lines of the second part of *Faust*:

> Alles vergängliche
> Ist nur ein Gleichnis

("All that comes to pass is but an image," or a "symbol" as it is often translated.)

It required a laborious effort of German critics of the beginning of the nineteenth century to distinguish the notion and especially the term *symbol* from that of *allegory*, which had so long been used for architecture, miniature painting, the poetry of the Middle Ages, and in the work of the greatest of medieval poets, Dante. Goethe himself does not hold firmly to that distinction. Friedrich Creuzer, in the long introduction that he gave in the first edition of his large work on *The Symbolic and the Mythology of Ancient Peoples* (1810–12), distinguishes in Platonic and neo-Platonic contexts between mystical or religious symbols and plastic symbols. He saw in religious symbols a link that raises the human to the divine plane. He insisted on the power of suggestion the symbol must possess to stimulate our thought. Although this introduction had been translated in the voluminous adaptation in French that J. D. Guigniaut had done of the German work, it scarcely attracted the attention of French Hellenists and mythographers who used this very learned work on the religions of antiquity. It was certainly not even slightly known to any of the French symbolists unless they may have learned something of it through Ernest Renan, Louis Ménard, or Alfred Maury. Schelling's *Lectures on Art*, given in 1802–03, were published in 1859 and had no greater resonance in France. Wilhelm Schlegel in 1822–25 reworked his *Lectures on Poetry*, which had appeared in a journal in 1800, before his conversion to Catholicism. He included in it, perhaps under Schelling's influence, certain interesting views on the symbol and the imagination and on the correspondences between the human mind and the world outside and beyond it. But, here again, there is in all likelihood no case of direct or oblique influence of such theoretical views on the French symbolists of 1885–92. It is very much more likely, as is often the case in the history of ideas and sensibility, a matter of polygenesis, or the appearance, simultaneously or staged over several decades, of comparable aspirations or parallel answers given to questions of a like nature.

In all events, between 1790 and 1840, long before Baudelaire, various minds among German authors, without having absorbed Swedenborg, had already proclaimed that art is inevitably symbolic or even hieroglyphic (Schiller, who died in 1805, had said as much in his "Theosophy of Julius"). Carlyle had doubtless read it in the German authors. The German dramatist Hebbel had noted in his Journal (*Tagebücher*) on February 2, 1842, in terms that were to be recalled by the Abbé Bremond during the controversy over pure poetry in 1924:

> Every authentic work of art is a mysterious symbol and, in one sense, unfathomable. The more a certain poetic style derives from thought alone, the less of mystery it will possess and the sooner it will be understood. But its content will also be more quickly exhausted, and it will be cast aside like the oyster shell from which the pearl has been extracted. The didactic poet goes so far as to offer the unadorned solution instead of the enigma which alone is of interest.

Edgar Allan Poe was not the only one who, in 1845–50, might have been able to demonstrate to Baudelaire the wrongdoing of "the didactic heresy" in poetry.

2

BAUDELAIRE

It is far too easy and, in the long run, quite pointless to analyze piecemeal an author long reduced to silence and to write, for example, on Baudelaire's classicism or his romanticism, on the several declarations of love for form, devotion to art, and the cult of a majestic and indifferent beauty that make him a Parnassian poet. It is no less pointless to praise him, as one of his English admirers (T. S. Eliot) has done, under the pretext of enhancing his greatness, for having been a Catholic and a classicist born outside the age in which he ought to have lived. There should be some hesitation at calling him a symbolist, since he could not have adopted such a label for himself thirty years before it existed. The word *symbol* appears only three times in *Les Fleurs du Mal* (once as an adjective qualifying the gibbet on the Isle of Cythera—an emblem of the poet's horrible fate—and, other than in the well-known line from "Correspondences," as a substantive used to describe the tiny coffins, resembling cradles, of little, shriveled old women, half returned to childhood). Elsewhere the poet prefers, perhaps for the sake of rhyme or sound, the term *allegory*, used twice, or *emblem*, to which he assigns similar connotations, used four times. The swan, escaped from his cage during a drought-ridden Parisian summer, becomes, somewhat awkwardly, a "strange and fatal myth." In his prose works, Baudelaire alludes more often to what we mean today by "symbolic," and in passages here and there in his writings he qualified as "symbolic" Théophile Gautier, Victor Hugo, Eugène Delacroix, and Richard Wagner, as well as Rabelais and Sainte-Beuve.

Three of the most learned of Baudelaire critics have devoted their most detailed attention to this aspect of the poet's work: Jean Pommier, who pays particular attention to one of the elements of symbolism, correspondences, and synesthetic effects; Pierre Moreau in a learned and discerning analysis; and Lloyd Austin. To his book *L'Univers Poétique de Baudelaire*, Austin has added the subtitle *Symbolisme et symbolique*. He has, in fact, proposed quite ingeniously to his colleagues, to eliminate the confusion surrounding "that poor word symbol," to use Valéry's phrase, that they adopt once and for all a distinction between *symbolics* and *symbolism*. The first of these terms would be reserved for every poetics based on the notion that nature is the symbol of a transcendent truth. This notion is encountered sometimes in Baudelaire, more often in Mallarmé, and in the rarely modest theoretical writings, none of which hunger for clarity, of the symbolists of 1890 and their successors: Rémy de Gourmont, Gustave Kahn, Albert Mockel, Charles Morice, and Tancrède de Visan. We often designate as *vertical* the category of correspondences that rise from the world here below toward the heavens along "living pillars." On the other hand, if Austin's proposal were followed, *symbolism* would be reserved "for every poetics which, without posing the question of any mystical transcendence, seeks in nature symbols that translate the state of the poet's soul." The second meaning would not designate horizontal correspondences or synesthetic effects, but rather something like the "correlative objective" proposed by T. S. Eliot in an essay on *Hamlet*, that is, an object or a situation that may serve as an expression of a certain particular feeling and that also evokes that feeling. It would be a matter, then, of an indirect or oblique means of expression, as another English critic has put it. But the terminology (and even the entire attitude) of English-language criticism differs a great deal from that of the French. A wide gulf of incomprehension separates them, a deeper gulf, it seems, than the one that makes it difficult for one people to transmit to another an understanding of their respective novels, poems, or paintings. It is doubtful that the distinction proposed by Austin will be adopted by his colleagues in other countries or that it will make a great deal of sense in their eyes.

The history of the fortunes of Baudelaire's work in France seems calculated to surprise readers of the midtwentieth century who have read and reread, and often, from their early school days, commented upon the most diverse of the poems from *Les Fleurs du Mal*, as well as upon a number of aphorisms or striking statements in the prose works. Even those who, during the fifty years after the poet's death, expressed loudly their admiration for his verse works, usually kept to the least original pieces and, with the exception of the sonnet "Correspondences," to the least symbolic: "Benediction," "Man and the Sea," "Don Juan in Hell," "Sadness of the Moon," and a few other poems popularized by their musical versions. The decadents isolated and, at the same time, deformed the satanic aspects of Baudelaire. The young Paul Bourget surprises us when, more serious and inspired than others, he expresses his preference for "A Martyr" as one of the most beautiful gems in the book. *Esthetic Curiosities*, which groups together the three "Salons" and other articles on art, had indeed appeared as the second volume of the so-called *Complete Works*, in the "definitive edition" of 1869. Very few remembered them. *Romantic Art* had been published the same year, but the long articles on Delacroix, on Constantin Guys, or, with reference to the latter, on Wagner, on Gautier, had not made a much greater echo. The *Posthumous Works*, published in 1887, gained wider recognition only after the appearance of the considerably augmented reedition that the *Mercure de France* devoted to them in 1908. We would like to know if Rimbaud truly read *The Artificial Paradises*, published in 1860 by Poulet-Malassis, and what Verlaine, Mallarmé, Villiers, and Laforgue thought of it. But, here again, we are faced with uncertainty. It indeed seems that the minds of that time were not ready to extract all their meaning from nonetheless illuminating remarks on hieroglyphic art, on the man-God, or on music and painting reciprocally augmenting their respective powers, even when these passages derived in part from Poe or from Thomas De Quincey. It was still much later before it could be understood from the poet's heartrending letters to his mother, from a few quips, or from feverish outbursts of sincerity in his letters to friends or to M. Ancelle what a tragically torn life had lain at the source of the poet's work. The element hailed as being "symbolist" in advance of the actual movement, which was discovered by Baudelaire's earliest posterity, was therefore that of synesthetic effects. The success at the same time of Wagnerism, won after many struggles and thanks to the young artists of 1890 who imposed it upon the traditionalists and the officials of the Paris Conservatory and the Opéra, helped to popularize the correspondence of the arts as essential to the esthetic revolution of the day.

The history of the idea that various sensations may correspond to one another, reinforce one another, and be transposed one into the other was written after Baudelaire, Rimbaud's sonnet "Voyelles," and Wagner. The only predecessor where this kind of idea was concerned and who truly counted for Baudelaire was Hoffmann. We know from the 1855 essay "On the Essence of Laughter" that the French poet held a special esteem for the German writer's "absolute comic art" (as Baudelaire called it), his superior form of the grotesque. He revered even the tale of "The Princess Brambilla" as a catechism of high esthetics. Its author, at once profound in the Germanic mode and witty as though come from a sunny climate, knew how, as is the wont of comic authors, to be himself and another at one and the same time. He had a clear awareness of his comic genius and, simultaneously, gave the appearance of being unaware of himself. Hoffmann's fantastic aspect, which had deeply impressed Balzac at the time he was writing *La Peau de Chagrin*, was less striking to Baudelaire, who was little attracted to whatever tends to go beyond the human realm. But on several occasions, he insisted on what had most caught his attention in the work of the author of *The Devil's Elixir*: not the sense of the diabolic, but the correspondence or analogy between sounds and colors, colors and feelings. In the *Salon of 1846*, he cites the passage from Hoffmann, taken from *Kreisleriana*, that had particularly pleased him:

> It is not only in dreams, and in the light delirium that precedes sleep, but even awake, when I hear music, that I find an analogy and an intimate blending of colors, sounds, and odors. It seems to me that all these things have been engendered by a single ray of light and that they must join together in a marvelous concert. The odor of brown and red marigolds especially produces a magic effect upon my person. It makes me fall into a profound reverie, and I hear then, as though from afar, the grave and deep sounds of the oboe.

It is possible, depending upon the esthetic fashion—as changeable as any other—either to wax ecstatic before the ingeniousness of these transpositions of art forms or to smile at them as vain and a bit too obvious tours de force. A line from Baudelaire's "Song of Autumn" delicately alludes to Sainte-Beuve's poem, "The Yellow Rays," which was a clever variation on the color yellow. Many French schoolboys have admired the virtuosity and the evocative strangeness, in no way to be disdained, of the "Symphony in White Major," in Gautier's *Enamels and Cameos*. A certain puritanism, which is a part of our creed of the beautiful and causes us to find poetic what is serious and even pretentious, today

restrains our enjoyment of poetry that displays its lightheartedness and speaks its
joy in its own mastery of verbal or rhythmic inventions. Musset's best poems,
however, are not his songs of despair, but his lighter pieces; and Hugo is not great
only in his nocturnal sorrows and in the specter's revelations of "La Bouche
d'ombre." "The Steps" or "The Insinuation" of Valéry are more successful and
less pretentious than a certain stanza from "The Seaside Cemetery," on Zeno of
Elea, or a certain stilted invocation to the "salty power" in the "billow" toward
which the poet wants to run. Baudelaire's "The Fountain" is certainly not
inferior to certain of his invocations to the demon or to his denunciations of the
monster "Ennui." The tercets of the sonnet "Correspondences," which give
examples of synesthetic effects, obviously do not have the grave scope and the
revelatory tone of the quatrains that have a quasi-religious purport. They are nevertheless strangely beautiful and the idea, which they clothe with sumptuous
adjectives and images or with pungent comparisons, was well worth exploring. Our
latter-day estheticians have preferred to frown at the impurity that may reside in not
jealously respecting each art's own means of expression. The famous "Ut pictura
poesis" had in the past led to much artifice. The sonnet "Vowels" was celebrated too
quickly and, despite the newfound treasures in certain of its lines, it is in fact
permissible to see in it the paradoxical game of an adolescent desiring to shock.
Des Esseintes' language of colors and the music of his liqueur bottles ridiculed
still more the systematization of these horizontal correspondences between color
sensations and gustatory, olfactory, or auditory sensations. But on another plane,
as with Richard Wagner in his "Letter on Music" (1860), the Baudelairian
affirmation was defensible; every art form, having attained a certain level of
development, is tempted to borrow techniques from other forms. The best criticism of a painting, Baudelaire was to suggest, might very well be a sonnet. The
stanza of "Lighthouses," which characterizes Delacroix, translates the effect
produced by his painting in musical terms and compares it to Carl Maria von
Weber's music. In other poems from Les Fleurs du Mal, sensations similarly
cease being isolated; they turn in vertiginous movement, augment one another,
and "mystically" metamorphose. Colored auditory sensations may be the
privilege of only a very few psychic constitutions, and Hoffmann played upon
them with virtuosity. But there was a thicker shroud of mystery for Baudelaire to
tempt from transpositions of sensations and, sometimes, from transpositions of
art forms. These correspondences between the arts were to become one of the
features of symbolism attributable to Baudelaire. They were to constitute one of
the means by which the poet or the artist might seek to attain an underlying unity
behind the multiplicity of appearances. In his great and serious article on Delacroix (1863), Baudelaire praised his favorite painter for having above all rendered
the invisible and the dream world with lines and colors while conferring upon
these pictorial techniques the riches that the parallel arts of literature and music
have at their disposal. He saw in these new forces, which the various arts reciprocally lent to one another, "one of the distinctive symptoms of our century's
spiritual state." More peremptorily, a few years later, Walter Pater, the English

critic who provided the esthetic for what one might call British symbolism, more heavily imbued with decadent tendencies than the French movement, was to declare that "all the arts aspire to the condition of music."

The transpositions of art forms can in effect be nothing but an amusing game that certain metricians of symbolism were occasionally to practice in the manner of Gautier or Théodore de Banville. But such transpositions also furnished Baudelaire the means with which to produce much more profound effects. Far from being the high priest of a form of sensualism that was to cultivate rare sensations for their own sake, Baudelaire refined them and charged them with spirituality:

O métamorphose mystique
De tous mes sens fondus en un!

O mystical metamorphosis
Of all my senses fused into one!

cries the poet in "All in One," refusing precisely to describe one by one, in the manner of the Petrarchists or of certain Baroque poets, the beautiful features of woman adored more for her soul than for her body. Everything in her is harmony; even her voice "produces perfume." If eroticism often consists, as Valéry quipped, in taking the part for the whole, Baudelaire is one of the least erotic of French poets. "Her Hair" is in this sense the most evocative of the symbolic poems in *Les Fleurs du Mal*. If, in the first line, with the words *fleece* and *curling fleecelike* (*moutonnant*), and even with the word *withers*, one may momentarily think of a comparison between the woman and an animal, this correlative objective that is the mulatress' hair becomes very quickly a receptacle for purified memories, then visions of exotic lands that are the pretext for pungent dreams, ships harmoniously gliding over a sea bathed by the setting sun. From the gentle rocking of the waves, the imagination is invited to rise towards the sky for which the blue or deep black of the hair becomes the symbol. Dreaming and memory are joined finally in the last two lines, one of the most sumptuous and least carnal of the great Baudelairian evocations:

N'es-tu pas l'oasis où je rêve et la gourde
Où je hume à longs traits le vin du souvenir?

Are you not the oasis where I dream and the gourd
From which I imbibe in long drafts the wine of memory?

It is nevertheless in the vertical correspondences, the ascending ones (the movement being one of rising from the earth toward the heavens along "living pillars") or the descending ones (the spiritual being incarnated in the material, the angel attracted toward his fall), that Baudelaire best appears as a poet of original symbolic form. Some have spoken skillfully and prudently (Marc Eigel-

dinger especially) of Baudelaire's Platonism. Doubtless it was not through reading Plato's *Dialogues* or even through reading Swedenborg's works, which in all
probability he did not read firsthand, that he became acquainted with Platonism.
But for a long time, since Joachim du Bellay and perhaps somewhat by way of
Lamartine, a certain form of Platonism had been known to every cultivated poet.
Moreover, it is a natural inclination of the mind, or of certain temperaments, to
discover or rediscover in oneself the aspiration toward ideal beauty, toward the
permanent and the eternal that perhaps lies behind the transitory, toward the
archetypes beyond paler images, that are the essential characteristics of an
elementary Platonism. For that there was no need to have read the *Parmenides*,
the *Timaeus*, or the *Republic*.

At no point did Baudelaire expound systematically on what he meant by his
pursuit of essences or Ideas that symbols alone are able to render concretely or
imaginatively. But what one may call "symbolic" in his view leads to a few
positions that seem fundamental to him and his work.

The first of these is *not* scorn for what is real or even for external nature,
whatever he may have said about it in a letter in a moment of irritation. But he
does refuse to worship nature or the real world like a pagan or a materialist, to be
content with descriptive poetry, or even to seek to become one with nature like
the pantheists. In the play of appearances, in the splendor of forms and colors, he
seeks an ulterior meaning; he wants to decipher a secret, to arrive at the spiritual
hidden within the material and that is the generative cause of appearances. In his
intelligently generous and very perceptive article on Victor Hugo, in 1861,
Baudelaire best expressed his thoughts on this matter. He has just mentioned
Swedenborg and Johann Caspar Lavater, and, expanding their statements on
correspondences, adds:

> ... We arrive at that truth which says that everything is hieroglyphic, and we
> know that symbols are obscure only in a relative sense, that is to say, with respect to
> the purity, the good will, or the innate clairvoyance of souls. Now, what is a poet (I
> take the word in its widest usage), if he is not a translator, a dechipherer?

In a peremptory tone and as if he were stating (as Poe does in certain of his
writings) a scientific truth (he makes use, moreover, of the adverb *mathemati-
cally*), Baudelaire maintains that comparisons, metaphors, and epithets are
brought up "out of the depths of the universal analogy." He praises Victor Hugo
very highly for knowing how to take hold of external life and to absorb that life
into himself, while not confining himself to that alone. In his awe, he wants to
interpret that vertiginous reality by returning to the meaning that the Creator has
given it or that the poet will confer upon it. The poet's intelligence, which thus
becomes the decipherer of analogies, is quite different from that drier kind of
intelligence, closed to what is mysterious, too quickly carried away by "militaris-
tic petulance," which was Voltaire's. The poetic intelligence is able to put
imagination to its service.

In a letter of January 21, 1856, to Alphonse Toussenel, Baudelaire had in fact declared in a grave, revelatory tone, which is that of the sonnet "Correspondences":

> I have been saying for a long time that the poet is *sovereignly* intelligent, that he is *intelligence* par excellence, and that imagination is the most scientific of the faculties, because it alone comprehends the *universal analogy*, or what a mystical religion calls *correspondence*.

In the same letter, the poet did not reject nature, which his romantic predecessors had so celebrated as a consoling sister; he saw in it "a word, an allegory," at once the incarnation of a higher essence and the microcosm of the vaster world of which it is the mirror. The writer who is ignorant of that symbolicalness passes on by, distracted and uncomprehending. One who is fortunate enough to possess "the innate awareness of correspondences or of universal symbolism" goes on beyond. Like the narrator in Proust's novel in contemplation before flowers, hawthorn hedges, or Elstir's paintings, the poet perceives signs that seem to be addressed directly to him. His awareness is awakened as if by a problem, but something still more profound is stirred within him. In a very strong, emotive outburst, in a veritable ecstasy that is simultaneously active and passive, he calls forth and receives a quasi-mystical revelation. Wordsworth, in his poem written "near Tintern Abbey," described with precision that ecstasy in which "we are laid asleep in body and become a living soul." Our senses seem dormant as in a catalyptic state, the heart nearly stops beating; we see, then, by means of a second sight, into "the life of things." Baudelaire seems to allude to a similar psychological and even physical state in fragment XVII of *Rockets* (*"Fusées"*):

> In certain almost supernatural states of mind, the profoundness of life in its entirety is revealed in the spectacle, as ordinary as it may be, that is before one's eyes. It becomes the Symbol of it.

This poet, who in the eyes of some of his contemporaries passed for the poet of the flesh and the senses, is in fact (and almost to the same degree as Lamartine, though less casually), one who seeks stubbornly to raise the material toward the level of the spiritual, to wed substantives to adjectives carrying moral value: "mystical," "spiritual." The material, by contrast, is characterized as "stupid" in "Questioning at Midnight," and "the enormous idiocy" symbolically has "a bull's brow." In the opposite way, the debauchee himself aspires to a "spiritual dawning." Love for woman is love of her soul, even if in a few quips the poet, waxing sarcastic, seems to doubt the reality of that soul and would refuse women entry into churches. He thinks without doubt that it is the man's role to lend to her (or to give to her) that soul in order to be able subsequently to worship her. The soul of man unceasingly aspires to be elsewhere, to be an Icarus, to travel "anywhere out of this world." In its being incarnated in a body, the being, the idea, the form, or the archetype has denatured itself; it has, like Hugo's God (and like many mystics' speculations), left behind some kind of nonhuman perfection, its solitary unity. Nostalgia for that state before the fall thereafter haunts the creature, if it knows in any small way how to read the insufficiency of external meaning and detect the signs of a profounder significance reserved to the decipherers of symbols.

"The Irremediable," perhaps the most philosophically profound and also the most awesome poem of *Les Fleurs du Mal*, is where the poet expressed in the most suggestive symbols this feeling of irresistible descent into the abyss and of remoteness from the soul's first vocation, a feeling common to the Platonists and to Plotinus as well as to mystics of every religious persuasion, and even to mystics who do not believe in God. The first eight lines form a single sentence punctuated by semicolons. Each line adds to the impression of mournful despondency that weighs upon humanity, ailing and without remedy. There is no "I" or "you," as in many other of Baudelaire's pieces, or even a collective "we" as in "The Irreparable"; there is no suggestion of a concrete setting, no lament, for this evil; there is no respite that might be derived from the use of refrains or repetitions of lines to cast thereby a spell over evil by singing of it; there is no seeking out of any musicality. There is a minimum of adjectives, a concise firmness in these imperious octosyllables. The title indicates the abstract subject of the piece. This abstraction does not need to be explained at all; it is translated immediately in a series of symbols. The three imposing substantives of the first line, each written with a capital letter, "An Idea, a Form, a Being," are the various names of the Being-in-itself, of the creative principle, of the original model who, like Vigny's angel Eloa or the Lucifer to whom Victor Hugo was to grant final salvation through love, has tumbled into a hell in which he is bogged down. A series of four symbols confer a concrete reality upon this philosophical or theological fall: an Angel weary of beauty without risk and of his paradisiacal sojourn is pulled into a whirlwind where he gesticulates like a madman; the captive of a snakepit, assailed by remorse, contemplates, powerless, his annihilated will; a creature who is damned descends the infernal staircases, ambushed by monsters who squeeze him in the grip of their tentacles. The fourth symbol is that of a ship locked in ice but endowed with sufficient consciousness and humanity to wonder why and how it has incurred this fate. The eighth stanza finally explains, in a bitterly ironic tone, that these nightmarish images were the "emblems" of the irremediable (*l'irrémédiable*) and that the expert machination of the Devil (*le Diable*)—the rhyme was expected—has devised these moral torments.

A second part of the poem, in eight lines, presents a contrast to the first. It introduces other symbols: that of the mirror (which has become the heart that pitilessly examined itself); that of a well that is at once black and clear, for it is the symbol of truth; that of an "ironic, infernal" lighthouse; and that of an altar candlestick from some black mass. The contemplation of this downfall of the One catapulted into multiplicity, of the celestial become subhuman, is no longer uniquely a source of anguish. The poet, a true spiritual brother of the most pitilessly lucid of the French *moralistes*, also derives from that confrontation with the profoundest self's remorse and nightmares, "unique consolation and glory." Like Pascalian man, he knows that he suffers and dies of it; he almost extracts pride from what the poet, in the final and one of the most lacerating lines that resumes all the tragic force of his work, characterizes as "consciousness in the midst of Evil."

In such poems, which are exempt from every trace of virtuosity and from all toying with enigmas, Baudelaire best succeeds in laying a bridge between the material and the spiritual, in uniting the abstract and the concrete, the celestial and the infernal, and in following the principle he himself had formulated as the ideal of art for the moderns in the unfinished article, published only after his death, entitled "Philosophical Art":

> What is pure art according to the modern conception? It is to create a suggestive magic containing at the same time the object and the subject, the world outside the artist and the artist himself.

He sometimes gave the name of allegory to this process, but it is actually much more: a manner of feeling, of thinking, and of communicating by suggestion what he had experienced deeply. In *The Artificial Paradises*, he had called allegory "that so spiritual genre," and he had hailed it in one of the first *Salons* as "one of art's most beautiful genres." The spiritual or moral element, in effect, most often prevails in the relationships established between the two superimposed worlds joined by the living pillars of correspondences. This doubtless is one of the reasons why comparisons, which certain moderns might judge conventional, are more numerous and, as in the work of Claudel and Dante, more grandiose than the images in Baudelairian poetry.

At times, Baudelaire links these two worlds by use of the word *comme* ("as" or "like") strongly underlined, which gives to this or that couplet the geometric form of one of La Rochefoucauld's maxims. Such is the case in lines nine and ten of "Her Hair." More often, he prefers to retain the two terms and, departing from the concrete or the carnal, pass on by means of "comme" to an odor or a healing balm to the immensity of the sea, to the moon. Kisses, for example, become in "A Phantom" as powerful as an aromatic balm. In "The Ghost" they are cold as the moon. In "Jewels" the lover's desire, in a very purified form, however, for the woman, nearly inaccessible in her nudity enhanced by jewels, becomes a love "deep and gentle as the sea, / which swelled towards her as towards its rocky cliff." The conjunctive adverb *comme* appears four times in the first seven stanzas of "A Carrion." The third of the four "Spleen" poems is a long allegorical comparison introduced in the first line by "like the king of a rainy land," evoking Prince Hamlet of foggy Denmark hovering behind the bored and anguished poet. *Comme* is also the term of liaison between the sky and the weighty lid that configures it, between captive and blind hope and the clumsy bat that it becomes in the fourth and most famous of the "Spleen" poems. The women who offer themselves to Don Juan, sailing unmoved over the river of hell, are "like a great drove of victims." The lesbians the poet pities and claims to love appear in the very first line "like a pensive herd of cattle recumbent upon the sand"; but, more than whatever there may be of the bestial in them, it is their unrealized and vain love, yearning for an object never attained, that the poet stresses in these "seekers of the infinite." When Baudelaire avoids the small word *comme*, he replaces it by various paraphrases: "has the effect of," "recalls," "are the emblem" ("of your variegated spirit"), "one might say your look veiled by a mist." The anguished spirit of the poet, racked with remorse in "The Irreparable," is, according to a comparison dear to Baudelaire, "similar to the dying man" crushed by the horses' hooves, and, in "The Cracked Bell," it is his soul that "seems like the thick death rattle" of a forgotten casualty. Everything occurs as if Baudelaire insisted on maintaining the link between the two terms of the comparison in order to pass from one to the other in either an ascending or a descending movement. There is a Dantesque and weighty gravity, equal in beauty to the evocative force of certain images channeled into a cascading flow, to which Baudelaire has recourse in certain litanies of amorous adoration as in "Hymn" ("forever fresh sachet," "forgotten censer," "grain of musk"). The famous identifications of the character who chastises himself, with both the victim and the tormentor, the wound and the knife, the blow and the cheek on which it lands, or the compressed images of "The Irremediable" more closely resemble symbols in the traditional sense. But it is far from sure, in these poems with a more rapid rhythm (most often in octosyllabic verse), where there is immediate identification between the object and the subject, that there is a power of intellectual feeling communicated to the reader equal to that of Baudelaire's great image comparisons. Some modern spirits who are quick to condemn all rhetoric, like the poet Yves Bonnefoy in an article in the *Mercure de France* of September 1, 1954, have rather severely taken issue with "the conceptual development, as little concerned as possible with that which goes beyond words," in the diction, considered deceitful, of *Les Fleurs du Mal*. Certainly there are a few awkward phrases, sometimes monotonous repetitions in the recurrence of Baudelairian symbols: those of the elixir, of the angel, of the country inn (used in other poems and not always happily) in "The Death of the Poor," for example. But at other times the poet finds some imposing symbol to represent, both sensually and intellectually, the beloved woman. She is "the fine vessel that moves out to sea," the dream country toward which the ships of a vagabond disposition will set forth anew, but which now sit somnolent upon the canals of Holland after having returned from the far ends of the earth. Even more, she is all of Baudelaire's poetry, offered in homage to the beloved woman, set on a course towards posterity that she will one day set to dreaming, a "Vessel favored by a strong north wind."

For Baudelaire there is a "faculty of the soul," as old-fashioned psychology called it, that not only creates images and develops them into allegories or symbols, but that also perceives the insufficiency of reality and seeks in it a deeper meaning; that faculty is the imagination. It is well known that French poets and estheticians after Diderot and, perhaps, Joseph Joubert and the Comte de Rivarol, who did have a presentiment of the role of imagination in poetry and art, had rarely been given to speculation about the imagination. In this respect, note the contrast between them and the Germans and, especially, the English (Coleridge above all, as well as Blake, Wordsworth, Shelley, Keats), who paid high homage to the imagination as the poet's gift thanks to which he goes beyond the pleasant, ornamental quality of fancy and lays claim to domains inaccessible to reason. Except for a few of Hugo's prose texts (most of them published posthumously or, like that of *William Shakespeare*, little noted during the poet's lifetime), it is Baudelaire who set out in France to crown the imagination as "the queen of faculties." The symbolists, the surrealists, were to be his continuators in that regard. In so doing, Baudelaire owed something to various declarations of Poe, who was himself familiar with certain of Coleridge's statements, and to Delacroix whom Baudelaire quoted and interpreted.

He attributed to Delacroix (and borrowed from him) the celebrated phrase "Nature is a dictionary." He admired the romantic painter (in the same *Salon of 1846*, section IV, where he reports this remark) for having repudiated all realism despite the incomprehension of the critics who had attacked his savagery, and maintained that "a painting must above all reproduce the artist's intimate thoughts, which dominate the model." Like the painter, the poet, regardless of some of his offhand remarks, does not entirely despise nature and the real world; it was he, after all, who, already in 1845, had asked that artists show to what extent the moderns could be "great and poetic in their choice of neckties and their polished boots." Manet and Degas were to offer proof of this twenty years later. But in this finite the creative mind incorporates the infinite, and for Baudelaire the esthetician such was the function of art.

In the third and last of his *Salons*, in 1859, Baudelaire devotes all of section III to a fiery panegyric on the imagination. It is necessary to the moral sense itself and to virtue; it teaches man "the moral meaning of color." Especially, he says, "it creates at the beginning of the world, analogy and the metaphor." He adds later: "All the visible universe is but a storehouse of images and of signs to which the imagination will give relative place and value." All the other functions—or "faculties of the human soul"—including the intelligence must be subordinated to it. Doubtless for Baudelaire, more timorous than the adolescent Rimbaud, the imagination would be incapable of disrupting mankind's perceptions from top to bottom. He voiced his fear of such an obstinate and "rational derangement," expressed with regard to hashish. But the imagination does reorganize the immediate observations of the senses and the speculations of the intellect. It perceives on earth, this admirer of Poe was to say in his "New Notes on Poe," a correspondence with Heaven.

In this way, no doubt, Baudelaire is in fact an ancestor of the symbolists and, until Mallarmé came along, the most profound and reflective of the estheticians of symbolism. His symbols, or metaphors tending towards symbols, are sometimes rather lame. There is awkwardness in the too-celebrated "The Albatross," in "The Giantess," and in the tercets of "The Wicked Monk": "My soul is a tomb. . . ." Valéry would be able, taking Mallarmé of course as a paradigm, to speak of "the depressing banality" of many of Baudelaire's verse lines. But at other moments, when he found a less awkward form, Baudelaire, creator of symbols, deciphering a hidden and profound meaning behind the visible and the material object, deserves to have applied to himself (and he may be praised for having done so with genius) the noble statement he set down (*Salon of 1859*, IV) as the program for the imaginative mind as opposed to that of the positivist: "I want to shed the light of my mind on things and project its reflection upon other minds."

3

RIMBAUD, OR THE SYMBOLISM OF REVOLT

Even more than Baudelaire, Rimbaud would have been astonished at being labeled a "symbolist." It is known that his ambition at the time of his first youthful expedition to Paris was to be accepted among the Parnassians and that, later, in Abyssinia, he shrugged his shoulders when people wrote him from Paris that the symbolists claimed him as their precursor. Among all the interpretations that Rimbaud's work (which has become the object of a myth) has known, the least surprising is that which sees in him still a rebel against outworn poetic forms, a visionary recombining in his own way the elements of his dream universe, a metrical innovator, a symbolist. As much because of the singularity of his career of "remarkable passerby" as because of what was too disruptive in his genius, he scarcely left a mark on those poets or theoreticians of symbolism who read him between 1886 and his death in 1891. Claudel, in the great enthusiasm of his youth, Gide, and Valéry were nonetheless deeply impressed by their reading of Rimbaud during the dying years of the nineteenth century. Twenty years later, Jacques Rivière exempted him from the harsh condemnation that he had pronounced against the art of the symbolists. The surrealists appropriated him for a short time. If the centennial of *A Season in Hell*, in 1973, had been celebrated in the grave fashion that academic critics in our day have assumed, in colloquies (composed, to tell the truth, of written monologues), Rimbaud would definitively have been ranked as a classic, the most commented upon, after Mallarmé, of French poets.

It was inevitable that Rimbaud's adventurous existence and his repudiation of literature at scarcely more than the age of twenty should hold such fascination for posterity that careful study of his work would suffer from it. Successive generations of rebels have cherished in Rimbaud the very model of rebellion. Undoubtedly, it weakens the jolt we receive from the work and the elucidation of the elements in it that give it its unique strength, to affirm, as T. S. Eliot has done in Baudelaire's case—and as a hundred others, following his example, have done for Rimbaud—that the importance of these writers is due primarily to their remaining for us "the human prototypes of a new experience," and only secondarily to the fact that they were poets. Rimbaud was, nearly as much as Verlaine (though during a much shorter lapse of time), a man of letters and a technician of genius.

But our emotional feeling and even our admiration in reading *A Season in Hell* or certain of the *Illuminations* goes out not only to the artist in him or to the fabricator. Even if it is naïve to scrutinize each word of "Memory" or of any one "Illumination" in prose to find in them an allusion to the poet's childhood or to his travels, one cannot help but find the beauty of his verse or of his prose more brilliant because the author, to use Nietzsche's phrase, "wrote with his life's blood." The nineteenth-century symbolists had no knowledge of the voyant's two letters published in 1912 and 1926; a few expressions, considered once to be "striking," have since taken on the allure of clichés for schoolboy competitions: "I is another," or "the immense and rational derangement of all the senses." Doubtless, as Marcel Ruff has done in an excellent general study of Rimbaud, it is wise to reassert the true value—which remains great—of these remarks. Inspiration has for all time been considered by those on whom it breathes as a gentle visitation by the Muse or as a delirious god's imperious dominion taking hold of the inspired one. The identity of the poet is put into question; it is another who speaks through this poet-prophet. Praise of consciously sought mental disorder was, in 1871, far from being an absolutely new thing in the land where Pierre de Ronsard had been inspired by Pindar, where Nicolas Boileau had thought to perceive in this process "an effect of art," or where Victor Hugo, in his *William Shakespeare,* had scoffed at economy of expression and sobriety.

Other passages of the letter of May 15, 1871, to Paul Demeny may recall the preface-manifesto of Leconte de Lisle's *Poèmes antiques* and the enthusiasm of the adolescent Rimbaud for sunlight and the flesh and the Hellenic life proclaimed "harmonious." The peremptory distinctions between true voyants and nonvoyant poets proclaimed by the seventeen-year-old adolescent are too facile. He takes delight in heaping abuse on Musset's least good work, "Rolla," which he must have loved very much at first, before becoming irritated with himself for having been fond of it. He errs out of an excess of indulgence for François Coppée, René Sully Prudhomme, and the insignificant Parnassian Albert Mérat. But no one says that he should have been infallible. The viewpoint of more informed and more mature critics, that of Mallarmé, for example, ranking Gautier and Banville much too high, surprises us no less than that of Rimbaud. It is the fault not of Rimbaud, but of his commentators, if we have made these texts, hastily set down on paper by an impatient and impetuous young man, into a sacred text for all poetry to follow. Onto certain of these remarks have been grafted some rather ambitious estimations of Rimbaud as "a mystic in the primitive state" (this is Claudel's phrase) and in quest of "the true other life" in drugs, in dreams, and perhaps in death. More prudent Catholics, like Stanislas Fumet, have contented themselves with seeing in him "a thwarted mystic." Rivière went so far as to hail in him the being untouched by original sin, an angel exempt from the demoniacal spitefulness that Verlaine, with all the tenderness he felt for his star-crossed friend, could not help but point out and cherish.

All our notions about Rimbaud are obscured with very little gain in seeking to make him fit some preconceived idea or in labeling him with some epithet by which we think he can be summed up: "Rimbaud the child," "Rimbaud the voyant," "Rimbaud the hooligan" (supposed, besides, to have been impotent, for such is Benjamin Fondane's diagnosis of him), Rimbaud the mystic or the masochist, seeing himself as unhappy and "a great invalid, a great criminal, suffering under a great curse." He was all that and much more.

But before everything else, for posterity and among European writers of the

second half of the twentieth century, Rimbaud represents the rebel. "I am he
who suffers and who rebelled," he cried out in the most ferociously anti-
Christian of his early poems, "The Just Man." He rises like the Cain that Byron
and Leconte de Lisle had already taken as their spokesman, against the false
innocent (Christ) before whom his mother had thought she could make him
kneel. "Eternal thief of vitality," he calls Him in another blasphemous line.
Even earlier, a schoolboy impassioned by carnal, pagan goddesses in "Sunlight
and Flesh," he had cried out in a burst of joy: "No more gods! Man / Man is
God!" The new literature demanded above all the scornful rejection of worn-out
beliefs that had only served to reduce man to a slave state. Doubtless, the
adolescent had not yet heard of Marx or of Feuerbach. But he had rediscovered
certain of their frenetic negations, or perhaps come across some no less vehement
phrase in one of the French socialists, Jérôme Blanqui or Pierre Proudhon. To
achieve the creation of new forms and images he must first give free rein to the
forces of disintegration. Baudelaire, in the three or four of his poems that are the
most awesome in their evocation of the self-inflicted suffering of the poet who
seeks to be a martyr, had given form to this consent to destruction. Rimbaud
seeks to leap without the slightest remorse into a fall from grace, to demean
himself, to become as hideously monstrous as the hero of "The Man Who
Laughs," to make himself the scapegoat of his fellowmen and of all humanity.
Out of this inclination rises the heartrending cry of sincerity in the "Letter from
the Voyant." The romantics had enriched poetic language, had rid it of a
number of worn-out expressions. But their poetry was still discursive, given to
amplification, lay sermons set in verse; Leconte de Lisle's adjectives and images,
which Rimbaud admired at the time, are nobly moral and abstract. Rimbaud
does cite Punishments in his letter of 1871 (without rendering it justice), but he
seems not to have known Contemplations or even The Legend of the Centuries,
although there are those who have complacently seen in "The Satyr" a source of
the young poet's pagan verses. The different worlds, the external and the internal, that of the earth and that of the heavens, were not blended together through
a powerful cosmic inspiration. Everything remained apart, classified, organized.
In the famous "Alchemy of the Word," from A Season in Hell, Rimbaud makes
allusion to "worn-out poetic forms," while confessing that they had not been
excluded from the alchemist's experiments by the young destroyer. In barely one
or two years he succeeded in sweeping away all the tinsel of his predecessors'
poetic diction and in passing beyond personal poetry whose era he declared
henceforth to have passed away. French painters of the fifteenth century, like
those of the seventeenth, had already discovered this indirect lyricism that trans-
poses into the object and through it all the shimmering personality of the artist.
Jean Fouquet, Dumesnil de La Tour, and Jean Chardin, the impressionists, and
Paul Cézanne were soon to do the same and filter their vibrant exaltation
through a landscape, a bouquet of flowers, a few apples on a plate. But Rimbaud
had scarcely seen museums or art exhibitions before his stay in London where his
sister Vitalie's diary alludes to a certain visit to the National Gallery under

Arthur's guidance. His poems, moreover, are not oriented either toward painting or sculpture (as were those of Gautier and the Parnassians), or toward music, even though in his bound to surpass the timidity of his contemporaries he strives to "write vertigoes" and to "note down the inexpressible." Breaking out of the limits of verse poetry in "Movement" and in "Marine," then out of those of the *verset*, based on biblical verse, or overly cadenced and excessively genteel, vague poetic prose, he rejects all that contains and stagnates the torrent of sensations and images. He seems in no way to care about discovering by means of intellectual calculation a symbol by which to transmit them. All communication with the reader is broken off, or rather it will have to come about through an explosive shock that will overwhelm and floor the reader. "I withheld the translation," he said in "The Alchemy of the Word." The tyranny of good taste is shaken off. Simpleminded pictorial images and simpering refrains, the young rebel proclaims boastingly, have more certain charm for him than the saccharine art and intellectual pretensions affected by the bourgeoisie.

Too often people have sought to present Rimbaud as a Communard or even make of him a communist, which amounts to only slightly less a deformation than to caricature him as a pious Catholic. He knew moments of anarchist revolt against every established order; the poem "What for Us, My Heart, are Pools of Blood" cries it out forcefully. More regularly, he felt himself spontaneously in revolt against maternal tyranny and the prison of the family. His poems of early adolescence say this with brutality and verve. He ridiculed the patriotism of the bourgeoisie, which, after having voted en masse for Napoleon III, witnessed, fearful, the collapse of his army and had to fear, still yet, the social rebellion that rumbled in Paris. A few allusions in his verse bespeak his sympathy for the workers. But that goes little further than analogous allusions in Baudelaire or Coppée, whose attachment to social democracy was by no means either conscious or profound. Certain expressions in A *Season in Hell* are, however, more revealing and seem to hold out a much more reflective "no" to the notions that Cartesianism, the patriotism of the French Revolution, of Adolphe Thiers, and the positivism of Comte and Taine had all erected as idols: reason, the nation, and science ("Bad Blood"). Work, celebrated in the family and in the school by way of the most moralizing of La Fontaine's fables on the industrious ant or the plowman and in beautiful slogans condemning laziness as the mother of vices, is equally spurned by the rebel poet. Among the first in his half-century, which was also that of Gauguin, of certain writer-voyagers weary of Europe—Pierre Loti and others—of Rousseauists who were to take seriously the primitivism at which the utopians of the preceeding century had played in the salons, Rimbaud dreams of the impossible return to the past. A few sentences from those strange prose pieces "After the Deluge" or "Barbarian" suggest firmly that this hope is only a chimera and that this freshly innocent world is only a fantasy of tired minds. But for him, it is a question of incontrovertible disaffection with Western civilization, as was to be the case with the painter to whom he is sometimes compared, Gauguin. "I want the barbarism that is for me a rejuvenation," the painter was to write to Strindberg on February 5, 1895. Elsewhere he proposed a Rimbaldian cleaning of cobwebs, the return, beyond the horses of the Parthenon, "to the old wooden horse, his childhood's hobby-horse." Other poets, from the author of "Rolla" on, had envisioned this rejuvenation as a voyage in time toward that Greece whose gods lived among human beings. The Parnassians, and even Baudelaire, thinking for a time that he loved "the memory of those nude epochs," had thought of consoling the vicissitudes of the present with this same Hellenic dream. Rimbaud and some of those who were to come after him, seek to embark for real foreign lands, to flee in space and no longer in time, and to deny everything right up to the Judeo-Hellenic traditions so dear to the West.

But Rimbaud right at the outset surpasses everything that the end-of-the-century poets and theoreticians of symbolism were to attempt. Although most of them were to be content with a vague philosophical idealism, with Platonic declarations of devotion to beauty, and with technical discussions of the means and the rules to achieve renewed verse form, Rimbaud in his rebellion invades the domains of psychology and philosophy. With him, dreams do not merely flow into our waking lives, they blend with half-conscious reveries, with thoughts, impulses, desires. Rimbaud dips with both hands into what is most confused, sometimes the most pure and most deeply buried within himself and within us. The stars dance in his sentences like flowers; they emit the sounds of bells or of joyous fanfares; sounds and colors blend together, fused into a single poetic vision. Shimmering light of day and almost sexual rhythms, foam in the green night resembling dazzling snows (the poet says, more daringly, "dazzled"), phosphorescent snows that he hears sing while the dawn renders their awakening "yellow and blue," sky and sea, the earth recalled to mind with its tart apples and its old parapets united with the delirious ocean, cataracts of furious cloudbursts and suddenly tranquil rivers—everything is carried along in a strange and dizzying delirium in Rimbaldian evocations. The senses are no longer content to reinforce one another. The rational disordering of sensations they register overwhelms the vision and perception of the poet, who thus enlarges humanity's powers. Proudly, more demigod than man, he "sees what man believed he saw," and he imposes these whirlpools of visions on us.

Rimbaud's poetry becomes a means of exploring the depths that lie beyond clear consciousness and that the magician, with his omnipotent wand, causes to jet forth like geysers. It becomes equally a way to knowledge and invades domains before which science was abdicating. The adolescent Rimbaud wanted to reinvent love and perhaps reject the mutual incomprehension of the two sexes, unite the strength of the one and the other in a complete androgyny. He had doubtless been disappointed by woman, after his rebellion against a mother with whom he knew secretly he had many affinities. He had dreamed of finding in woman patience, gentleness, comprehension, consolation, as in the "domestic dream" that Verlaine sketched before meeting Rimbaud and even before his marriage. The lines of prose from "Deserts of Love" reveal how vulnerable the adolescent was in his avid need for tenderness and in the awkward brutality that badly concealed his appeal for sentiment. "All our embracing is nothing but a question," he declared in a more didactic tone that recalls Vigny or Baudelaire, in a poem from his seventeenth year, "The Sisters of Charity," in which, upon leaving childhood, he vents his disappointment with woman, who is incapable of perceiving the male's immense need for tenderness. The "Letter from the Voyant," written a short time later, does not exonerate men in this war of the sexes. Until now he had been "abominable." But her subservience will come to an end. She, too, can be and will be a poet if she ceases to be submissive. "She shall find the unknown. . . . She shall find strange things, unfathomable, repulsive, delightful" that the man will accept and understand.

Man thus extended and aggrandized will lay claim to his innocence. He will cast far from himself the biblical condemnation, push farther the limits of the human condition. This "intractable prisoner" will proclaim himself not guilty. Like Vigny's great rebels, the blasphemers of *Les Fleurs du Mal*, he will rise up against God and take by force the foreseen paradise. Baudelaire had retreated before so much audacity. Perhaps, as in Sartre's diagnostic analysis of him, he needed to feel guilty, to observe the rules set down by others even while guiltily violating these rules. He admitted, in his *Artificial Paradises*, that "every man who does not accept the condition of his life sells his soul." Rimbaud was also to submit during the last frighteningly pathetic weeks of his life. But he had at first sought to make his revolt total and metaphysical as well as social and literary. Symbolism, in England, Russia, even more than in France, was to be littered with pitiful failures: decadents, misfits, drug addicts, half madmen. Rimbaud had, like the romantics sixty or eighty years earlier, presumed too much on the power of literature "to change life." Therein also lies his greatness. He had wanted to believe that words and rhythms could change things and had turned his back on that "reality, rough in its embrace." Rather than join some coterie, with the inevitable compromises (success with the press, discussions of literary strategy debates in cafés and salons, the Academy for the more clever), Rimbaud preferred the complete repudiation of Western civilization. A century later, the youth of the entire world was grateful to him for it.

Symbols that reveal the workings of the Rimbaldian imagination can be easily garnered in the poems written before his seventeenth year. Several already evince a rare beauty: "The Poets of seven years" in a sarcastic mode, "Ophélie," less original and more descriptive, but already marking the appearance in Rimbaud's poetry of the victim of drowning, and that admirable, mocking, and joyous reverse *art poétique*, "What One Says to the Poet on the Subject of Flowers." "The Drunken Boat" is, among all of them, the symbolic poem par excellence. The virtuosity that the seventeen-year-old adolescent displays therein, his verbal mastery, the breadth of its development, have aroused many admiring commentaries. The most diverse sources have, of course, been assigned to it, most of them without any real relationship to the lines and phrasings of the text. Rimbaud doubtless had not yet seen the sea, but he had contemplated or seen images

of it in books; he dreamed of liberation and flight. He had no need to have read
Chateaubriand, Poe, or Coleridge in translation or to have noted any comparison whatever of the airborne ship to mankind in "Open Sky" from *The Legend of
the Centuries*, nor that in Baudelaire's "Voyage" where the soul is compared to a
threemaster, and still less that of the "Steamer" evoked by Mallarmé in "Marine
Breeze," which had been published in the first *Parnasse contemporain*. Above
all, the adolescent, who knew himself capable of poetic tours de force in French
(as he had shown in his sixty lines of Latin verse sent to the Prince Imperial on
the occasion of his first communion in May 1868) seeks to display his mastery.
He embodies in this symbol of the boat adrift and the unleashed universe all his
romantic fury. Throughout twenty-five stanzas of four alexandrines each, he
unfolds a power of inspiration and animated rhythm that Vigny or Baudelaire
might have envied. The drunkenness of the boat and of the adolescent dreaming
of his freedom becomes, thanks to the sounds, to the broken and sometimes
abrupt rhythm of the lines, to the clash of images, the reader's own. Hugo
himself rarely succeeded in orchestrating his eloquence to this point.

The organization is expert. The verb in "I was descending" ("Je descendais")—
in the imperfect tense in the first line—announces the movement of slipping
toward the ocean, of the blind plunge towards some abyss. It is reiterated
in the great trimeter of line eight when the boat leaves the river for the
boundless sea. Further along, and more lugubriously, a drowned man, who is
also qualified as "pensive" (Hugo had already called "pensive" the dead frozen in
the position imposed on them by "the form of the tomb," in his "Sadness of
Olympio"), descends, carried along by the currents of the blue-green sea. Beginning with the third verse, the sounds, the dislocations of the lines, and the
sonorous terms evoke the fury of a marine world where everything is carried
along in a saraband of the elements. The boat, or the child, by way of the small
word *I* (*Moi*), rises against all constraints, joyful in his disobedience, for he
knows he is still a child ("more deaf than the brains" of children who refuse to
obey), and already the weariness of one who will compare himself to a woman on
her knees, who will finally long for his familiar "still puddle," seems to forecast
the fate of the adventurous skiff. The remembrances of the land and of familiar
landscapes will surge forth at various moments in the images: the sea is compared
to the taste of sour apples while it tosses the boat, then invades its planks quickly
bereft of direction and defenses. Later, a flight of doves, white, half celestial like
those that embody the Holy Spirit, joyfully scattering themselves in flight, is
assimilated to the dawn over the sea. Rimbaud, only yesterday a schoolboy, will
even insert a few memories from his reading, as sarcastic as the tone may be, to
bring together (in one of the poem's most artificial passages) the "purple clot-
tings" of the sun setting on the water to "actors in very ancient dramas." Toward
the end of the long journey, the lichens of sunshine and the bluish nasal mucus
on a wall brought to mind by the reddening sun becomes, in a phrase that seeks
to be repulsive, an "exquisite marmalade for good poets."

For six stanzas, the pronoun *I* will proclaim with conviction everything that the boat and the voyant fused into one, like the prince and his guardian spirit in the *Illuminations*, claim to know from having seen, dreamed, followed, collided. Nothing is immobile or stable in these visions of the sea, the sky, the watery downpours, the bursts of sea foam. The young poet takes delight in linking all these to a fermentation (the word appears twice), an intoxication of rot pregnant with fertility, an amorous rhythm of ascending dreams and muted desires. The colors themselves are caught up in that moving rainbow. "Gleaming" red, the rust color of rotting things, purple, yellow, and the blue from the phosphorous bubbles at the bottom of the sea, the Homeric sea color, and especially green are lavished by Rimbaud. The azures that devour the sea in the sixth stanza are green, as is the night in the tenth. The poet takes pleasure in these evocations of hideous monsters and catastrophes. Momentarily—for the space of three stanzas, slower in rhythm, more caressing in tone—he stops, moved by the beauty of bronze-toned fish, the foam that seems to proffer itself like flowers, and the gentleness of the winds.

He would like children to share in the magical beauty of these visions. The sea that rocks him seems itself to weep. The boat, henceforth reduced to a few wave-tossed planks, has become drunken from its apparent freedom—apparent, because it was only the plaything of capricious hurricanes. Like the adolescent Rimbaud returning home after his first ardors, like the explorer of Abyssinia dreaming of a life of security in his native Ardennes, the boat regrets "Europe with its ancient parapets," fortified, guarded, imprisoned. He sums up these cosmic visions of intermingled isles and stars that have dazzled him and poses the moving question to which his later poetic writings seem to seek the answer: from where draw future vigor, from where seize upon the magical golden bird, the superhuman strength that would permit him to renew the whole of poetic expression, of love, of life? The pronoun *I*, the adjective *my*, will return in the final stanzas, but no longer with the exaltation of victorious freedom. Now, let that sea upon which he still rides swallow him up, his keel burst open; or let him return to his childhood dream of the liberating voyage, more radiant than this tiring escapade had been. He can no longer struggle with the merchantmen or the naval vessels, make mock of the hulks that transport imprisoned convicts. The admission of defeat, anticipating the one that closes "Memory," is pathetic. The violent rhythm of the poem has yielded to a nostalgic melancholy. From behind the adolescent in revolt, the child has reappeared.

"The Drunken Boat," colored, leaping, intoxicated with its verbal richness, imperious in its near Hugoesque eloquence, is still turned towards the past. Émile Verhaeren, Claudel at times, Pierre Emmanuel, and Jean Grosjean will know moments of impetuous inspiration and sometimes biblical anger that will render their works akin to the adolescent's romantic masterpiece. Rimbaud's true technical innovations and his art of rendering mystery and shadows unfolds with more secret intensity in his other long poem, a masterpiece of symbolic poetry, "Memory," probably written the following year. There, the oratorical tone is broken; unity no longer lies in that flight that blows like a tempest across the

conquering stanzas; the lines are often segmented with virtuosity and run insolently into one another. The stanzas within each of the five sections, clearly
differentiated by their tone and visual arrangement on the page, do not enclose
impressions and regrets in a rigid mold of four alexandrines; they, too, flow into
one another and carry with them, like the river that is at one and the same time
the setting and the actor in the poem, the flow of memories and regrets. To
emphasize better that gentleness in the continuity of a dream or reverie charged
with mystery, the poet did away with capital letters at the beginning of each line;
his use of exclamation points was even more sober than in his preceding masterpiece. We no longer have the seer whose eye deforms reality in order to enlarge it
and make it whirl about furiously. The sensations recalled are here suggested
with lightness; the flamboyant or livid colors have disappeared; the green is no
longer a raw green but veers toward grey ("the little girls' dresses"); the blue is
symbolic and sentimental; the adjective *grey* describes the sky in line sixteen and
the surface of the water in line thirty-one; it is also the color of the willows lightly
set to trembling by the flight of a bird. The yellow, perhaps the symbol of family
life, is an almost abstract yellow and, in two places, Rimbaud uses, out of
preference, the more conventional word—but one that is evocative of all that is
precious, Lamartinian (and later, Mallarméan and Valéryan)—*gold*.

Everything is mystery and shadow in this poem, and everything is symbolic;
from the outset, one is seized and intrigued by the polyvalence of the senses. The
title, "Mémoire," is feminine in gender—a more original, more obscure noun
than *souvenir* would have been. It is the very faculty of recalling what is designated and of recreating through the act of recall. The poem will be constructed
entirely of feminine rhymes, and the two terms that are to dominate, *river* and
mother, both designate what psychologists would call the "feminine principle."
Water, the first word in the poem, will be omnipresent as the river that flows or
tarries, as a window pane or a sheet of water, as watering the plain that borders it,
then as a symbol of stagnation, of sadness, of mire in which the child's dream of
liberation bogs down. The beginning appeared entirely radiant; the lines themselves take off in flight; the child's tears on which a ray of sunshine glistens are set
in opposition to the waters of the Meuse, caressed by the sun. In a repetition of
sibilant sounds, the poet imagines women in summer dresses on the green banks
of the river, taking the sun by storm. He evokes, perhaps at the sight of a flag
flying from a tower or from the mast of a boat, the banners of his history books in
which Joan of Arc took Orléans by assault and organized the defense of the city.
Are they then, the women and the children who doubtless are playing alongside
them, a completely pure and joyous vision of angelic revels? The denial breaks
both the tone and the idealizing reverie: "no." The river, with arms that it seems
to agitate as the sun sinks and the evening breeze makes the leaves of the trees
vibrate, describes seeming gestures of denegation—these same arms will reappear
in lines twenty-five and thirty-four. This river is woman, also, as the pronoun *she*
emphasizes at the end of line six. She runs toward the hill and the arch of a
bridge as toward protection, as does the mother, protected in her bed by a dais

and curtains. But no protection of this kind can retain the husband who has fled never to return, the sons who have dreamed of flight, and of whom one, the eldest, has also left for good, the other of whom, the young poet, dreams of his imminent freedom.

The vertical movement of the first stanza is succeeded by the horizontal movement of the second. It is no longer toward the heavens or the angels that our sight is directed, but toward the river and its banks under the noonday sun. The expressions of line nine are no doubt less fortunate and, a rare occurrence in Rimbaud, just the slightest bit overused: "the damp pane," "limpid bubbles." The river bed and the conjugal bed are united in one single allusion; the hollows from where the sunlight-gilded water is deep bring to mind perhaps the bed of some engulfed Ophelia. The greyish-green willows intermingle, in a daring line, with the dresses, pale in color as well, of Arthur's sisters no doubt, and the birds, free creatures, jump from branch to branch. The water is gilded, the marsh marigolds that grow there are yellow as well, and it is from there perhaps that, for the child whose dreams the adolescent relived, the color of the family household was derived. That humble flower is at one and the same time a gold coin, a louis d'or, an eyelid, and the symbol of the fidelity promised by the Wife (*Epouse*), written with a capital "E" as if to suggest the Wife par excellence, the feminine principle. She envies the sun, "the rosy and beloved sphere," the male element that might have brought love, security, joy.

This polyvalent symbolism soon gives way to a more concrete picture, sarcastic in tone. The lines, less tender, are broken; three times the sound *elle* is repeated. The poet's mother, stiff and proud, or the mother in general, is now more real, indifferent to what surrounds her, as in a painting by Seurat. Children, hers perhaps, have their prayer books in their hands. But "He" ("Lui"), the sun, and also the male, recedes in the distance. The bundle of the sun's rays appeared for a moment to the imaginative child like a flight of angels dispersing. She, the river, the mother, "cold and dark" in that day's end, seeks to hold back the husband, and soon the son, who are escaping towards their freedom.

The fourth stanza again varies the tone; it becomes pitiful and nostalgic. Two abstract substantives begin two verbless clauses: *Regrets, Joy*. The grass and the river bed, evoked earlier, are henceforth memories that one might wish in vain to retransform into realities. The tenderness of spring nights when the moon gilded the river and appeared to bless the union of the couple has disappeared, the poet seems to be saying in a mysterious line (line twenty-six). The heat of August, which bestowed life and fecundity upon the plants or insects that inhabit the abandoned fields, it, too, a source of joy, is no longer anything but a memory. The abandoned woman weeps; the tall, bold poplars evoked here instead of the willows, tremble or breathe for the wind alone that carries afar their vain complaints. Everything has become stagnant, as if dead.

The poet, reliving his childhood memories, speaks in the last movement, resigned almost to desolation. As in his childhood games, when Rimbaud amused himself by drawing on the chain of a moored boat to give himself the illusion of sailing free, he now admits the defeat of the wild dreams set forth a short time before. The "damp pane" has become a "mournful eye of water" that mocks him; he cannot get a hold on either the yellow flower that resembled a "gentle eyelid," or the blue one, the friend of the now grey and funereal water. Two interjections punctuate his regrets: nothing matters to him any longer, neither the willows nor the flowers of the reeds or rushes; the beauty of the spectacle does not overcome him, and at the bottom of the "eye of water" that holds him prisoner, he sees only mire. It is on this word, symbolic of his despair, that this admirable poem closes, more dramatic, more human, richer still with associations and polyvalent suggestion than "The Drunken Boat."

It is regrettable that at the period when criticism might have approached with seriousness the very precise study of Rimbaud's mythopoetic imagination in the *Illuminations*, it should have been distracted by controversies over the dating of those prose poems. Whether the poet repudiated them or not, whether he retracted this repudiation, and whether he did not pronounce his "farewell" once and for all, but was repossessed by his creative demon, is all really of very minimal importance for other than a few biographers. The metallic splendor of these texts, sometimes brilliant in their diamondlike hardness, sometimes sorrowful and closely akin to "Memory" in their nostalgia, should be received passively at the very first by the reader. He shares in Rimbaud's fleeting visions all the more in that he sees with the eyes of the author. The interpretation comes only afterwards, and it ought not to consist of assigning a single meaning, revealed by dint of intellectual subtlety, to this or that image, to which Rimbaud no doubt gave none: that of the hare catching sight of the world amid the sainfoin and praying through a morning spider web in "Deluge," or that of a goddess pursued by the joyful adolescent in "Dawn." These two poems, and several others, evoke a return to the youthfulness of a world cleansed of adult lies to which Rimbaud aspired. "Dawn" expresses the exaltation of the child who believes that he in truth commands the day to rise and participates in the life of nature as if he were the demiurge. He creates the flowers by giving them names that they echo back to him by way of a greeting. He laughs in cascades. The dawn, all of nature, is a woman or a goddess from whom he lifts the veils of night or the garments that cover her body. He believes, in his dream, that he unites with her in making love. All that is a dream abruptly dissipated, while at the same time it is a picture made up of small dabs successively added in short, clear sentences. Like "Dawn," "Mystique" is a picture, divided into two or three planes like certain paintings of the Last Judgment or even of the mystical Lamb. But evil, cruelty, "the homicides," and war have entered here. The angels that move about the meadows are fallen angels. The noise of avid and fearful humanity rises while there descends from heaven, in a vision of gentleness, that sheaf or basket of flowers by which Rimbaud often symbolizes the stars. It is through naïvely felt mystery, rendered with an explosive force and without the intervention of anything whatever of the abstract or the sought-after effect, that Rimbaud is a symbolist and a poet.

At times, he more directly turns into symbols his childhood life, his loneliness within the family, the setting of his native province, the women of whom his puberty dreamed, sometimes with brutality and sometimes with gentleness: in "Childhood," for example. In this piece, he accumulates a chaos of impressions and fables that nourished his childhood imagination, but within three astonishingly well-ordered paragraphs. The second movement of "Lives," which contains five paragraphs, evokes the intruder, Death—the death of a young girl, the death of her mother, the dispersion of the family, the deserted house. Rimbaud's familiar landscape (slopes, meadows, the river with its locks and islets, flowers that hum and, sometimes, sweat or speak, cloudbanks) is captured; tears (another frequent element in his poems of desolation at a world that could not remain virginal and pure) that seem to compose the seas, far away and beyond. Further on, finally in the fourth section of "Lives" and in one of the most personal poems of this collection—a collection that generally seeks (in accordance with the precept from the "Letter from the Voyant") to repudiate subjective poetry— Rimbaud announces the various personalities in which he symbolically incarnates himself: the saint at prayer, the scholar or the thinker in some library, the hiker who proclaims melancholically the "golden wash of the setting sun," the lonely child, confused, misunderstood. Then everything on the subject comes to a halt. The sources of which he often dreamed in his poems are dried up, the "future vigor" of birds is no longer even coveted. There is the celebrated conclusion of disenchantment: "It can only be the end of the world if one goes forward." It is in "Lives," practically alone among the *Illuminations*, that Rimbaud traces a symbolic painting of his real life transposed along with other lives glimpsed in dreams. On a less sarcastic note, with more detachment and while looking at himself with a half-amused smile, he traces there a transposed portrait of himself that recalls that of "Bad Blood" or "Night of Hell" in *A Season in Hell*.

It is after this end of the customary world, or even from "out of this world," that Rimbaud, in "Barbarian," calls forth the return to chaos. However, on four different occasions the word *delights* (*douceurs*) punctuates his evocation of primitive barbarism. On the silky moire of northern seas, among flowers that do not exist (twice stated), a blood-red color, a red flag perhaps, symbolizes the spilled blood, the flesh of a sacrificed animal. The poet has rejected everything from the civilized Western world—military marches, prudent morality. After the musical chord, "Delights," a clash of cymbals supervenes that announces mixed fire and rain and a burst of diamonds that are nothing other than the heart of the earth, "eternally carbonized for us." The infinite sufferings of human beings seem to be exhaled from there. A vertiginous music, soft and powerful, rising from the chasms, goes to collide with the stars as if it were hurling icicles at them. All at once, everything is caught up in the chaotic whirl: sweat, heads of hair, the eyes of dream creatures. A last mysterious sentence adds a note of tender softness, that of tears from a child or from mankind, which this spectacle has caused to flow. A feminine voice will perhaps be consoling. It is no longer said that she sings, but she seems to have quieted the volcanoes and the caverns of this arctic landscape. As in a round, in this very strange poem whose arrangement on the page appears to be skillfully calculated, the most mysterious sentence from the beginning returns as a refrain. Rimbaud amasses fires, diamonds, icicles, jets of sea spray, furiously to demolish and then recreate himself the world he condemns. The poem does not conceal a hidden symbolic meaning, or several, although various ingenious readers may have sought to lend it one. It imposes upon us a vision and the confused avowal of a failure, for once the old world is demolished, the new one evaporates like a vain dream. Every precise equivalent of one of these mysterious details to some real object that Rimbaud might have been able to perceive and recall (the colors of the red and white Danish flag, the rain of diamonds and fire from an Icelandic geyser) serve nothing except to exercise the intellectual subtlety of the interpreter.

"Tale" has the appearance of a brief narrative, almost that of a fable, and throws us less off course. A prince, come forth from fairy tales the adolescent recalls to mind, is also the all-powerful and capricious sovereign of oriental tales who is given to cruelty and the adolescent poet who seeks to step out of himself and unite with a genie in order to learn of reinvented and complete love. Weary of the world's mediocrity, of the monotony of love, he puts to death all the women he has known. Dying, they bless him, but this was only a dream massacre; they reappear and understand him no better. He kills those in his cortège, cuts the throats of the animals in the hunt and in his garden, and with the fury of Flaubert's Saint Julian puts palaces and cities to fire and blood. No one murmurs against his whims, worthy of Caligula. But he has not found the sought-for rejuvenation.

One evening, however, a genie "of an affable and even inexpressible beauty" appeared to him. Could this be the new, total love? Too splendid to be tolerated? Both disappear. But all that is only a vision from a voluptuous dream. The prince dies exactly as everyone else does. He was the genie and the genie was he. He has encountered only himself, or the creature projected by his own desire. Once again, a vision is dissipated. On the word "desire" this Illumination ends, that desire that demands a power of creation, an almost superhuman "learned music," in order to achieve satisfaction. But the poet states this with lucidity and irony. In A Season in Hell, it will be done (for "Tale" appears to have been written earlier) with more bitter sarcasm.

The sonnet "Vowels," "The Drunken Boat," and a few pieces from A Season in Hell excepted, Rimbaud's work and its revolutionary significance escaped the symbolists of the literary coteries of 1885–95. Too many legends had been woven around the man, his adventures with Verlaine, his career as a merchant and explorer in Africa. Verlaine, haunted by his former friend, whom he had understood better than some like to admit, was barely able, by virtue of his temperament, to explain critically the meaning of Rimbaldian poetry and of that, to his eyes, diabolic rebellion against literature. The Illuminations published in La Vogue were able to touch a dozen or so readers open to the technical innovations that they read in them or who were capable of submitting themselves to Rimbaud's vision and to the brilliance of his images: Gustave Kahn, Félix Fénéon, among others. What was needed was for a few enthusiasts of the work to have had the time to penetrate it and then to convert younger generations to their admiration. Such has always been the process by which a truly new work (that of Shelley or Keats in England, of Hölderlin or Nietzsche in Germany) has been able fruitfully to exercise its influence. Mallarmé, who alone might have been able to make Rimbaud's work known or to speak of it with communicative warmth among his Tuesday listeners and his young correspondents in the provinces, remained curiously discreet on the subject. His most striking critical texts (the Oxford lecture, his declarations to Jules Huret) remain silent about the one he must have felt had surpassed all his contemporaries by his genius. His letter of April 1896 to Harrison Rhodes bears scant witness to any familiarity with anything but "The Drunken Boat" and a few of the very earliest of Rimbaud's pieces.

It was the same "Drunken Boat" that was first to attract Valéry to Rimbaud. On April 5, 1891, he praised him very highly to his new friend Gide and copied the text of the work for him. He refused to immolate this poetry of vision and trance to that of Mallarmé, which he placed so high. Doubtless, as when he later felt attracted by the young surrealists of the "Littérature" group, he realized that an entire part of his nature (that which affirms that sometimes "the dream is knowledge," and that the first lines of verse are on occasion "given by the gods") secretly united him to the most violently inspired of poets. In "Remarks concerning myself," which precedes André Berne-Joffroy's volume, *Présence de Valéry* (Plon, 1944), Valéry recalled the shock that the discovery of Rimbaud, following quickly upon that of Mallarmé, was for him: "I was as if intellectually overcome by the so sudden appearance on my spiritual horizon of these two extraordinary phenomena. . . . I vaguely compare Mallarmé and Rimbaud to adepts of different species: the one creating I don't know what symbolic calculus, the other having discovered I do not know what unprecedented radiations." Gide, for his part, confided to Valéry that he had, around 1894, become imbued with Rimbaud and had acquired from him the taste for a certain "turbulence of life." Later, on June 4, 1911, he confessed this to Paterne Berrichon, as reported by Yvonne Davet in her *Histoire des Nourritures terrestres:* "The *Illuminations* were my viaticum, nearly my only sustenance during the most important months of convalescence of my life." The third great writer born, like Gide and Valéry, around 1870, Claudel, proclaimed still more loudly his unconfined admiration for the man who had, he said, prepared him to accept Catholicism at the same time as a new kind of poetry. His literary debt to Rimbaud, openly admitted and publicized, exaggerated by him no doubt, is immense and has been the object of important studies.

One is astonished by contrast at the surrealists' relative silence about one whom they placed with Lautréamont in the first ranks of their literary gods. René Char, who was one of them before a rupture that he wanted to be more discreet about than that of others of the excommunicated heretics, is, among all of them, the most Rimbaldian and has written several remarkable pages on the poet.

André Breton never pretended to imitate a poet he venerated too much to dare invite comparison with him. None of the most highly visible of the surrealists, moreover, was tempted to imitate the silence of the author of *A Season in Hell*; suicide was the refuge taken by two or three of them, but for reasons that were often extraliterary. Breton, however, asked in his later days about the reason that had led him to speak so rarely of Rimbaud, recalled in his *Entretiens*,[1] the decisive year of his life, that in which, as a boarder at school in Nantes, he had met Jacques Vaché and discovered Rimbaud's work. Walking through the streets, the city parks, possessed by the poet, he thought he saw the settings, the images of the *Illuminations* rising up on every side. He pressed Apollinaire and Valéry with importunate questions about the poet whom he devoured with passion. It is no doubt Breton who, in no way devoid of critical spirit and flair (he was among the first to see through the deceit of the fake texts of "La Chasse spirituelle"), has best defined the feeling of love that brings twentieth-century readers to Rimbaud more than to any other poet. To understand such a poet is valuable, but the need as well as the capacity to understand is limited. "The virtue of a work is manifested only secondarily in the more or less scholarly exegeses to which it gives rise; it resides above all in the passionate adhesion that, in unceasingly growing numbers, young minds unhesitatingly show him. . . . At the outset, it is not a question of understanding, but rather of loving."[2]

4

THE TRAGIC IMPRESSIONISM OF VERLAINE

Verlaine, vulgarized for a time, ridiculously mutilated (because he was reduced to a few graceful but facile poems), caricatured in inaccurate biographies, had become in the first half of this century a great unknown among French poets. Even today, at a time when Nerval's most ephemeral works, Mallarmé's most artificial and distant ones, and the most amiable ones of that Verlainian poet that Apollinaire sometimes was are explained to excess in international colloquies or wantonly obfuscated in learned journals, the great poems of Verlaine receive relatively very little attention. For that reason, their freshness has at least been preserved. In his work there remain perhaps the greatest number of discoveries to be made by lovers of poetry, and even the greatest number of technical secrets to be elucidated, especially in regard to prosody, for those who truly wish to know symbolism.

Happily, the edition of Verlaine's poetic works prepared and edited by Yves-Gérard Le Dantec (and since reedited and published by Jacques Borel) provides a carefully established and easy-to-consult text. Jacques Robichez's edition of Verlaine's poetry (published by Garnier) is no less valuable. The two extensive volumes, containing up to their date of publication both the poetic works and most of the prose works, published in 1959–60 by *Le Club du Meilleur Livre*, with provocative introductions by two fervent students of Verlaine, Octave Nadal and Jacques Borel, are both elegant in format and of great usefulness. However, a suitable edition of the correspondence is still lacking, and the careful presentations of this or that segment of it (the letters exchanged with the painter F. A. Cazals, skillfully brought to light by Georges Zayed) do not suffice to fill this void. Although he was not the superb letter writer that Mallarmé was, Verlaine's letters sometimes enclose secrets about his personality, his intentions, and even his technique. Most fortunately, some French professors (Antoine Adam, J. -H. Bornecque, Claude Cuénot, Octave Nadal) and others, Swiss, Italian, British, and American, mentioned in more detail in our bibliographical note (Cecil Hackett, Ruth Moser, Karola Rost, V. P. Underwood, Marta Vogler, Georges Zayed, Eléonore Zimmermann) have, since around 1935, completely renewed our knowledge and appreciation of Verlaine. As early as 1933, in his book *De Baudelaire au surréalisme*, now a classic, Marcel Raymond suggested that "a slight modification in the present-day orientation of poetry might suffice to bring about a renewal of Verlainian influence." He himself has since considered Verlaine with admiration in other writings. To speak of Verlaine's influence on the poetry of 1930 or 1970 would scarcely make any sense. These later poetic works seek and find their way by themselves; they aim most often to be unadorned to the point of dryness, biting, sometimes reduced to an imperious aphorism, rarely inclined towards humor or smitten with musicality. Moreover, they show no greater evidence of Rimbaldian or Mallarméan influence or of any desire to redo Valéry or Claudel (two poets, incidentally, who have spoken quite well in praise of Verlaine). Verlaine had reflected on the art of poetry as much and quite as well as other French poets. It has been demonstrated how skilled his art is and to what extent he was a "man of letters," that is, at times knowingly calculating and anxious to place, and therefore to sell, his poetry. But he was not a man to prefer those enigmatic and disturbing formulas on the essence of poetry and on the Orphic explanation of the world that were enunciated by Baudelaire, by the seventeen-year-old Rimbaud, or later by Mallarmé. Now, it is by way of these handy formulas, quickly digested, more than through their more mysterious poems, that poets often attain the posterity of handbook readers—alas! the most influential of all.

He wrote too much, and many mediocre things. Those less prolific than he, like Coleridge or Baudelaire, or those who died while still writing, or who disappeared young, like Rimbaud and Keats, have in the last resort found themselves more fortunate. What is worse, Verlaine repeated himself; J. S. Bach, Antonio Vivaldi, Goethe himself, Hugo, and Claudel did the same, the latter taking the precaution of frequently contradicting himself. Verlaine often fell into vulgarity or into inconsequential platitudes. But criticism came to the final conclusion that there were some very fine works, fervent with youthfulness, in the poems of the fiftyish Victor Hugo and even in the works of the elderly Tennyson, or in the last canvases of Monet and Renoir. In Verlaine's case, it has taken much longer to revise lazily arrived at opinions that set the final limit of his important production at *Romances without Words* (1874; he was then thirty years old) or, at the furthest extent, at the religious verses and the laments emitted in prison and collected in *Wisdom*, written between 1875 and the date of their publication in book form in 1881. But the greater Verlaine, certainly the most tragic, is the one of the fifteen or so pieces in the volumes that followed: *Long Ago and Not so Long Ago* (1885), *Love* (1888), *In Parallel* (1889). And the very last of his poems, from 1895, "Mort," is not the least moving or the least artistically orchestrated.

If being called a "symbolist" meant above all to have recourse to symbols and to insinuate that a mysterious meaning resided behind the appearances of expression, Verlaine would be a symbolist only occasionally. But Verlaine occupies a considerable place, both in the history of the symbolist movement (his "Art poétique" and his sonnet on decadence have served much more effectively as rallying banners than all the manifestoes) and in the spiritual and technical enrichment of French poetry that occurred between 1870 and 1890. One often forgets today that it was he first of all, through his work and his early innovations, who initially fascinated the adolescent Rimbaud and contributed to showing him his way; the younger man very quickly showed more fierce boldness than the older one. Even then, Verlaine, so malleable and unresisting, revealed a certain independence in refusing to let himself be seduced by the voyant's theories and in accepting to serve as the target for his sarcasms. He understood that neither free verse nor the biblical *verset* nor the poem-in-prose suited him, and that objective poetry, if he had been capable of it, was not in itself superior to the other. Nevertheless, and better than any of those who are called symbolists (Mallarmé included), Verlaine proclaimed the superhuman or inhuman genius of his young friend. In truth, in several of his judgments or his remarks uttered somewhat casually on Baudelaire, on Poe (by whom he refused to be captivated), and later in his admittedly hasty articles on the *poètes maudits*, Verlaine revealed flair and perspicacity. As others have already remarked, he remained faithful to poetry and to a rather elevated idea of art, refusing to abandoi literature as Rimbaud did, or to toy with it in graceful "futile petitions" or witty quatrains that might be deciphered by the postman.

With respect to the psychological imbalance that is at the source of his poetry, Verlaine let it be understood more than once that he knew very well what was involved there, even if he lacked the will and perhaps the desire to discipline himself. "I have the rage to love. My so weak heart is mad," he pathetically admits in the fifth of his pieces entitled "Lucien Létinois" in *Love*. His avowal in a letter to Cazalis has often been cited: "I am a feminine person, which explains many things." Antoine Adam, as early as 1936, in one of the most subtle and most convincing studies in which psychoanalysis has served literary appreciation, then Guy Michaud in his *Message poétique du symbolisme* in 1947, have shown how well Verlaine's work can be elucidated by the deciphering of his temperament and by a character analysis of the poet's self. He knew himself to be profoundly, and no doubt incurably, "double," vacillating between the faun and the angel, the occasional tiger and the small child crying out his need to be commanded and loved. The perspicacity of his self-image is keen in a different way from that of many so-called personal poets, from Lamartine or Musset to Laforgue. He knew the strength of that "amativeness" within him that he could not resist. There is yet to be extracted from his prose and poetic works (in the former, often under the cover of characters into whom he projects his own self or behind whom he conceals himself, Gaspard Hauser or the condemned husband rising up from Hell in "Grace") a self-portrait of Verlaine that would be astonishingly accurate.

Verlaine's work is so closely entangled in his life that critics who have devoted themselves to it have hardly been able to avoid explications based on his heredity, his parents' indulgence, the keen awareness of his ugliness ("They did not find me handsome," Gaspard Hauser says of women), a first love for his cousin Eliza, broken off by death, and finally, homosexuality. Sensual rage and ecstatic rapture alternated in him, or rather coexisted, along with gentleness and contrition. Antoine Adam has shown what one can read into declarations by way of which the poet seems to rediscover old symbols of sexuality that on one occasion profess guilt and on another pride themselves on being unorthodox. "A falcon I soar, and I die a swan," he exclaims in the most inverted and daringly inverse of his sonnets, "The Good Disciple." He finds it delightful to abdicate, to allow himself to be engulfed in the vertiginous sensation of the swing that rocks him, of the carousel horse that turns, of the jig that he dances. He knows that he is like the dead leaf carried off by some ill wind, like the butterfly, like the pilotless vessel. At the moment, that forgetfulness is delightful, that langorousness is voluptuous and propitious to dreaming. Afterward, reality will take its revenge and remorse will gnaw him:

> Le ver est dans le fruit, le réveil dans le rêve
> Et le remords est dans l'amour: telle est la loi.

> The worm is in the fruit, the awakening in the dream,
> And within love is remorse: such is the law of things.

From this vertigo, from these bouts of repentance, will spring forth, however, confessional poems scarcely less bitter than those of Baudelaire, almost as uninhibited in their unabashed display of a dislocated self as the avowals of Dostoevski's characters. In marriage, in his liaison with the imperious dominator that Rimbaud was, in conversion, sometimes even in a childish patriotism, in promises to himself (set down in his diary) to "pray morning and night" and to attend mass everyday, Verlaine would seek the stability to which he aspired. All in vain. He was never really to find that discipline except in his craft as a poet and in the constraints he was able to impose on himself.

"This innocent," Paul Valéry, the most conscious and least undisciplined of verse writers, wrote of Verlaine, "is an organized primitive. . . . Never was there a more subtle art than this art that supposes that in it one flees from another and not that one precedes him." In the area of language, first of all, Verlaine joins the example to the precept, or rather furnishes examples well before formulating the precept, by wringing the neck of eloquence. Eloquence, to be sure, did not die of it; from "The Drunken Boat" to the "Five Great Odes" and the remarkable poets of 1950 or 1960, it survives and creates the merit of several of the most moving works of French poetry. But Verlaine broke with the somewhat encompassing unity of tone and style that characterized Les Fleurs du Mal almost as much as the works of Hugo or Leconte de Lisle. There is nothing stilted in him. He dared introduce familiar speech, popular turns of phrase, and even low-class words (*peuple*) in his verses, to write as one speaks among friends—"You! you've got your head someplace else" ("Toi! t'as du vague à l'âme"), to use "ça" repeatedly instead of "cela," to omit the pronoun before the third-person verb in the present tense ("faut pas"), to introduce the exclamatory "tiens" or "hein," or call wooden horses "dadas." Historians of the symbolists' language, such as Charles Bruneau, have pointed out provincialisms in the poet's verses, popular archaisms, the unselfconscious omission of "ne," which, in a negative expression, should precede the "pas," charming grammatical inaccuracies such as "faisez le beau" (for "faites le beau"), "plus pire" (for "pire" or "plus mauvais"). Odd poetic effects sometimes result from these insolent manipulations of speech, as in the celebrated lines of "Reversibilities" that set to dreaming one English poet, very much like Verlaine in his way of life, Ernest Dowson:

Ah, dans ces mornes séjours
Les Jamais sont les Toujours!

Ah, in these dreary abodes
The Nevers are the Always!

Similar effects are achieved with other adverbs, "Encores" or "Déjàs," put in the plural like substantives.

The French reader is so accustomed to demanding a certain purity of tone and to taking offense in numerous ways at the mixing of the genres, that Verlaine's semivulgarisms clash with the need for dignity and even for formality that he brings to the reading of poets. Verlaine, without affectation and with a knowing dose of humor and poetic vision, as an amused observer of others than himself, achieves an almost unique success in nineteenth-century poetry in pieces like "It's Jean de Nivelle's Dog" or "Brussels: Wooden Horses." The symbolic meaning of this last piece does not have to be emphasized by the poet, desirous of losing himself in the circular motion. Adroitly, following a few lighthearted lines ("It's wonderful what a buzz you get, going to that silly circus"), in the final stanza he dares evoke poetically the coming of night that sees the departure of the soldier and the maidservant, their Sunday diversion at the carnival ended:

Tournez, tournez! le ciel en velours
D'astres en or se vêt lentement.

Turn, turn! the sky, velvet-clad,
Slowly adorns itself with golden stars.

He would later advise the poet to avoid "impure laughter," which French poets have traditionally—and quite regrettably—in fact avoided in their works, especially the romantics. But Verlaine in practice frequently accepted it and did not judge it impure. Laforgue, Apollinaire, and various "fantasy poets" of our century were not to forget this precedent.

But still more than in the area of language and style (although an in-depth study of Verlainian metaphors deserves to be undertaken and ought to prove rich in possibilities), it is through his metrics that the poet showed himself to be a sometimes innovator and a very great master. As early as 1931–32 a very keenly precise article by P. Mathieu in the *Revue d'Histoire littéraire* analyzed the various lasting changes that Verlaine had brought to French prosody, still timorous among the romantics (Hugo excepted) and with Baudelaire. A book by Eléonore Zimmermann, impressive in its sharp subtlety and its erudition, has analyzed Verlaine's work very closely in its musicality, its stylistic methods, as much as in its inspiration and its affinities with other forms of poetic expression, notably that of Rimbaud.

The example of his more deliberately revolutionary young friend, it is readily admitted, prompted the author of *Romances without words* (1873) to put behind him what had been facile and traditional in his previous collections. Verlaine himself, always generous in that regard, stated this to be the case. To tell the truth, it is not at all certain that the elder of the two poets, frightened by the audaciousness of the younger man, and especially by his theories (which he considered demoniacal), was not made more cautious because of that. Verlaine was already, before knowing Rimbaud, the author of Sapphic love poems published in Brussels in 1867 under a quite transparent pseudonym, and also of the collection entitled *Fêtes galantes*, judged by the schoolboy Rimbaud in Charleville, as early as August 25, 1870, "most strange, very odd and truly... adorable." Free verse, in any case, suited Verlaine no more than Mallarmé, Apollinaire, or Valéry, and he did not deceive himself on that score. Aggravated at the end of his career by the innovations of young poets who seemed to reject him, he spoke out as a conservative embittered against those who thus claimed "to lay a hand on verse."

More than any other, nevertheless, Verlaine worked to alter the profound character of the alexandrine by multiplying the number of ternary lines, by boldly varying the cesura, by accumulating odd run-on lines that broke out of the verse mold and came close to certain prose poems: dialogues with God or Christ in *Wisdom*, an astounding piece in the same volume that invokes the voices of Pride, Hate, and the Flesh in order to entreat them to die and to make way for the voice of Prayer and "the terrible Voice of Love." He will vilify rhyme in a celebrated line from his "Art poétique." The most skillful of rhymers (and the most discreet of them when he wanted to be), Verlaine makes light of rhyme at other times, forming couplets that end with the two words "choisi" and "quasi," "gai" and "guet," playing with bizarre words ("up-chucked" ["débagoulé"], "tribades"), in the hardly edifying "Saturnian Poem" from *In Parallel*. Above all, he modifies the alexandrine while rendering it more supple with such virtuosity that the ear no longer knows if it is hearing ten, eleven, or thirteen syllables or where the verse line, segmented by run-on lines and odd divisions, begins or ends. Verlainian metrics often seem to reject any kind of syllabication and are based on combinations of very expert stresses, so expert that they often fall on conjunctions or on particles astonished to find themselves thus ennobled. With a daring that few French poets have had, Verlaine took delight in composing poems made up of odd-syllable lines: five syllables ("In the Interminable," in which frequent recurrence of rhymes reinforces the impression of monotonous boredom), of seven or nine syllables (the former very frequent and most often admirably successful, as in "Wooden Horses" and "Art poétique"). But it is mastery of the eleven-syllable line, for example in the most grandiose of all Verlaine's poems ("*Crimen Amoris*"), and in the thirteen-syllable line ("A Tale" in *Love*; less happily in the pious poetry of 1893 that begins with "Little Jesus who already suffers in your flesh"). Often, running every risk, Verlaine triumphantly won. Ronsard had been able to endow certain heptasyllabic poems with a hesitant and seductive grace; but it is Verlaine who imposed upon French ears both this line and the nine-syllable line from this or that "forgotten arietta." After

him, Frenchmen have recited "It is the langorous Ecstasy" or "I detect through
a Murmur" quite as familiarly as though it were a matter of one of Villon's or
Gautier's lines, or one from Baudelaire's "To Her Who Is too Gay." The very
new stress combinations of the Verlainian hendecasyllables (two groups of four
syllables and one of three in a number of lines from "*Crimen Amoris*"), the
fragmentations of the verse line when the poet uses the article *les* to form the
rhyme, the words that the article announces ("seven sins") being, for the eye
alone, carried over to the following line, makes the poet the first in France who
cannot be reduced to a system based on syllabic count. With him, French
versification at last proclaims that it rests on individual combinations and not on
a mechanical counting of syllables. Later in his career, the aged poet was to feel
himself outdistanced by the young symbolists of 1885 and made fun of their
innovations. But since Rimbaud was not known, and since Mallarmé remained a
traditionalist in matters of versification, it was Verlaine who had made their
attempts possible.

Verlaine's mind was without doubt not the most disposed to construct coherent and rigorous doctrines. Nonetheless, and paradoxically, no French poem in
the latter quarter of the nineteenth century and for some years to come in the
twentieth, not even Baudelaire's "Correspondences," has had more striking effect
as a poetic manifesto than "Art poétique," composed in 1873–74 and published
in 1882 in a review and in 1885 in the volume *Long Ago and Not So Long Ago*.
In that volume the poet sets forth, in the form of precepts (or rather of advice),
what his work, from before 1873 (and even before he had known Rimbaud), had
put into practice. Did he write it under Rimbaud's influence? It is generally
stated that he did, but gratuitously, and without doubt by way of a too elementary
simplification of the very mysterious concept of "influence." Other recollections
that some have thought to find there (from Shakespeare's *Twelfth Night*, for
example) are even more problematical. The piece, if worthwhile for its content
and its doctrinal statements, is no less significant for the emotions with which it is
charged (this defense of freedom and imagination by a prisoner) and for the
exquisite art of its vocabulary and its rhythm. Several commentators mentioned
in our bibliographical note, in particular J. -H. Bornecque in a review published
in Turkey, have shown this to be true on the basis of evidence.

Verlaine states first of all, not in a didactic counsel but in an impassioned cry,
the primacy of music in poetry, and foreshadows, without knowing it, the symbolists and their successors, Pierre Louÿs and Paul Valéry, who chose later to
consider music as the rival necessary to despoil to the profit of poetry. Image,
symbol, are at one blow relegated to a secondary level. This music will be above
all that finer, newer one born of the odd-syllable line that melts away as did poor
Lélian's will and that rejects pose and affectation, and weighty stability if, indeed,
Verlaine meant to play with the double meaning of the verb *qui pose*. That kind
of ambiguity Verlaine calls "misapprehension" ("méprise"), and he recommends
it: it forces upon the reader an active way of reading that Mallarmé was soon to
demand by asking the reader to seek out the key to poetic mystery. In the very

graceful third stanza, by way of three metaphorical evocations, Verlaine offers a
few illustrations of this mystery while taking care himself, as one of the clearest of
poets, to use the adjective *clear* ("clair"). For, Valéry was to say later, what is
more obscure and more profound than clarity? In the same stanza, the adjective
trembling ("tremblant") is no less important; beauty for the poet is inconceivable
without mobility or without vibration.

Like the painters who, shortly after the composition of this poem, were in
1874 to take to themselves the term *impressionists*, by which people had thought
to ridicule them, Verlaine forcefully lays claim to the nuance, mother of dreams
and of soft spiritual harmonies in place of color. At the home of Nina de Villars, he
had often encountered Manet who asserted: "The principal character of a painting is light." The prosaicness of the artful conceit and of clever wittiness is
banished, though not that form of it that comes from recourse to the familiar that
Verlaine practiced. Eloquence is vilified in the well-known outcry. Rhyme,
which Verlaine in practice never renounced (although he may have treated it
with disrespect), is condemned if it is too rich. Before everything else, let poetry
be escape, adventure, unceasing aspiration towards the new: let it suggest, like
music, the unexpressed; it does not reject precision, but prefers it to be limited
and to serve as a foil to ambiguity.

This pursuit of vagueness that is "muted" ("en sourdine"—also the title of one
of the poems from *Fêtes galantes*), of the half-light, of grisaille, or "morning
twilight" ("crépuscule du matin," the orginal title of "L'Angélus du matin") or of
evening twilight—is quite another matter and much more than a technique for
Verlaine. It translates his rejection of brutality, of the too-neat choice between
the flesh and the soul, between angelism and the mire, between the drunken
man's brutality and childlike gentleness, and even between one sex and the
other. Verlaine's poems on lesbians are much more than an erotic game on a
theme that Gautier, Baudelaire, and many others since Sappho had touched
upon. The "Songs of the Ingénues" in Verlaine's first collection, these artless
young women who know themselves to be "the future lovers of libertines," allude
to the hero of sexual transvestitism, the gracious and cunning Faublas. Another
piece, in *Les Fêtes galantes*, has as its title "The Ingénus," male this time, but
their words are "specious," the autumn evening is "equivocal," and even their
sex is vague, as are the commentators of many poems who are undecided
whether to read Mathilde or Arthur behind works like "Forgotten Arietta" or
even "Water Color," in which the author dreams of letting his head roll upon a
young breast. In more than one domain, Verlaine spontaneously translates the
deep secret of his vacillating nature by avoiding the clear-cut, the decisive, the
choice that was later to disturb the Gide of *Fruits of the Earth* because it forces
one to renounce what one has not chosen and some potentiality within oneself.
In his old age, and like so many others turned conservative (Baudelaire, also
weary, had indeed conceded to his younger friend Manet that he was foremost,
but "in the decrepitude of his art"), Verlaine treated his "Art poétique" lightly in
1890, while sounding this warning—tinged however with a rare modesty—to the

young: "Do not take my 'Art poétique' at face value; after all it is only a song." At
that time he made himself the apostle of common sense, especially against the
dogmatic doctrines of the technicians. That "Art poétique," so undidactic, so
lilting and mocking, remains the only one still alive among the ten or fifteen
poems of the same, or almost the same, title that, since Gautier and Mallarmé,
French poets have written (Tristan Klingsor, Francis Jammes, Max Jacob, J. -M.
Bernard, André Salmon, Jean Cocteau, André Spire, and various surrealists).

Around this period in his life, between 1871 and 1874, Verlaine was equally
seminal in creating (or nearly so, if Victor Hugo's poems that can be called
impressionist, such as "Evening Things" in *The Art of Being a Grandfather* are
excepted), in the poetic domain, literary impressionism. Here again, his
originality seems complete. He was scarcely touched by the example of Edmond
and Jules de Goncourt, and very little by that of the painters, even those
like Monet and Pissaro whom he might have been able to see in London in 1871
or in Ignace Fantin-Latour's studio. The very tempting and very dangerous
parallels that critics strive periodically to propose between the three forms of
impressionism—pictorial, musical, literary—do not help very much. The practitioners of these three art forms are conditioned by the techniques of expression,
the medium, the autonomy peculiar to each of them. It is more natural to expect
of the poet that he pierce or tear away the veil that he draws over reality or over
the canvas on which he traces it, and touch upon the secret or the import that lies
beyond. The exaggerated claims to the synthesis of the arts and to an ambitious
and heady orphism count among the least fortunate aftereffects of the symbolist
movement. The transpositions of art dear to Gautier and even the synesthetic
effects described in the tercets of the celebrated Baudelairian sonnet scarcely
went beyond the picturesque or the piquant. It would amount to a kind of
purism, however, to seek to raise an insurmountable barrier between writers,
painters, and musicians who, in Paris especially, live, discuss, and create in close
proximity to one another. Prudently, in the last great article that he had written
on Delacroix, Baudelaire had observed that the arts are incapable of taking one
another's place, but that they could in our times "reciprocally lend one another
new strengths."

Verlaine did not venture to formulate the theory of any certain literary impressionism. He wrote from London to Edmond Le Pelletier at the end of 1872,
when he was making an effort to learn more about English art (for which he
cared little, but which he was perhaps to like better in the long run): "In the
meantime, like Mérat, I am collecting impressions." After so much classic,
romantic, and Parnassian poetry that explained, proclaimed, reasoned, or, in
any case, went beyond sensations, Verlaine, out of temperament, had preferred
to let himself be lightly touched and sometimes invaded by landscapes and
objects, refusing to interpret them or to ask them their secret. The frequency of
expressions of his ignorance, of his uncertainty, of his refusal to know, is revealing: "what?" "who?" "we don't know why," "I am unaware." Often he avoids
organizing sketchy details in an ordered landscape, not from lack of skill, for he is

the author of one of the best composed landscapes there is, in the very beautiful poem contained in the collection *Love*, "Bournemouth," but because he wanted only to enumerate, to juxtapose, while omitting verbs and adjectives, as in the graceful Belgian landscape entitled "Walcourt," composed in lines of four syllables with two tonic accents. Realism? Not precisely, for this reality is permeated with phantoms ("Charleroi"); the sounds of wind, of some forge, the whistling of grass in cold blasts, trains that thunder, even odors; all of these are "sinister," and the poet renders this shuddering of things and of his entire being. Above all, everything there moves, runs, flees. Few poets have so well rendered in French this feeling of something ephemeral, disturbing, in which the self is dissolved, which Joseph Eichendorff, Nikolaus Lenau, or an impressionist like Edward Moerike have captured in the German language. "Simple Frescoes" in heptasyllables and in entirely feminine rhymes, in *Romances without Words*, is a slender, graceful, and disturbing masterpiece:

> La fuite est verdâtre et rose
> Des collines et des rampes,
> Dans un demi-jour de lampes
> Qui vient brouiller toute chose.

> The flight is greenish and pink
> Of hills and slopes,
> In a dim lamp's light
> That comes to confuse all things.

In *Romances without Words* as well, and also in heptasyllables, the untitled piece that opens with "The ordered ranks of the hedgerows" ("L'Echelonnement des haies") is one of the most original works of Verlaine the impressionist. The verb *unfurls* ("moutonne") brings together from the start the plain dissected by hedgerows and the image of foamy waves. Everything is in movement—hills, trees, young horses in the fields, lambs, and the swirling rain. No feeling, no lament is suggested. The masterpiece of this type is doubtless "In the Interminable/Tedium of the plain," in pentasyllables. The word *tedium* ("ennui") brings together the impression received by the poet and the feeling of dreary monotony that weighs upon his soul. The blackness of the sky is interpreted through comparisons, to the moon, for example, that seems to live and die. The oaks appear to float like storm clouds in the grisaille that blends together sky and earth; the thoughts of the poet, who does not want to complain in his own name, transfers to imaginary animals, in the form of questions, his internal desolation. The real is grasped but never immobilized or materialized. Verlaine does not try to take hold of this reality as Rimbaud does, to incorporate it into a construction of his own like a demiurge recreating the world. He does not seek, like a voyant, to supplement it with a superreality. He translates the astonishment of his sometimes childlike soul and that headiness born of the void into which he feels himself perpetually upon the point of sinking. Beyond external notations that are a form of realism (but a magic realism in the manner of the German romantics), one denotes Verlaine's effort to forget himself, to escape life's wounds and his feeling of guilt—from before the time of the pistol shot and the prison at Mons.

It would be idle to exaggerate the similarities between Verlaine the poet and this or that one among the painters who were his contemporaries. He is not, like them, a colorist; he does not have their luminosity or the serene patience of their attention to the out-of-doors. More than they, he feels himself to be a musician and inclined towards gently soothing reveries. There is in truth a literary impressionism that runs parallel to the need to harden and stiffen reality that was typical of Flaubert and Maupassant. The Goncourts are the prose authors who had the clearest awareness of it and who, in passages that one would prefer to isolate from the rest of their work, have given remarkable samples of it in prose. Mallarmé, as early as March 1865, wrote to Henri Cazalis, alluding to his "Hérodiade": "I have discovered there an intimate and unique way of sketching and noting very fugitive impressions." Hugo, we know, called him, in a surprisingly exact remark: "My dear impressionist poet." There are those who sometimes seek to limit Verlainian impressionism to a brief period in his career—1872-74—and to convince themselves that afterwards he went beyond it. He certainly changed, and he understood the danger of monotony that that kind of art runs. But there remains much of this feeling of the fluidity of all things and of what is elusive, in poems from which neither the inner life nor feelings in which impressions complement one another are banished. Other than the very well-known sonnet of the summer of 1873, "Hope gleams. . ." (Wisdom), in which impressions and discreet symbols are wedded (a piece of straw that is perhaps grace, a wasp that could be woman, consoling water, the pebble in a hollow place), several of Verlaine's most beautiful poems are still impressionistic, but composed rather than juxtaposed and incorporating within them the dramatic element of time that flies and and that overlays impressions of the present with nostalgia for the past and anguish before the future. We would include among these poems that ought to be the very first to represent Verlaine in an anthology of French impressionistic poetry: "The Morning Angelus" from Long Ago and Not So Long Ago (published under a different title in the first issue of Le Parnasse Contemporain), "Kaleidoscope" from the same collection that dates from the prison years (October 1873), and, later, that subtle poem on the imagination that bears the title "Limbo" in In Parallel (1889).

Artists and art critics who, around 1885, turned away from pictorial impressionism, like the very remarkable and short-lived Albert Aurier, reproached it with being a surface art, a kind of realism too slavishly submissive to the visible appearance and the color of things and landscapes, uninterested in the absolute and in being. The pursuit of that absolute and the disdain for the concrete and the fleshly did not always succeed, moreover, for the English pre-Raphaelites, for the philosophical painters of Germany, or even for Gustave Moreau, Odilon Redon, and Puvis de Chavannes in their less good moments. But if, in effect, the absence of the tragic can be deplored among painters such as Monet, Renoir, or Alfred Sisley (whose daily existence amid poverty and among general incomprehension nonetheless skirted tragedy more than once), this reproach cannot be addressed to Verlaine. More than Rimbaud, who was less gnawed by remorse and less haunted by the flesh than Verlaine, more than Mallarmé whose torment was metaphysical and literary, Verlaine lived tragically; it is he who could most accurately be seen as a parallel to Van Gogh. "Kaleidoscope," "Bournemouth," and "There," another poem inspired by the section of London called "Angels," stand among the greatest poems in French of throbbingly painful memories, of anguish, and of visionary dreams welling up out of reality. In the first of these pieces, past and future are confounded in an irresistible whirlwind, as often in Verlaine. The setting is that of the large city that had fascinated the two friends vagabonding among the streets of the British metropolis, though here it is a "dream city," a "magic city" (lines one and nine). The rupture, the one's scorn for the pitiful "mad virgin," the other's exasperation, and, then, his "cellular" life emerge. Will he be able to relive the past? "A slow awakening after many metempsychoses?" The poet sees again in his mind the vulgarity of the city and its hideous festivities, which were nonetheless dear to him; of the future he expects nothing. He calls upon death, but directly, without romantic rhetoric. Will it be the awakening from a dream, the dream of life, "life's unquiet dream" to use Shelley's phrase? Then, again, the descent into the dream and into the same pitiable weaknesses?

> Ce sera comme quand on rêve et qu'on s'éveille,
> Et que l'on se rendort et que l'on rêve encor
> De la même féerie et du même décor,
> L'été, dans l'herbe, au bruit moiré d'un vol d'abeille.

> That will be as when one dreams and when one awakens
> And goes back to sleep and dreams once again
> Of the same fairy tale and the same setting
> In the summertime, in the grass, to the shimmering hum of a flight of bees.

The word *kaleidoscope* contains within itself the adjective that signifies "beautiful," and Verlaine tried to see as beautiful, through the darkness of what lay in wait for him, his dream of the future. He cannot believe in it. He knows himself to be the slave of his destiny, and he bows his head. "It will be so ineluctable that one will think to die of it." A few years later, he wrote "Bournemouth," when he was teaching in England. In his *Confessions* of 1894, he recalled that visit and the landscape. Modestly, he added: "I also wrote an entirely insignificant poem, entitled 'Bournemouth,' that people are quite pleased to find good." Octave Nadal was to say correctly of that admirable work, which is symbolist in more ways than one: "It is the roar, the death rattle, and the stubbornness of the sea that find their correspondences in the tortured and patient heart of the poet." Claudel, who had had the courage in his youth, when it was not fashionable to do so, to celebrate Verlaine, declared in his later days (in his *Improvised*

Mémoirs from his eighty-second year) that this poem was "one of the most beautiful pieces of French poetry." With a worthy independence of taste, he added, rightly in our eyes, that it was not in his Catholic collection, *Wisdom*, but in *Love* (published in 1888) that Verlaine had attained the summit of his art.

"There," from the same collection, entirely stamped with the memories of London, and transpierced by the passage of grace while he recalls his "old sins," a symbolist poem in its own way, is discreetly haunted by Rimbaud's memory. It is in the twenty or so poems that form the Rimbaud cycle that Verlaine attains the tragic. These pieces range from a few ariettas from the beginning of their liaison to the most immodest lines, "Verses for Being Vilified," and "Lusts" in *Long Ago and Not so Long Ago,* and to the two pathetic sonnets of *Dedications* (1890), addressed to Rimbaud (the second, inserted later in *Dedications,* is from 1893) "Mortal, Angel AND Demon," "You, dead, dead, dead."

People have evinced distaste for certain of these poems. There are those, in fact, like numbers IV, V, and VI of the "Old Coppées," interlarded with slang and very free in their language, that wallow in obscenity. The inverse sonnet "The Good Disciple" flaunts insolently, as no poem in any other language has dared, the physical ecstasy sought by the two companions. But the very brutality of that frankness which seeks to make a display of itself only barely hides Verlaine's secret remorse, recalling past pleasures and knowing with what regrets and what abandonment they were followed. "Laeti et errabundi" is a poem otherwise radiant with beauty in its boasting. Verlaine, so feminine himself, and whom the need for feminine tenderness and understanding always pursued, takes pleasure in crying out his disdain for orthodox love: ". . . detached / From women taken pity upon / And from the last of prejudices." No doubt he is echoing certain of the mocking remarks about his need for women and grace, and on the subject of his very real suffering at the time of his divorce, that his young partner must have often repeated. The piece is swept away by an inflamed outburst; it closes with the admirable verses in which the poet celebrates his forever absent friend as a "god among the demigods" and refuses to believe him dead. "He lives his life," and that exalting love burns his veins and radiates in his brain. Verlainian eroticism is one of the most ardent and the most splendidly expressed in all literature, equaled by neither the Marquis de Sade nor Jean Genêt in prose nor Victor Hugo or Pierre Louÿs in poetry. Verlaine is the poet of the flesh, as he was at other times and in other pieces, the poet of virginal reveries and of the soul's longings.

But this exaltation of the flesh is very far from being joy alone. Verlaine knows that desire is insatiable, and he recalls this in another very beautiful piece of insolent avowal ("These passions they alone still call love"); he boasts of being the apostle of that reinvented love. He knows as well, however, the weariness and disgust of both rapture and sensual satisfaction. In his boldest collection, *In Parallel,* he included two sonnets of "Explanation" in which he confessed "satiety to be an obscene machine," and a "Saturnian poem" in which he depicts himself sinking into the mire, jeered at by hooligans in the street, fallen to the lowest degree of abject humiliation.

It is in certain ones of these poems from the Rimbaud cycle that Verlaine reached the depths and the summit of the tragic, on a par with Baudelaire, and better than any other poet from what is called the symbolist movement. It has become fashionable to declare as outmoded the verse tale, of which Musset, Keats, and Matthew Arnold in England had given some very fine examples. It is not even certain that these verse tales, a kind of indirect lyricism avoiding the self and its laments, may not be preferable, in Musset's case, to the "Nights" and "Hope in God." More than one poetry lover, rejecting passing fashions, may have regretted that French symbolism and its immediate successors should have abandoned poetic domains where free rein could be given to narrative account, drama, inventive fantasy, and humor. Poetry did not as a matter of course gain anything in being reduced to lapidary aphorisms and to abrupt discontinuity. To be sure, some banalities slip into the hundreds of alexandrines of "Grace" or "Final Impenitence" (*Long Ago and Not so Long Ago*). But Verlaine embodies therein the torment that is his during those years when he is unable to resign himself to the abandon upon which Rimbaud has decided and to bury his memories of complete joy experienced with him. The claims of the flesh are less plainspoken than in the more directly personal and vulgar pieces in the late-published collection, *Flesh*, in which the poet wants to make himself believe that the pagan times regretted by Lucretius can be reborn, the bodies of lovers embracing one another in the forests like does and stags. The battle between the Devil and salvation, the headiness of knowing oneself to be damned, and the vague feeling that it is to the damned (as in the novels of François Mauriac and Julien Green) that grace prefers to go, renders these tales lugubrious and tragic. "Don Juan Duped," in decasyllables, shouts blasphemies: "The Flesh is holy, we must worship it," and contains something of the fearful boldness within revolt of Balzac's novella *The Elixir of Long Life*. But the masterpiece of the genre, and perhaps Verlaine's masterpiece, is the great symbolic and apocalyptic poem to which he gave the Latin title "Crimen amoris." Verlaine recounted in *My Prisons* how he composed this diabolical tale in the early days of his incarceration, using a small piece of wood and on paper having served to wrap his meager food ration. He later reworked it a great deal. Some Baudelairian memory wandered about his brain when he incarnated in his sixteen-year-old friend (Verlaine several times attributed that age to the urchin-genius who invaded his life in 1871) the most beautiful of angels, Lucifer. In an oriental palace in the midst of an orgy where the Seven Deadly Sins flaunt themselves, during the course of an enchanted night, the adolescent suddenly appears. There, he cries out impudently his rebellious will against conventional morality, against narrow and timorous love, against God: "Oh, I shall be he who will create God!" He wants to marry the Seven Deadly Sins to the Three Theological Virtues, good and evil, heaven and hell. He lights an immense cauldron of fire in which "Satan, his brothers and his sisters" die as (in certain of the *Illuminations*) the victims of the capricious prince die. He offers to some new and maleficent divinity this sacrificial conflagration.

Punishment comes in a lugubrious twilight of the gods and of men. "The

sacrifice had not been accepted." Verlaine cries out the terror that his friend's
monstrous pride inspired in him. In a very beautiful finale, the night becomes
once again serene, an "evangelical" softness (Verlaine used this adjective) has
succeeded the harsh Rimbaldian colors: black, red, gold. Nature once again at
peace "professes / The clement God who will guard us from evil." Verlaine,
fraught with fear, aspires to punishment and peace. He cannot brace himself to
go beyond "morality, that weakness of the intellect" vilified by his friend, and
resolutely bypass the distinction between good and evil, the better and the worse.
He already senses the submission, if not the denial, to which his friend was to
resign himself, far from the Western world, and, on his deathbed, having
perhaps murmured childishly, "Then, it was evil." The form of the poem of
twenty-five stanzas (one less than the "Femmes damnées" of Baudelaire of which
it makes one think), Verlaine's most brilliantly colored and most dramatic, and
the originality of his hendecasyllabic lines divided after the fourth syllable, then
after the seventh—sometimes the sixth—make it the most successful of Verlaine's works and perhaps the most tragic of all the poetry that is called symbolist.

5

MALLARMÉ

It is almost certain that, in the second half of the twentieth century, Mallarmé's glory has risen to a peak from which its brilliance shines more ardently than that of Baudelaire or of any other French poet. He is the most beloved among young poetry lovers. His work, more mysterious, has guarded its secrets more jealously even than that of Hugo, Verlaine, or Rimbaud's prose poems. It is more tempting (and easier) to memorize and recite for oneself with quasi-voluptuous pleasure "L'Après-midi d'un faune" or "Other Fan" than almost any other French poem. In them, sensual pleasure and intellectual enjoyment are harmoniously joined. But what surprises present-day Frenchmen whose grandparents so ridiculed this incomprehensible and unfathomable poet is that the most expert and the most diligent among the fervent admirers of Mallarmé's work are, at least half of them, foreigners. Of the exegetes who have done the most to elucidate the very abstruse poems, a great number are found to be Germans, Swiss, North Americans (R. G. Cohn is in the first rank among them), and especially Australians (Lloyd Austin, A. R. Chisholm, Gardner Davies, James Lawler, Kevin O'Neill, and still others). Mallarmé would have been amused if someone had told him that the most carefully detailed explication of "Prose for des Esseintes" or for the sonnet "yx" would come from Australia and New Zealand. This author, who was so Parisian, so little traveled, so bourgeois even in his modest professor's existence, discoursing on Tuesday evenings in his dining room, surrounded by the buffet, the clock, and the bowl of punch (bourgeois, it has been said, in the way that Bach, Kant, and Flaubert were), has, since 1870, come to be perhaps the most universal of poets. Happily for him—and for them—he has had few imitators. But James Joyce's reflections quite as much as Valéry's and then the speculations of linguists and stylisticians are greatly indebted to him.

This cult that counts only a very few heretics no doubt contains a certain danger. One hardly dares formulate any reservation concerning so slender and exceptional, but nonetheless uneven, a body of work. The young are likely to be attracted to it because they believe they thereby enter into a chosen circle that sets them apart from the common herd, "that dreary mob." The Mallarméan religion of Poetry as the sole legitimate way to attain the Absolute has contributed to turning away from French poetry a number of readers of taste and goodwill whom the hieratic ritualism of the Master leaves cold and whom his interpreters have taken hardly any pains to enlighten. What is more, precious hordes of ingeniousness have been lavished by a number of critics to elucidate such and such a sonnet or this or that quatrain, some mysteriously symbolic image, some rare word, or one diverted from its "impure" meaning. It seems sometimes, to read these critics, that only with naïveté may one derive enjoyment from that poetry or bring to it a value judgment, prefer Verlaine's "Tomb" to that of

Baudelaire, consider certain "Little Airs" puerile or certain other pieces too sophisticated in their preciousness.

Above all, each new exegete thinks himself bound to reconcile earlier interpretations (sometimes radically opposed) of a poem or a line, or, on the contrary, of undertaking a formal refutation of explications offered by his predecessors and of showing that he surpasses them in subtlety. "To the best minds / What errors are promised!" say two of Valéry's lines of verse. Certain of the interpretations offered by very erudite academic critics throw out a challenge not only to common sense but to intelligence and taste. The most abstruse sources find themselves assigned to the verse of a poet who read little: the Kabbala, Eliphas Lévi, and others. Now, Mallarmé, professors ought to know, had somewhat to prepare his classes, his compositions to correct in addition to his family life, his life as a sought-after and obliging friend, that of a lover perhaps, and his life of reverie incurred upon by his detested daily work. Some persons believe this work can be read only with the help of laborious commentaries, but this is not the case at all for at least two-thirds of the poems, and these not the least beautiful or the least profound for their not being the most tortuous. As the result of carping so much over the others, we have neglected the reading, which might prefer to remain naïve and, so to speak, purely hedonistic, of some admirable prose poems of Mallarmé, of his *Correspondence*, about fifty of the letters that are probably among the most beautiful ever written by a French poet. One who took no pains to hide his disdain for the critics (whether they were favorable or hostile to him) and for all commentary on his poetic works finds himself seventy-five years after his death buried under a heap of exegeses, often more foolish, but alas less poetically and less tragically so, than the oddities of which the author of *Igitur* accused himself.

The problem with this heaping up of explications is serious. Mallarmé, doubtless, did not want an art for everyone, which he had lucidly repudiated in one of his first writings. He knew very well that, like every innovator, he would have to create his public little by little. But he did not want this public to be composed only of professors and scholars, and even less of psychiatrists, psychoanalysts, and students of eroticism, which might appear to be the case ever since the deciphering of his verse has been undertaken with a seriousness that might well have caused this master of irony that he knew he was to smile. To be sure, as every successor of Baudelaire and Balzac was free to do around 1865, he was pleased to scatter a few allusions to courtesans. His very Baudelairian "anguish" caused him, in the sonnet so entitled (*Angoisse*), to evoke one "who knows more about nothingness than the dead." Barren like her, but more tormented by his betrayal of an inaccessible ideal, he is, he says, "afraid of dying when I go to bed alone." The poem on the Negress buffeted by the demon of lubricity is excessively lacking in ambiguity and, moreover, in originality, but it shows that Mallarmé could amuse the artists' studios or feed the jokes of frequenters of cabarets as Théophile and Antoine de Saint-Amant had done long ago, or later on, the author of "A Carrion." It is permissible to read immodest riddles in "Introduce

Me into Your Story," and it has been done. People long speculated whether the crime (as it is called) of the Faun was in wanting to separate two lesbians or in wanting to caress both of them at one time, or whether the two nymphs that he wants to perpetuate represent only abstract and metaphysical values. This game of the commentators is vain indeed and serves only to spoil the enjoyment of one of the most delicately sensual poems in French. An erudite foreigner, Austin Gill, goes so far as to see in the two young persons, entwined and then divided, two ethics between which Mallarmé hesitates or, still more unlikely, two women, one a mystic in her own way and the other more carnal, from George Sand's novel *Lélia*, a work that the poet had undoubtedly never opened.

People have speculated with no less indiscreet learning about the loves of Mallarmé himself. They were no doubt prompted to do so by the fact that, no less than Baudelaire had, he slipped into his poetic work many allusions to real women: his own wife to begin with (in "Gift of the Poem" for example), the young Englishwoman Ettie Yapp, loved and left intermittently by his friend Henri Cazalis, later married to an eminent Egyptologist, Gaston Maspero. She died in 1875, and it is probably she who speaks from beyond the grave in Mallarmé's very beautiful sonnet "On the Forgotten Woods..." It is probable that Mallarmé in 1861–62 had felt some tenderness for this young and, we are told, charming foreigner: "Ettie and you were one of my dearest surviving dreams of the future," he wrote to Cazalis in July 1862, expressing discreet regret over their falling out. It is she who doubtless inspired in the poet his first perfect poetic success, "Apparition," in 1862, much less revised than any other of Mallarmé's poems in later versions, notably in the one he gave Verlaine in 1884, for his *Poètes maudits*.

Finally there is an entire cycle devoted to Marie-Rose Laurent, married very young to a bourgeois who worked in the grocery business; he quickly abridged and poeticized her name into Mary or Méry. She gave herself to Coppée, to a few other poets, and to Manet. The sardonic Irishman George Moore, who then haunted the studios of the Batignolles painters, called her "the whole gamut" ("Toute la lyre"). Her titular lover, or protector, was an American dentist. Her hair is immortalized in Mallarmé's verses on several occasions. She reflected a dream of a blond beauty who had always touched the imagination of the poet who, already at the age of twenty, had celebrated in his "Futile Petition," in the only line in this sonnet that he was to preserve intact throughout all its versions, that "Blonde whose divine hairdressers are goldsmiths." It is true that the piece was addressed to two other women before finding its more-or-less definitive form in the *Poètes maudits* of 1884. Moreover, we know very little about the role this lady of rather doubtful literary taste—comparable in several regards to Madame Sabatier, whom Baudelaire thought he loved and whom he celebrated (among others)—played in Mallarmé's life and perhaps in his inspiration. One likes to believe that after the death of Manet, the poet's friend, she granted to Mallarmé all the satisfactions of which he could have dreamed. A Belgian writer, Robert Goffin, had it from Edouard Dujardin (who had it, it appears, from Méry

Laurent) that, whether through weakness on his part, whether through the lady's adroitness, Mallarmé "had never been able to carry to a completely carnal resolution the great love that he dedicated to her."[1] Such might be the sense of the more than tepid sonnet "Lady Without Too Much Ardor" on a love become friendship and the anniversary of which revives untumultuously "All our native monotonous friendship" in the last line.

The detail is of slight importance for the admirer of Mallarmé's poetry; but the question that every critic, Sainte-Beuve maintained, should pose in order fully to understand a writer, "How does he love?" is not totally without interest. Mallarmé's feelings toward the woman who became his wife, when he made up his mind without great enthusiasm, at the age of twenty-one, in London (April 1863), "to legalize the beating of their two hearts," was to play a role in the anguish, the despair, the moral solitude that assailed the poet at Tournon, Besançon, and Avignon, no less than his meditations on the absolute and on nothingness. Mallarmé's poetry is far from being impassive in the Parnassian mode or totally objective as that desired by Rimbaud. A psychoanalysis of Mallarmé has been sketched out and it is customary to praise, for it is in fact of great value, the *Vie de Mallarmé* by Mondor; but, as a matter of fact, a spiritual biography of the poet is yet to be written.

The youthful letters of the poet are revealing and marked by an exquisite simplicity, as are those to his young German fiancée (the most touching in French since those from Victor Hugo, also twenty years old at the time, to his fiancée, Adèle) and those to his friend Cazalis in which the poet reasons with himself surrounding the excellent motivations he has for deciding upon this marriage: "She is as intelligent as a woman can be without being a monster. It is up to me to make an artist of her." The verb, conspicuously, is not put in the future tense. He adds, like every male bourgeois: "After two years spent with me, Marie will be my reflection."[2] She is poor, and they would be poor together; his children, at least, were not to have any merchant's blood in their veins. Her father was a schoolmaster and that comforted him immensely. He was not to feel in her hair the touch of a hand that had rolled grocers' paper cones (p. 55).

The elder M. Mallarmé, the poet's father, died on April 12, 1863. Stéphane, having only recently attained his majority, married Marie Gerhard on August 10 of the same year and his daughter Geneviève was born in November 1864. To his letters, rich in intimate and poetic confidences to the future physician and poet Cazalis (Jean Lahor in poetry), are soon added other letters, no less remarkable, to the future Egyptologist Eugène Lefébure. Curiously, in February 1865 Mallarmé reproaches this correspondent, whose letters reveal a fine lucidity and a talent for friendship, of devoting too much of his poetic attempts to love. Mallarmé's confession is revealing:

. . . . If it is not seasoned by a rare condiment, lubricity, ecstasy, illness, asceticism, this vague feeling does not seem to me poetic. For my part, I could not pronounce this word, except smilingly, in verse. . . . What has particularly indis-

posed me against this word... is the silliness with which five or six jokesters...
have constituted themselves the priests of that fat boy, red and chubby as a butcher's
son, that they call Eros, seeing themselves as martyrs each time they accomplish his
facile rites, and climb upon women they have seduced as upon the piles of wood at
the stake.[3]

Later, in a very long and very important letter of May 17, 1867, on his poetics, on the revelation of his duty or of his poetic mission, Mallarmé, in very Baudelairian terms, details his tastes where women are concerned: either blond and plump courtesans who "give the distinct impression that they have battened on our blood" or, on the other hand, "it is necessary that a woman be slight and slim as a licentious serpent" (p. 249).

Woman's role is far from being insignificant in Mallarmé's poetry, and it was to be considerable as well in that of Valéry, who expressed himself with no less disdain for this poetic theme of days gone by (Renaissance, baroque, classic, romantic, and Baudelairian). Refined eroticism touched with irony will add a certain charm to the sleeping woman or the courtesan in repose in her "sleep without men" ("Anne"). Herodias and Valéry's "Young Fate" will be able to speak in the most sensual of lines their "horror of being virgins." But the elegies and the invocations to women, the tenderness of relived memory or "the art of evoking happy moments," cease with Mallarmé to be one of the central motifs of poetry. The symbolists we consider minor today, on the contrary, proliferated images of languid softness, visions of ethereal women bedecked with flowers, and incorporeal loves.

Mallarmé is without doubt the most difficult of all the poets who have written in French. Since the appearance of his work, and thanks to him, his obscurity and, even more, the reasons for that determination to be difficult, which has been given the name of "obscurism," have been examined. Retrospectively, the reputation he has slowly acquired has led poets and critics to reinterpret certain poets of the past in the light of his accomplishment: Luis Gongora and Maurice Scève especially, the Greek Lycophron to whom professors compared him out of derision, the English Euphuists, the successors of John Lily, the author of *Euphues*, or certain French *précieux* of the seventeenth century. It is natural—and T. S. Eliot has brilliantly formulated the theory thereof—that a new artist of very great talent modifies our vision and the whole heritage of the past into which his work is incorporated. It is also inevitable that his revolutionary novelty evaporate little by little and that he, like every herald of the avant-garde, soon be claimed by tradition and rendered somewhat inoffensive.

Twenty other French and foreign writers have been, or have appeared, obscure in their time and have doubtless remained so: the Dante of the *Vita Nuova*, the Shakespeare of the *Sonnets*, the English Metaphysical poets, Hölderlin, the Goethe of the second *Faust*, Nerval, Hugo, Lamartine himself, Blake, and Robert Browning. In many cases, the obscurity has been dissipated through the efforts of commentators and textual critics. In others, it has, on the contrary, been thickened by those who have sought, for example, to associate Dante with some scholastic doctrine, Hugo or Nerval to some arcane tradition, the Tarot deck, or Kabbalistic doctrine. A certain kind of obscurity can derive from chaotic thought, too hasty or too excessive in the sudden eruption of its inspiration to yield to any elucidation. The intermediate links in chains of thought are bypassed by the prophetic minds of the Old Testament, by Pindar, or by Hugo. Such seems to be the case sometimes with Claudel's obscurity, the very same that made Gide exclaim in his *Journal* of October 30, 1929, with respect to *The Satin Slipper:* "Dismaying!"

Mallarmé's obscurity is, of course, entirely different. Its sources and the forms it takes are multiple. It is not impossible that there may have been in it a share of mystification, and that the poet may have taken a malign and quite innocent pleasure in mocking those readers for whom he cared little: those who withhold all effort, who rarely have a sense of irony, and for whom any novelty must resemble that of day before yesterday. He loved to laugh at journalists to whom, before permitting them to leave with the text of a particular address he had just made, he declared: "Wait until I add a bit of obscurity there." Jérôme and Jean Tharaud have reported that he amused himself by responding to the young Maurice Barrès: "Seek, and at the end you will find pornography; that will be your reward." To another somewhat intemperate admirer, who praised him for having condensed into one stanza the mystery of the universe or of being, he replied: "But not at all! It was the sideboard in my dining room that I thus described."

It has been possible to have the mechanism of obscurity dismantled by those who have assiduously studied the poet's literary expression; comparing carefully and skillfully the various uses of a single term (haggard, abolished, missel, diamond), or of a certain image in Mallarmé's verse and prose, they have tried thus to clarify the meaning of a disconcerting sentence. To be truthful, neither Mallarmé's vocabulary nor his syntax nor his versification nor the mannerisms of his prose have yet been fully studied. Like every poetic language, Mallarmé's language plays, sometimes barely consciously, with ambiguities; it is naïve for commentators to want to isolate therein a single meaning to the exclusion of all others. We know that Mallarmé, like other poets labeled obscure whom admirers and exegetes interrogate, refused to elucidate the meaning of his poems. However, he did sometimes outline its meaning in letters to friends from his youth (Cazalis or Mockel), but not for his most abstruse works. He preferred to require of the reader an active or, as our contemporaries would say, creative participation that makes them reconstruct the vision in which the poem had its origin and that he had, by dint of searching and condensation, tried to transpose. The concise and very clear remarks the Goncourts say in their *Journal* they heard him pronounce are very convincing; many prose writers and novelists in our day might adopt this: "A poem is a mystery to which the reader must search for the key."

Doubtless there was in this modest professor whose ancestors had exercised from father to son the most bourgeois of professions (in the registry office) a certain aristocratic disdain for artistic forms of thought that might be plebeian, facile, placed within the reach of anyone. Emilie Noulet has, among other claims to the gratitude of Mallarmé scholars, that of having emphasized the importance of a youthful article from Mallarmé's twentieth year. It had appeared in L'Artiste, September 15, 1862, and had as its title "Artistic Heresies: Art for Everyone." "Everything sacred that wants to remain sacred envelops itself in mystery," the first sentence states. Religions, music, have functioned thus. Poetry owes it to itself to operate in the same way. It is not made to be taught in schools. Nor is it poetry's place to chide the public for its incomprehension. What do the philistines matter to poetry, and why strive to convert them. Let no one speak to us of poet-workers, or seek to be understood by the masses! The young man of twenty who cites Hugo several times and has, to be sure, read Gautier ends proudly:

> Let the masses read the moralists, but do us the
> favor of not giving them our poetry to spoil.
> O poets, you have always been proud; be more than that,
> become disdainful!

Already, in this four page manifesto, the future poet of "Saint," in which the *Magnificat* unfolds, and of the "book clothed in iron" from the "Prose for des Esseintes," cries out lyrically his desire that poetry isolate itself from the common herd, as Horace had once asked in the First Ode of his Third Book: "O golden clasps on old missels! O inviolate hieroglyphs on rolls of papyrus!"

There is some hieratism in Mallarmé's attitude (and there will be equally as much later in St.-John Perse) toward poetry. It is a little like entering a religious order to cultivate that very secret Muse, and it is with a pious reverence that it must also be approached by the reader. To communicate directly an impression, a sentiment, a thought, would be too easy, almost brutal. To describe some object (a vase as Gautier was able to do, a caged wild animal as Leconte de Lisle did, a person like Lola de Valence seen by Manet, as Baudelaire had evoked her) also risks being banal. As early as 1864, Mallarmé set down, in a letter to Cazalis, the essential base for the poetics of which he wanted to be the initiator: "Paint, not the thing, but the effect that it produces." Even so, these effects might risk being banal sentiments, accessible to the common herd of mortals. In "picturing" them one would therefore have to endow them with rarity.

The familiar procedures of the poet are diverse and may be discerned, but less ambitiously applied and rarely as convergent, in all poetry of any value: private associations of images, of memory, of experiences, or of dreams; allusions to a sideboard or a console, to a lamp become "angelic," to the odor of the oil burned by the lamp ("burned glass of aromatic spices and gold"), to the setting sun illuminating the pane of glass of an ancient palace, to a given musical instrument (a mandola, a harp that has the form of a wing, a viol, etc.). Ambiguities and periphrases have always been dear to every form of "preciosity." They bestow on the reader the joy of piercing the secret of a riddle or of discovering an analogy that tears him away from the flatness of the world of habitual routine. The rain shall become "the shower's dishevelment at my windowpanes." Decorative elegance is also seen, as is the gracious poetry of the flower, or the half-real flower, or "the one absent from all bouquets." Mallarmé had no fear of turning to a symbolic language of flowers: "the too grand gladiolus," or the "family of the irides" from the "Prose for des Esseintes," the "Lilies" of which the awakening faun, "erect and alone," feels himself the equal "in ingeniousness." Imprudent or overly precise commentators have taken the risky course of establishing scales of rather ridiculous allegorical correspondences; hence, the rose would regularly signify virginity or the female genitals, the diamond the supreme moment of voluptuousness, and so on. This too quickly reduces Mallarmé to some kind of Jean de Meung. Others, Charles Chassé especially, familiar with the nuances of the English language that the poet taught without knowing it too well, have sought to translate certain of Mallarmé's terms into English and so rediscover their true meaning: *résumée* juxtaposed with *toute l'âme* would mean not "abridged" or "reduced to the essential" but "taken up anew"; *grief*, from "The Tomb of Edgar Poe," would be the English "grief"; *un âge ignoré* (Hérodiade") would have the sense of "ignored," unknown, misunderstood; the *croisée vacante* is simply the "open window"; *aucun* has the sense of the English "any"; *la plume* of the punished clown is his *panache*, "the plume."

There is a certain piquancy and sometimes even a bit of truth in these ingenious glosses. But they all make the initial mistake of trying to be too systematic and, what is worse, of reducing obscurity to clarity by force, as if Mallarmé, with some kind of perverseness, after having conceived something clearly, had then expressed it obscurely. He was thus playing with his reader by concealing a second or buried meaning within some labyrinth. Every exegete ends by yielding to the temptation to reconstruct, as if it were a matter of a composition in Latin or German, Mallarmé's syntax by reestablishing it logically. He cannot keep from paraphrasing in prose what was said in sensuous verse lines and he can believe that in so doing (like a certain colonel who has in the same way rewritten "The Seaside Cemetery" in flat speech) he has rendered a service to the reader and to the author. What is more important is to reconstitute and embrace the obscure vision from which the poem was born, as one esthetician has wisely noted.[4]

It is an error to see in Mallarmé's obscurity only a premeditated plan or an intellectual game. Certainly, his verses do not give the impression of having sprung from the first burst of inspiration as, in the view of certain people (who, moreover, are mistaken), Rimbaud's or Hugo's do. If, unlike the poet of "The Young Fate," he did not sketch out a great many drafts, he often came back to his verses to correct them or to modify them. Albert Thibaudet maintained that there was in him much of the Parnassian, but that he departed from that "school" in order to contradict it. Gide, in his *Pretexts*, has been more boldly adventurous in stating that "one could in a way see in him the last and most perfect representative of the Parnassian school, its summit, its ultimate realization, and its consummation." His verse, however, is less narrative, less attracted to vast mythological epics, less oratorical and less sculptural than that of the Parnassian poets. The same Thibaudet seems nearer the truth when he recognizes in his book on the poet that he thought more by way of images than of ideas. He had already emphatically made the same declaration with respect to the first dissertation on symbolism (by André Barre) defended in France in the first of his *Réflexions sur la littérature*, published in book form by Gallimard in 1938.[5] The poet's thought proceeds by analogy, as this "demon of analogy" himself has profoundly and amiably evoked in the most interesting of his prose poems. He took pleasure in the quaintness of unexpected associations of ideas. This tendency did not in every case prove successful. One may, if one wishes, find well developed the quatrain from the "Tomb of Baudelaire" in which gaslight becomes the accomplice of sordid loves in some furnished hotel room, even if the poet is recalling *Les Fleurs du Mal* in which the debauched fly to their pleasures or return from them in the early morning by the light of street-lamps. The reader of 1960 or 1990 is not required to know that the gas flame of days gone by was called a "butterfly" and is thus linked to the idea of flight; and the eighth line, "Whose flight strays according to the lamplight," is one of the most mediocre in French poetry. It is undoubtedly useless to seek to make Mallarmé's verse limpid, that is, to deprive him of its personality and refuse to join in the vision he had of the world that is at the source of his expression. But it would be ridiculous, in order not to stand apart from "the happy few" or the snobs, to abdicate all value judgment. Obscurity is sometimes in Mallarmé the source of a beauty unknown before him. Sometimes as well, it led him to pretentious monstrosities and to alienating from the enjoyment of his thought and his art "the idle person, delighted that nothing there concerns him at first sight," while a little respect for such a person might have easily won to that form of poetry and to poetry in general, to "the unique spiritual task," readers whose secret desire is to be won over.

Mallarmé invited the comparison between the poet and the alchemist in his magician's robe, to slow gestures, to profound, ceremonious, and remote reckonings. "I believe," he confided to the reporter Jules Huret in 1891, "that poetry is designed for the pomp and the supreme ceremonies of an organized society." It was a strange social or decorative role assigned to the poet as master of ceremonies that, half a century later, Paul Valéry was to assume. Shrouding himself in mystery, then, disdainful of the tribal vocabulary, renewing it by the inhabitual placement of its words in his extremely subtle phraseology, the poet aspires to some kind of chemical purity through elimination and condensation. As early as 1867, in his long confidential letter to Lefébure (May 17),[6] he stated with the seriousness of a young man of twenty-three: "I have created my work only by elimination, and every acquired truth is born only of the loss of an impression which, having sparkled, had consumed itself." The work he already dreamed of accomplishing would be, after the Venus de Milo and the Mona Lisa, the third "great scintillation of Beauty on this earth." Its beauty, purified by the conjunction with Nothingness, laboriously achieved through a daily duel with powerlessness, ill luck, the temptation of sterility and death, would be a tragic beauty. Breaking the ties with everyday reality, it reposes on a play of almost structural relationships. In the declaration to Jules Huret, which Mallarmé made into a veritable literary manifesto, he praised, as he always did in all sincerity, Zola, the master of an "evocative art" and unequaled painter of movement and of the masses. But, he added, as a precursor to a kind of structuralism:

> But literature has something in it more intellectual than that: things exist, we do not have to create them; we only have to grasp their relationships.

The secret of things, once pierced, or as Mallarmé put it more exactly on the same page, "the threads of these relationships" once in his wizard's hands, it remained only for him to join them together. Much earlier, in the admirable letter to Théodore Aubanel on July 28, 1866, he had described himself as a sacred spider weaving at the transections of these threads "of marvelous pieces of lace." They already exist, he added in Platonist fashion, "within the bosom of Beauty." Poetry thus takes on the wildly ambitious task of deciphering the dark secrets of the universe. The terms of the autobiographical letter to Verlaine on November 16, 1885, are well known and tell of the seriousness of the office that, as high priest of the beautiful, he judged it his duty to fill "with an alchemist's patience": to create The Book in which would be formulated "the Orphic explanation of the Earth which is the poet's only duty and the very essence of literary skill."

There will be discussion for a long time to decide whether this stubbornly dreamed of book is "A Throw of the Dice," as Robert G. Cohn maintains, which the aging poet showed to his young admirer Valéry as an irrational ambition, or whether we possess the fragments of it in the notes published by Jacques Schérer in Le Livre de Mallarmé, [7] or still yet, whether that immense dream, challenging all accomplishment, terminated in a failure or an abdication. Little matter, and if there is such a thing as a relative failure, it was sublime and seminal. In what one has to call Mallarmé's symbolism, there is not so much the recourse to symbols or the suggestion of correspondences between heaven and earth, reality and the beyond, as an almost superhuman effort to unlock and recreate the meaning of the universe by expressing it with a radiant purity. On June 27, 1884, [8] in a short letter to Léo d'Orfer who had asked various poets for a definition of poetry, Mallarmé answered with the most ambitious definition ever offered, worthy of The Defense of Poetry written with ardor by Shelley a little before his death, but more elliptical:

> Poetry is the expression, through human language reduced to its essential rhythm, of the mysterious meaning of the aspects of existence: it thus bestows authenticity on our sojourn and constitutes the only spiritual task.

People have attempted sometimes to discern in that high conception of poetry traces òf mysticism inspired or reinforced by esoteric readings or by a patient study of Hegel. But the poet who announced early in his youth having "struck down God, that old panoply," never accepted that anyone try to bring faith to bear upon his work. His essay "Catholicism" (1895), included in *Divagations*,[9] and "Likewise," which follows it and which originally bore the title of "Solemnities," embroiders with rare ingeniousness on the ritual, the liturgy, the external ceremonies of the church, but gives evidence of no sympathy whatever for the faith or for the efforts at Catholic renewal among writers. In no way attracted by the esotericism of certain of his contemporaries and by the lucubrations of Sar Péladan or Stanislas de Guaita, Mallarmé leaned rather toward a simplistic materialism.

As for Hegel, Villiers de L'Isle-Adam spoke to him of the German philosopher whom he seems, however, not to have known very intimately. Did Mallarmé ever read him? And what works by him? He often uses great words like *infinite*, *absolute*, *nothingness*, which every Frenchman who has passed through his philosophy year at the lycée can lavish. He was probably struck by a few phrases (that he could have found in Taine or Renan or in lesser popularizers of a certain Hegelianism) presenting the universe as the Ideal in the process of accomplishment or the individual self as the realization of the Idea. He took pleasure as a very young man in alluding to the universe that thought itself through him, Stéphane, without his having had to read Arthur Schopenhauer or being plunged into some kind of Germanic pantheism. At twenty-two he had made himself the promise, he confided to Cazalis, of remaining always faithful "to the strict ideas... of his great master Edgar Poe";[10] it was an allusion to "The Philosophy of Composition." He was later to read *Eureka* and perhaps wax enthusiastic for that strange cosmology that Poe's English and American compatriots hold in very mediocre esteem. In 1885, still, in his autobiographical letter to Verlaine, Mallarmé was in no way embarrassed to admit that he had "learned English in order better to read Poe." It is to Poe more perhaps than to Hegel that he might have been indebted for the notion that the mind of man, thinker and poet, is capable of understanding, or at least of interpreting, the structure of the macrocosm that is the universe. It is not from his complacently magnified self, as with Hugo, but from the universe or from the Absolute that the poet would depart in order to reflect in his verses that Absolute.[11] To caricature him as a metaphysician is to betray him. His philosophy is above all that of an esthetic.

One would like to know whether, in the presence of his Tuesday listeners, Mallarmé sometimes happened to specify what he meant by *symbol*. But his admirers have been most reserved about specific details on the subjects that were approached or treated in the modest setting of the Rue de Rome. Doubtless, the master preferred to improvise on the spur of the moment, caring little about teaching a coherent doctrine to his submissive disciples. It is his personality that seems to have fascinated the young symbolists who thronged there (Henri de

Régnier, Francis Viélé-Griffin, the younger Valéry, and the fierce Claudel, whom the master chided for having spoken ill of Victor Hugo), or a few foreign visitors: Stefan George, Vittorio Pica, the Dutchman W. G. Byvanck.

The one who was the first to report what he thought he understood of Mallarmé's ideas, Camille Mauclair, does not seem to have enjoyed his complete confidence, and it is perhaps the irritation felt by Mallarmé that is expressed in the last line of the enigmatic "Little Air—Warlike," in which there is an allusion to "that nettle / Mad with friendliness." Like other great men to whom understanding by the young has come only very late, Mallarmé liked in his last years to feel himself surrounded by disciples. He was not unaware that the most sovereign indulgence toward them, as toward their elders and toward every rival, requires distributing praises among them to avoid any acrimonious polemic and to avoid being distracted from a determined reverie. He thus lavished "Toasts" and compliments upon Gustave Kahn, René Ghil, Jean Moréas, and Henri de Régnier and was generous towards Verlaine (Rimbaud, the great absentee, is the only one toward whom he did not try to be fair or charitable); despite all the explanations people have sought to give for them, his very high praises of Gautier, Banville, and Madame Desbordes-Valmore continue to astonish us and to inspire some doubts about his critical judgment.

By contrast, we are grateful to him for having shown himself so strangely patient toward the skillful journalist Jules Huret. It is in the latter's *Enquête* (which placed him, in presenting his interview, on the same plane as Catulle Mendès!) that Mallarmé came closest to an elucidation of what he meant by *symbol*. After having paid homage to the Parnassian craftsmen of traditional verse and especially to Banville, he comes to the point of justifying the innovations in form by the young (this was in 1891) and to the theoretical poetics he attributed to them or that, generously, he conceded to them. The passage is a celebrated one. It situates in the first rank, in poetry, the necessity of preserving or of enlarging the mysterious; and to that end, not to name or to state outright, but to suggest and (the formula is a little too facile, but it was a question of simplifying for a newspaper article) evoke by way of an object a state of mind:

> ... The Parnassians, they take the thing as a whole and show it; thereby they miss the mystery; they withhold from keen minds that delightful pleasure of believing that they are creating. To *name* an object is to suppress three-quarters of the enjoyment of the poem which is designed to be revealed little by little: to *suggest* it, there is the dream. It is the perfect employment of this mystery that constitutes the symbol; to evoke an object little by little in order to show a state of mind or, inversely, to choose an object and bring forth from it a state of mind through a series of decipherings.[12]

In the same text, Mallarmé came back once again to distinguish his poetic ambition from the ordinary pretensions of those who are content to enumerate, to describe, or to align sumptuous words and believe that they have thereby produced poetic gems. One must first of all depart from the "human soul":

Poetry consisting in *creating*, one must grasp certain states within the human soul, gleams of a so absolute purity that, well sung and well illuminated, this gives form in fact to mankind's own precious jewels; in that there is symbol, there is creation, and the word poetry here possesses its meaning. It is, in sum, the only human creation possible.

The symbolist process for the poet is, then, an act of creation, and the poet's gesture repeats anew that of a creator-demiurge or replaces that of God, whom the still young poet had prided himself upon having "struck down in his terrible struggle."[13] One of the most faithful reports from one of Mallarmé's contemporaries who listened to him speak, Gustave Kahn, set down in his *Origines du symbolisme*,[14] identifies such use of the symbol to a great effort of creative synthesis:

It was Mallarmé who had above all spoken of the symbol, seeing in it an equivalent to the word synthesis and conceiving that the symbol was a living and embellished synthesis without critical commentaries.

The domain of poetry thus envisioned was to be limited to a point that modern civilization may legitimately regret. There have been a few exceptional moments (as during the years 1940–42) when poetry rediscovered a vast audience, and not necessarily by demeaning itself. A few good poets at the time returned to Lautréamont's formula ("poetry must be written by all, not by one"). But, in general, a great part of the public that lacks neither intelligence nor sensitivity has seen itself more and more excluded from access to poetry. Poets have lost thereby no less than readers. In various Mallarméan declarations poetry is raised to so exalted an empyrean that all human feeling is excluded from its narcissistic enjoyment. "Poetry for me takes the place of love because it is smitten with itself and because its pleasure in itself falls delightfully into my soul."[15] Poetry, the poet proclaimed in his youth, banishes love and friendship. It also banishes the other arts. "There is only Beauty—and it has only one perfect expression, Poetry. All the rest is a lie." Painting, music, are the puny rivals that poetry must despoil; or, rather, the other arts will be united to poetry or swallowed up in it in a grandiose fusion. In the philosophical jargon that the master did not disdain to use and on which certain followers, from Charles Morice to Camille Mauclair, gorged themselves, the latter, interpreting the views of the admired poet, advocated not just the ordinary synesthetic effects or the delightful correspondences between the arts with which Gautier and some of Baudelaire's contemporaries played, but a much more ambitious synthesis. Poetry became for Mauclair the One from the Platonic *Parmenides*:

The question of unity within multiplicity is the root of all philosophy, of all art, of all science, of all criticism, and, finally, there is only one subject: it is that one.[16]

But, and happily so, if it is true that poetry loses nothing in being the work of poets who, from Lucretius and Dante to Goethe and Mallarmé, have thought assiduously and profoundly, it is no less true that it would be a betrayal of Mallarmé to seek in his work "the debris of some grand design" and the elements of a system. The peremptory declaration of his admirer Valéry, made to Frédéric Lefèvre in 1926, could have been that of Mallarmé himself: "The essence of poetry is the search for poetry itself." That search led him towards glacial summits far beyond the sway of "Ruhe," the serenity in which Goethe, possessed of a strong physical constitution and accepting more easily the perhaps salutary limits to art, was able to find repose. Like his Hérodiade, the French poet, in love with purity and the absolute, must have murmured to himself: "I want nothing of that which is human." As in the case of Flaubert totally disillusioned, of the Goncourts haunted, like Mallarmé, by nothingness and wondering unceasingly why there had been no collective suicide of the human race, Mallarmé needed to erect another religion in the place of the one in which he appreciated only the entirely hieratic exterior: the religion of poetry that would place at a great distance from its sanctuary the unworthy mob of the noninitiates.

There is no lack of gratitude towards the devotion and pioneering heroism of Dr. Mondor in declaring that his *Vie de Mallarmé* and, especially, his edition of the *Oeuvres* in the Pléiade edition are, thirty years after their appearance, in need of being redone. Only on the basis of an edition that would include the successive versions of the poems, that would elucidate the circumstances that gave rise to many pieces of prose, that would establish the relationships between the various uses of forms of expression and terms particular to Mallarmé, could an evaluation of what the poet might have owed to the use of symbols be established. Even then, to be sure, there would persist a vast margin of divergence among Mallarméan scholars, not only on the way in which one might reconstruct with logical but banal clarity a particular sentence of typically Mallarméan syntax—a supreme heresy toward the master—but divergence on the esthetic appreciation of a given stanza or of any given symbol. Perhaps never will so great a number of so ingenious and so fervent Mallarmé scholars come together and grant so generously their collaboration to a work that would be the poet's "solid sepulchre" and the necessary base for new work on his verse and, perhaps even more importantly, on Mallarmé's prose.

Until now, in their proud, pioneering enthusiasm, exegetes have lavished their attention on the most enigmatic poems that stimulated their ingeniousness all the more. To some extent, no doubt, and dangerously so, it is the function of the symbol to constitute a series of riddles on which the intellectual subtlety of the commentator is exercised and deployed. Nevertheless, it is too bad that the play of the intellect, proud of its agility, is substituted completely for a more innocently naïve enjoyment. A sentimental enjoyment also, if by that we mean the power of dreaming over poetry in the way that Mallarmé dreamed over Wagnerian music. One can take pleasure in the late poem that Mallarmé placed as an introductory "Salutation" to his collected verses, while at the same time finding arbitrary and even a bit facile the association of images that passes from the glass in which champagne bubbles to a troup of sirens to a voyage of the Argonauts to the threats of winter and old age for him who had just been designated (in 1893) the Prince of Poets. The prow of poetry buffeted about by the pitching of the waves is not very striking in its originality. The most beautiful line is doubtless the twelfth, "Solitude, reef, star," evoking the artist, lonely pilot at grips with the reefs and guiding himself by the stars or aspiring to the highest reaches of the firmament. But once again, every explanation amounts to excessive clarification and to transmutation of poetry into lowly prose.

In their ambition to distinguish themselves as much as possible from the mediocre herd of those "who do not know how to read," and whom Mallarmé ridiculed, critics have comparatively neglected the poet's more "Baudelairian" works, which preceded his revelation before the "Hérodiade." "Azure" is not any the less a tragic and anguished poem for all of its being as though the Mallarméan "artist's Confiteor," striving to "wrestle to the earth pitiful sterility," as he described it. "Sea Breeze" is not spoiled, as "The Voyage" and other poems by Baudelaire are, by prosaic impurities and the lapses that spoil the unity of impression and effect that Valéry deplored in too many of the pieces from Les Fleurs du Mal. The forty lines of "Windows" have few equals in French poetry and the symbol of the casement or the "golden panes" that the sick man goes to embrace to discover there, far from too-commonplace life, art and the mystical, is set forth at the same time with both delicacy and strength. "Weary of Bitter Repose" is marked by a pre-Raphaelite grace and a fortuitous expression that makes one regret that Mallarmé did not write more in that mode. He did not always gain in going back over the first versions of his youthful poems (there are four versions of "Alms," two of "The Chastized Clown," between 1864 and 1887), and many readers refuse to be convinced by the conventionality of scholars and editors who reject the text of the first version in favor of what the author, in his subdued, old man's corrections, timidly substituted for them.

In other cases, pieces of relative simplicity and of sovereign beauty have been spoiled for many readers innocently prepared to be captivated by their charm, by the flood of often trifling commentaries. Such is the case with "The Gift of the Poem" and the four or five sources (The Bible, the Georgics, Vigny's "Suzanna at the Bath," and "Hérodiade" itself, which the sonnet seeks to give as an offering) that have been assigned to the phrase "night of Edom" or to the word palms. With regard to the latter, the poet stated quite simply to Henri Roujon that he had placed it there "in order to evoke the idea of glory" and, to be sure, for its sonority and for that clash of cymbals at the beginning of the sixth line. One has the right, however, not to be totally overcome upon reading the next-to-last line and its allusion to his then young wife rocking her first-born, Geneviève, to the mother's numb and chapped finger, and to the mystery of maternity:

... Avec le doigt fané presseras-tu le sein
Par qui coule en blancheur sibylline la femme. . . .

> ... With your withered finger you will press the breast
> Through which flows in sibylline whiteness the woman....

The "Précieuses" of the seventeenth century would have relished that suggestive periphrase. One of the three "Fans," the second, that of Mlle. Mallarmé (1884), is irreproachable and perhaps the poet's symbolist masterpiece in the minor mode. In it, the young girl, dreamy, is evoked during a summer's evening. She is dreaming perhaps of the male ravisher who is one day to appear; her lips, like the air stirred by the fan, suggest a kiss, but one "born for no one" and that prolongs itself in vain. The fan unveils the world and yet remains prisoner of the hand that plays with it. Life is glimpsed with all that its reality contains of the seductive, but also of the brutal. To refuse to live it and to prefer the kingdom of the dream would be better. The last stanza, with its charm of rococo art and in which Mallarmé, writing for and about his daughter, did not wish to insinuate any commonplace ambiguity, is one of his purest successes. There is neither search for the absolute nor analogy with the supreme object, poetry, in this symbol, accessible to every reader. In his *Divagations*, Mallarmé also evoked a fan that he was pleased to compare to a wing and, in its closed form, to a "unanimous fold": "The fan ... that other paper wing ... hides the site in order to bring against the lip a mute painted flower like the dream's word, intact and nil, appropriated by the beatings." The grace of this little poem is enhanced by the malice with which, at the end of the two most evocative lines, he slips into the rhyme scheme the ordinary words of conversational style: "that's it" ("ce l'est"):

> Le sceptre des rivages roses
> Stagnants sur les soirs d'or, ce l'est....

> The scepter of the rosy banks
> Stagnant over the evenings of gold, that's it....

The poet's method of writing is apparent in the correction he imposed on line thirteen where space, compared to a long kiss, was followed by "which, proud of being for no one" ("qui, *fier* de n'*être* pour personne"). "Proud" ("fier") has been happily replaced by "mad" ("fou") and "n'être" by an analogous sound ("naître") but a more exact and at the same time more suggestive meaning.

It is not sacrilegious to insinuate that, beneath many enigmatic allusions, there has not slipped an ironic smile from Mallarmé. Too little has been made in his case of the irony softened by kindness in his life as well as in his writings. In many cases, it would have been easy for him to direct his listeners towards the unilateral explanation of a given obscurity that he preferred to leave within the shadows of its ambiguity: Anastase and Pulchérie from the famous "prose" or "Vasco" in the final line of "To the only care of traveling." In this latter case, one thought to perceive all sorts of phantoms behind that name, including that of Chateaubriand, and meanings no less sundry than the naval term *bearing* ("gisement"), until a more knowledgeable researcher recalled that the piece had appeared first in a volume for which it had apparently been composed: *Commemorative Album for the Four Hundredth Anniversary of the Voyage of Vasco da Gama.* [17] On the other hand, it is too bad that the English translation of "The Tomb of Edgar Poe" should have been rediscovered just as he had sent it to Mrs. Sarah Whitman in a letter of July 31, 1877. [18] The "naked scepter" ("sceptre nu") of the second line is there rendered by "a naked hymn" with the explanatory note, "When words take on in death their absolute value." The angel of the fifth line is defined as being "the poet named here above"; "O grief" is rendered by "O struggle," one does not quite know why; "dazzling" ("éblouissante"), daringly placed before Poe's name, becomes the prosaic "Poe's dazzling tomb" with the explanation (if indeed it is one), "dazzling: with the idea of such a bas-relief." Neither the translation nor the various explanations show evidence of a very sound mastery of English, and Mallarmé treats this grandiose sonnet as if he were addressing a fourth form English class. One sighs with relief that the idea did not come to him, on the occasion of his lectures at Oxford or his conversations with George Moore, Arthur Symons, or York Powell, to translate more often his remarks into the Briton's language.

The sonnet "yx" that Mallarmé had already announced to Cazalis on July 18, 1868, and that, modified, was given its present form in 1887, has been, with "The Virgin, the Vivacious, and the Beautiful Today," the most frequently explicated of his poems. The author had indeed indicated to his friend in 1868 that he would not take it amiss at all if the piece had no meaning whatever, "thanks to the portion of poetry that it encloses," and that this meaning was "evoked by an internal mirage of the words themselves." Commentators (among the best of whom have been a Belgian, Emilie Noulet, and an American, Robert Cohn) have elucidated its enigmas and the terms by which Mallarmé had been fascinated (*ptyx, nixe phénix,* and *septuor*), which, moreover, are not impenetrable. In "The Virgin, the Vivacious... ," people have been able to read in various ways the symbol of the icebound Parnassian poet, the symbolist poet, or Mallarmé himself, a prisoner not of life but of the ideal that is his tormentor (Emilie Noulet), therefore an affirmation of aggrieved pessimism or, on the contrary, an almost joyous exultation and deliverance (Jacques Duchesne-Guillemin and, especially, James Lawler and the English critic C. Chadwick). But the splendor of the poem is such that any exegesis that does not immediately lead the reader to take delight in the form and the music of the verse would be futile.

The most subtle of Mallarméans, who are perhaps the most authentic ones, have noted their entirely special predilection for the works most charged with enigmas: the final "Throw of the Dice" or the "Prose for Des Esseintes," "Hérodiade," among the poems of some length where, in our opinion, the poet was able to give more freedom to his genius and was less limited to a play of ellipses that, in the sonnets and madrigals, attracts the preference of those who seek to isolate their lyricism from any too personal suggestion and eliminate "the real, because [it is] base." Less exclusive admirers, including this writer, take more pleasure in "The Afternoon of a Faun" and in "Funeral Toast." The former (the first version dates from 1865), better than "Hérodiade," on the subject of which Mallarmé set down the following lines, approaches his youthful idea, which was "to paint and to note very fleeting impressions, . . . following upon one another as in a symphony."[19] This was the poem of his summertime; "Hérodiade" was that of the cold winters of Tournon and Besançon. The mobility with which the images are changed from one into the other justifies in effect the name of impressionist poet that Thibaudet affixed to its author with respect to certain ones at least of his poems. For a first, more oratorical and dramatic version (Mallarmé had dreamed of seeing it performed on the stage), he substituted a second more touching, dreamy, and delicately sensual one. To the other of his two close friends, Lefébure, in July 1865, the poet declared: "My subject is ancient, and a symbol." A symbol of the artist who thought himself able to materialize his dream, to seize a fleeting vision of beauty, glimpsed for a moment, to prolong or "perpetuate" a delightful vision? No doubt. "Art is desire perpetuated," Jules Laforgue was later to say. The Faun finds himself once again alone; he has caused the nymphs to flee as he has trampled the reeds. The bite he thought he had felt on his "breast, innocent of proof," is owed only to "some august tooth," that of poetry, of the "tart lime of the bitter ideal," mentioned in another poem. But this voluptuous dream was beautiful and the Faun wants to prolong it "through idolatrous paintings" as when, having sucked the clarity from grapes, he blows in their skin and relives a sweet giddiness. He consoles himself for his disappointment, confesses what he calls, without believing it, "his crime." He had wanted too avidly to caress the two nymphs while savoring "the secret fright of the flesh." He will carry his desire elsewhere, still higher, even as far as the goddess of love. Or, drowsy, he will possess in his dreams its almost equally voluptuous shadow. To extract, with maladroit insistence, an intellectual and philosophical symbol from this so delicately sensual symphonic poem would be to betray it. "All words [must] fade in the face of sensation," the poet warned in November 1864, with respect to "Hérodiade," which he was slowly bringing into being along with his "Faun."[20]

"Funeral Toast," written for the *Tombeau de Théophile Gautier*, a collective volume, resounds with a song of triumph. In 1872, his metaphysical and esthetic crises momentarily surmounted, less anguished by poetic impotence and sterility (which he had exaggerated to excess by complaining of them), Mallarmé is strengthened in his proud conviction that poetry alone can vanquish death and nothingness. He knows henceforth that, appreciated by Hugo, by Verlaine, by the Parnassians who celebrated Gautier in the same volume, and who had invited him to render that homage, he would himself be counted among the great French poets. The piece, majestic in the development of its three parts, is severe in its setting (the gates of the tomb, funerary libations, confrontation with nothingness, the vehement rejection of any other consolation than that of art) and in the diction of its ascending and descending groups of alexandrines. It does not play with enigmas[21] and has no need to torment syntax. It unites the power of suggestion to a gravity worthy of Vergil or Milton. Mallarmé, whose language elsewhere was often inclined towards substantives and infinitives rather than the softness of adjectives, here attains, by the choice and placement of the epithets, a classic splendor: "magnificent, complete, and solitary... ," "the lucid horror of a tear," "the irascible wind of words that he has not said," "a solemn movement of the air." One would almost think, knowing that Leconte de Lisle and especially Hugo were themselves also writing a poem for this same *Tombeau* (Hugo's long poem with the celebrated allusion to "the oaks being cut down for the tomb of Hercules." has been highly—perhaps excessively—praised by Valéry), that he wanted to raise himself even higher still than they and put into that piece where the "I" is pronounced only at the beginning, the shudder of grief-stricken friendship and the vibration of a victorious struggle with the angel of death:

> ... Le sépulcre solide où gît tout ce qui nuit,
> Et l'avare silence et la massive nuit.

> ... The solid sepulchre where lies all that harms,
> Both miserly silence and massive night.

People have spoken of failure, and some of the poet's nobly stoic plaints, in his verses or in his letters, have inspired his commentators to take up that refrain and to speculate whether Mallarmé died pursuing his dream of The Book and conscious of his not having been able to realize it. It matters little. The "throw of the dice," which can appear to be meaningless, is, as it happens, among all his poems the most admired by intrigued connoisseurs; he opened the way to a whole new form of poetry to be read and seen and no longer heard, a form whose possibilities are even now far from having been completely explored. The poet was intoxicated by the "sumptuousness of the void" and, from his youth, rejecting Baudelaire's lament, disappointed by a world in which action is not the sister of the dream, he wanted to pursue obstinately and perhaps realize his dream. He placed it always ever higher. He pushed further than any other the ambition to create through poetry and, like the phoenix, stubbornly to be reborn after having consented to a symbolic death. He has had not imitators, but successors. The entire conception of the creative act and of "literature or the right to death," according to Maurice Blanchot's somber remark, among the men of the second half of the twentieth century, reflects the example and the probings of this great mind "addicted to dreaming," as he wrote to his friend Villiers de L'Isle-Adam.

6

THE SYMBOLISTS

Battle, mêlée: such are the terms by which the survivors of the years 1885–95 liked to designate that period of the symbolist movement about which several have been pleased to count off their memories. The combat, in truth, was less vehement than that which the realists, the romantics, or even the men that one groups under the label of the "classic" generation of 1660 had had to sustain. The Parnassians were able to reject some of their finest poems (those of Mallarmé and Verlaine) for their third collection; but after that collection of 1877, quite mediocre at that, their influence quickly declined. Moreover, François Coppée and Catulle Mendès and, later, Laurent Tailhade or Emmanuel Signoret, more or less Parnassians, were linked with the combatants of symbolism and often found themselves confused with them. José María de Heredia was not Mallarmé's enemy, and at least two of his sons-in-law, Henri de Régnier and Pierre Louÿs, appear to us today, if these classifications mean anything, to have been closer to Parnassus than to symbolism's vague idealism. The naturalists did not concern themselves any more with engaging in battle with the symbolist poets and dramatists who in no way threatened their effort to hold sway over the novel. The Goncourts and Joris Karl Huysmans were very close in their novels to the symbolists' impressionistic grace or to their inclination towards decadence and the diabolic. André Fontainas and a few talented Belgians (for the poetic originality of their rejuvenated Walloon literature dates from symbolism), Ernest Raynaud, Paul Valéry, later liked to evoke the fervor of those Parisian youths smittem with poetry, thirsting after the ideal and the absolute, and impassioned over questions of technique and prosody.

All that has given birth to a few diverting volumes of anecdotes in which foreigners appear to take particular delight, for the details of the worldliness of the salons or of the Bohemian life of Montmartre always seemed to them typically Parisian. But this has not aggrandized in our eyes the symbolism of around 1890. The more serious history of letters and the arts cannot be constucted uniquely, or principally, according to that perspective of groupings, cenacles, of exclusiveness, duels, rivalries between the habitués of cafés from one bank of the Seine or the other. It is too easy in Paris to gather five or six people around a café table, draw up a grandiloquent and bellicose manifesto, don a label ending in "ism," and obtain thus the attention of the daily and weekly press. The people who think of themselves as the most individualistic have a fondness for these groupings; and rare indeed is the unusual person who refuses to put his signature on a petition or a declaration of principles, especially if it vituperates against the authorities in power or against the elders who occupy positions of importance and influence. No one has yet collected in book form the various symbolist

manifestoes (only in the selection of documents that closes the great work of
Guy Michaud). There are those of Jean Moréas and of his short-term allies, of
the eight or ten reviews that competed at the time through effects of style and
mysteriousness, the decadents, the hirsutes, the hydropathics, the clients of the
Café du Chat Noir, and so on. To read them is, moreover, depressing. Their
clearest merit would be to allow the historian of language to study the oddities of
vocabulary and the syntactical contortions that were the trademark of this kind of
writing. For the rest, the works themselves must count; and it must be admitted
that of the one or two hundred little books and volumes that flourished then,
scarcely any survive. The little reviews express their fervor and sometimes also
the exacerbated search for originality of youth of the time. It happened that
important texts found a place in Vogue or Lutèce (Rimbaud, Verlaine), in the
Revue indépendante (Mallarmé), in the Entretiens politiques et littéraires, and
that ephemeral sheets such as La Conque gave Valéry the opportunity to
start on his literary career. But it is not possible to maintain that any one of
these reviews was representative of a true poetic current or even had any doctrinal unity. There is a little of everything in La Plume (1890–1902), in
L'Ermitage (1890–1905), and in La Revue Blanche (1890–1900), which, moreover, sought in the beginning to be eclectic. There was very little of "symbolism"
in L'Occident (1902–14) and much more than symbolism in Le Mercure, which
explains its longevity. It was a long time after symbolism was extinct that there
appeared, in 1905 and 1906, respectively, two reviews that undertook to revive, elucidate, and spread its doctrine: Vers et Prose and La Phalange.

The latter, inspired by Jean Royère, himself the founder of "musicisme" (a
form of symbolism seeking to be musical), counted collaborators of talent, including Albert Thibaudet. But its very approximate definitions of symbolism
gained nothing in clarity for having come twenty years (or nearly so) after the
height of the movement: "very individualistic literature... in this sense...
naturalism broadened and refined," says Henri Hertz citing Rémy de Gourmont
on February 20, 1913, in La Phalange (pp. 97–104). The same Jean Royère had
been the editor-in-chief of Ecrits pour l'art, whose preliminary manifesto (March
15, 1905) declared in the jargon of the period: "Poetry will be the intuition of the
All manifested by Rhythm." In 1905, one of the well-meaning, good poets of the
day, who had been close to Mallarmé, had stated unsmilingly, in the first issue of
Vers et Prose: "I am a poet if I express in accord with harmony, the vital truth
that shimmers within me.... Poetry is only a Love superior to that of the lovers'
embrace" (pp. 95–103). And yet again: "Poetry... is the ineffable and vivifying
joy in which the reason, the heart, and physical trembling are no longer distinguished from one another, where, from the senses themselves, thought seems to
be born, moves, and moves us, and confounds itself in the harmonious plenitude
of a heart that swells and a soul that sings" (pp. 95–103). Two years later in the
same review, Saint-Pol-Roux, known as The Magnificent, in a brief article
entitled "Poesia," gravely affirmed: "Poetry is Science itself in its initial stage."[1]

In 1906, in a volume *Vues d'Amérique*, written upon his return from a visit to the Saint Louis Exposition, the novelist Paul Adam showed that he knew how to manipulate the jargon of the cenacles of 1890:

> Art is the work of translating a thought by means of a symbol. . . .It desires to eternalize the almost abstract idea of magnificence rendered corporeal in this setting at this moment. Prior to the work itself, a concept is born that will explain it. . . . Art is the work of inscribing a dogma in a symbol.

Rather strangely, he admired this symbolism notably in the canvases of the least literary and least cultivated of painters, Claude Gelée.

Moréas's style in replying to the silly, mocking chronicle of a journalist for *Le Temps* by way of his manifesto in *Le XIXe Siècle* of August 11, 1885, is more excusable, for the fiery Hellene was devising the defense of his colleagues. He called forth the examples of Vigny and Baudelaire and cited Edgar Allan Poe's definition of the "beautiful," which Poe's first French admirer had appropriated as his own. The following year, on September 18, 1886, he gave to *Le Figaro* his celebrated manifesto, several sentences of which were to pass into anthologies and manuals of literary history:

> We have already proposed the name of Symbolism as the only one capable of designating reasonably the current tendency of the creative spirit in art. . . .Symbolist poetry seeks to clothe the idea in a sensitive form which, nonetheless, would not be an end in itself, but which, while serving to express the Idea at the same time would remain subject to it. The Idea in its turn must not be allowed to appear deprived of its sumptuous robes of external analogies; for the essential character of symbolic art consists in never going so far as the conception of the Idea in itself. . . .Tangible appearances [are] destined to represent their esoteric affinities with primordial Ideas. . . . For the exact translation of its synthesis, Symbolism needs an archetypal and complex style; uncontaminated words, rigidly constructed phrases alternating with phrases marked by undulating lapses, meaningful pleonasms, mysterious ellipses, suspended anacoluthons.

Further on, he calls for "rhymes that are illucescent and hammered like a shield of gold or bronze, in conjunction with rhymes of abstruse fluidity." Some years later, in a curious review, *Entretiens politiques et littéraires*, founded in 1890 by Paul Adam, Henri de Régnier, and Viélé-Griffin, Viélé-Griffin wrote, under the title "Qu-est-ce que c'est?", while promising himself to strip the term *symbolism* of its tinsel:

> The symbol which cannot have any existence except correlatively to the object of symbolization is the synthesis of a series that is hypothetically anterior to the latter; symbolism, then, as an esthetic doctrine, would entail in principle the symbolic realization of a dream of art that synthesizes settings and ideas. . . .It is necessary to translate the self, an unconscious synthesis, into symbols which express this self in its harmonious consciousness.

One may allege that Moréas was Greek, Viélé-Griffin American, Mockel (and a few others) Belgian, and that they all were taken, as foreigners who are fascinated by an acquired language often are, with rare words and garlands of sumptuous and sonorous sentences. They were, however, in their attempts at definition of the aims of their poetic revolt, neither more nor less clear than the French, very few of whom deserve the reputation for lucid minds and manipulators of sober prose that they have made for themselves. The truth is that, for about fifteen years (and Mallarmé incurs in this a share of responsibility) French men of letters gorged themselves on pretentious phrases and views that are often worse than confused. It is not to them that one must go to acquire some notion of what may have been the philosophical substratum of symbolism—if indeed such a substratum was necessary to it.

Rémy de Gourmont, a Norman whose skill at dissociating ideas was once worth some prestige, Charles Morice and Tancrède de Visan who were Lyonnais, Gustave Kahn who was Lorrain, and the grumpy and scrappy Adolphe Retté, born in Paris, have not been a lot happier in their attempts at elucidation. The first of these has emphasized to the point of satiety in his novels the incurable solipsism of human beings, which was to be one of Proust's obsessions, but which was rendered by Proust with an entirely different tragic power. No more successful was Barrès, who appreciated Moréas (this was not his only error in judgment), who formulated the *Culte du moi* and slipped into his *Jardin de Bérénice* the then fashionable phrase, "It is we who are creating the universe." He could not, however, create the symbolist novel. In his *Livre des masques: portraits symbolistes* (1896), made up of rapid and often very inane vignettes, he gave to the term *symbolism* a whole little jewel case of synonyms: "individualism in literature, freedom of art, tendency towards that which is new, strange and even bizarre . . . , idealism, disdain of the social anecdote, anti-naturalism . . . finally, free verse." Such an accumulation does not clarify much of anything. But it is the principle of the world's ideality on which the critics were to insist, and several of his contemporaries echoed him. "In relation to man, the thinking subject," he adds in the preface to the same work, "the world, all that is external to me, exists only according to the idea that is conceived of it."

Much more than Hegel, very little read even by those who mentioned him (without ever citing him with precision), it is evidently Schopenhauer who lies at the source of this philosophical view or of that cliché, drawn from the title of his great work, that says "the world is my representation." Every pupil of the philosophy year in the French lycée—as Alain Fournier and Jacques Rivière were to be at the Lycée Lakanal—has been, in juvenile fashion, shaken during the course of a few weeks by the discovery (by way of Leibniz or Berkeley) that the external world is perhaps only the representation that one makes of it. Propitious perhaps for music and a certain ethereal poetry, this philosophical idealism is assuredly not so for the novel.

Charles Morice was perhaps to leave a name and to gain, in the editions of Verlaine's works, a note for having been the object of the dedication of "Art poétique" (after, moreover, having attacked the poet, who pardoned him for the attack). The son of a very Catholic family, Morice sank quickly into alcoholism, the Bohemian life, and misery and acted as literary "slave" to Paul Gauguin and Auguste Rodin. Some attention was given in 1889 to his pretentious and muddy work *La Littérature de tout à l'heure*, [2] which J.-H. Rosny printed in *La Revue indépendante*. [3] He intoxicated himself with words then in vogue: *synthesis, unity*. The concluding sentence gives the tone of this long manifesto, in which certain people have found some lineament of thought:

> The Synthesis returns the mind to its homeland, reassembles the inheritance, recalls Art to Truth and also to Beauty. The synthesis of Art is: the joyous dream of the real truth (p. 359).

His subsequent book, though shorter, is no less pompous. He cites therein a letter from Mallarmé addressed to him and sums up its essence by "Art is Life," but it surpasses life and dwells in eternity. [4] He praises the new poetry for having penetrated and conveyed correspondences, and he proclaims with pride: "The symbol is the fusion of our soul with the objects that have awakened our sentiments, in a fiction that transports us out of time and space" (p. 47).

The Lyonnais who adopted the beautiful pseudonym of Tancrède de Visan published, especially in *Vers et prose*, various articles that he assembled later in *L'Attitude du lyrisme contemporain*. [5] He possessed some philosophical culture, and he may have reflected at length and with some distance on symbolism, belonging as he did to the second generation of the movement (he was born in 1878). He praises in his book the internal and central, and no longer peripheral, vision of the symbolists: "By means of successive images, they externalized lyrical intuitions." He tries to distinguish the symbol from allegory and inserts several clichés that Nietzscheism had rendered fashionable around 1905: the celebration of Life and the necessity for art to attain Beauty through Life (therefore no longer turning one's back on it like Villiers de l'Isle-Adam and the invalid of Mallarmé's "The Windows"). He develops at last a theme that had been launched earlier by Jean Thorel on the analogies between French symbolism and German romanticism, and he is one of the first to link symbolism to Bergsonian philosophy.

Thorel's article had appeared in the third volume (1891) of *Entretiens politiques et littéraires* (pp. 85–109). It had a promising title: "The German Romantics and the French Symbolists." The author sought to show therein that the symbolists, probably without knowing it, had had ancestors in Germany at the beginning of the century; that Villiers and Mallarmé were in their own way "Fichtean," for the true master of idealism had been Fichte; that these same romantics had been attracted by the symbol (that of Ondine, for example) and that Creuzer's *Symbolic and Mythology* had appeared while certain of them were still writing, in 1812 (not Novalis nor Schiller, however, nor Heinrich von Kleist, nor Friedrich Hölderlin, already gone mad); finally, that they also had sought to express the inexpressible, aspired to vagueness, and even (Ludwig Tieck especially) practiced an irony which that of Jules Laforgue resembled. The article is intelligent and competent. But Maurice Maeterlinck, the translator of Novalis excepted, the symbolists do not seem to have been struck by it or even to have been very concerned with explaining their affinities with the predecessors that one sought to assign to them. These analogies between the two groups of poets, sometimes mystics and souls caught up in religiosity (Wilhelm Wackenroder and Friedrich Schleiermacher on the German side), are in fact real, but there cannot be any question of sources or influence. It happens that a family of like minds finds itself thus, a hundred years and a thousand miles removed from one another.

Schopenhauer, who made such a mark on Richard Wagner and Thomas Mann, who had even been commented upon in France by Challemel-Lacour, and of whom Henri Bergson was to say in 1915, in his little book on French philosophy, that he was "the only German metaphysician to have also been a psychologist," was easier to read than Fichte or Schelling. He had written essays full of subtlety and verve on art and literature. His posthumous book with the very pedantic Hellenic title was composed of mordant aphorisms, a genre always appreciated by the French. If the self-creator alone is real and the idea alone is living, one deduced easily from this, and with oversimplification, that it was fitting to create a new language and a new art to preserve and express that subjectivity. This could nourish various manifestoes and contribute to the religions of art and (especially) music; but the poetic work of the symbolists was not very much enriched by it.

Around 1910, when Bergsonian philosophy had suddenly become fashionable in Paris, it was tempting to claim, in retrospect, as did Tancrède de Visan somewhat lightly, that Bergson was the philosopher of symbolism just as Fichte had been that of German romanticism—two equally adventurous statements, the first of which is an impossibility for anyone who is attentive to chronology. Nothing so much attracts the novices of scholarship as imagining (and, if possible, establishing) relationships between the literature of a period and the reigning philosophy, or a philosophy that in retrospect is supposed to have been such. It was attempted for Descartes and classicism, and for Comte or Taine and realism or naturalism. But it is especially Bergson who has been the victim of this scholarly game, and it is Claudel, Proust, and Valéry (among others) in whom "Bergsonism" has thus been detected. In their lifetimes they protested, Proust perhaps to excess (and, moreover, contradictorily), Valéry with vehemence in writing to Thibaudet his firmly negative position on this point. Bergson, the son of a Polish musician and an English mother, who, perhaps, had helped him respond to the romantic poetry from across the Channel, took hardly any interest in the literary struggles of his times. Among the cenacles and the authors of pretentious manifestoes, he would probably have seen, as did Renan in replying to the queries of Jules Huret, "little children sucking their thumbs." It was in Charles Péguy later and in the critic Thibaudet after World War I that he recognized faithful interpreters of his thought and, perhaps, disciples. His first book, *Time and Free Will* (*Les Données immédiates de la conscience*), appeared in 1889 when the symbolist movement was already launched and victorious. His third, *Laughter,* the only one that includes a few pages on art—admirable ones, moreover—dates from 1900. Those he might have affected (Gide, Valéry, Proust) paid it scarcely any attention, and their work was already underway or in gestation. All the studies on the relationships between symbolism and Bergson are obliged to fall back on analogies or on rather cumbersome hypotheses.[6]

To be sure, some of the terms, let us say some of the concepts or clichés, that were current around 1885–90, are met both in the symbolists and in Bergson: the unconscious, intuition, synthesis, soul state, and "the unknowable," which Herbert Spencer, who had at first attracted Bergson (Spencer, the least poetic of philosophers), had bestowed on the symbolists. But the meaning that Bergson conferred on several of these terms has nothing in common with their use by the poets or the polemicists of symbolism in the little reviews. The first sentence of one of Bergson's best books, *La Pensée et le mouvant* (1934), was to be praise for what had been the most cruelly lacking in the young poets of symbolism, precision: "What has been most lacking in philosophy is precision" (p. 7). In the same work, far from vaticinating on the synthesis, as youthful symbolist reviews had done, Bergson assimilated it to analysis: "The spirit of synthesis is only a higher power of the spirit of analysis" (p. 231). Elsewhere again in the same work, taking up a communication given to the *Congrès de philosophie* in Bologna in 1911, Bergson praised above all simplicity:

> The essence of philosophy is the spirit of simplicity. . . . Always we find that the complication is superficial, the construction an accessory, the synthesis an appearance: to philosophize is a simple act.

The thinker required such simplicity equally in the writer's style, and he would no doubt have scarcely encountered it in the poets and the prose writers of 1890, Mallarmé included. "One has to have pushed to the end, the decomposition of what one has in mind in order to arrive at being able to express oneself in simple terms";[7] and in *L'Energie spirituelle:* "The art of the writer consists especially in making us forget that he is using words" (p. 49).

It is not just the word *symbol* on which agreement would be difficult to reach between Bergson and the poets who had made such repeated use of the term. For him, the symbol is a form of knowledge or an abstract and conventional representation that very much resembles a cliché. It is the opposite of intuition, which sets aside symbols and asserts itself at the interior of the object. True metaphysics nourishes the ambition of doing without symbols. Therein is a misunderstanding or rather a different usage of a poorly defined term. Bergson did not take the trouble to inform himself about those symbolists who created some stir in Paris when, a little before his thirtieth year (he had been born in 1859), he returned to the capital. His speculations were leading him elsewhere. These poets and their friends who had tried to theorize had in no way preceded or prepared the way for his reflections on duration, memory,[8] or art.

It often happened that Bergson spoke of art and of seeing in it, through a master he had loved, Félix Ravaisson, "a figurative metaphysics." He often repeated that "it is the same intuition, diversely utilized, that makes the profound philosopher and the great artist."[9] The celebrated developments of *Laughter* that reply to the question, "What is the object of art?" (p. 115), and the praise of those "souls more detached from life . . . , who have, in some sense, a virginal manner of seeing, hearing, and thinking" (p. 118), would perhaps have attracted the symbolists if they had been written in 1880 rather than two decades later. Such as they are, they seem to reconsider certain declarations about poetry, its incommunicability, its privilege of tearing open the variegated veil "that those who live call life" (Shelley), which had been that of the English romantic poets and of Lamartine. But neither Bergson (and for good reason, since the dates make it impossible) nor any other thinker furnished any substratum of thought or any system for symbolism, which, moreover, had no need for any. "Sustaining criticism," as Thibaudet called it, had not greatly assisted romanticism or realism and later would be of little help to surrealism.[10]

Apart from a very small number of interested persons (Gabriel Mourey, translator of Algernon Swinburne, Gabriel Sarrasin, devoted admirer of English poetry, and especially Théodore de Wyzeva, who read several foreign languages), the symbolists moreover hardly knew directly their Germanic predecessors or those of English expression, Poe being an exception. In fact, they were not only closer to the French romantics, they were nourished by them; and the one whom, above all, the somewhat vague and fluid, langorously melancholy poetic writings in vogue in 1890 most often recall is Lamartine. Moreover, they did not hide the fact from themselves. If there existed a history of that poet's fortunes, one might in all likelihood read there that, despite the scorn of Leconte de Lisle (who, however, had the flair to sense the epic grandeur of *The Fall of an Angel*) and that of Rimbaud, Lamartine was the source of inspiration and the model for much of the poetry of 1885–90; and the latter is not always equal in worth to "The Vine and the House" or even "Ischia." Paul Morand has viciously called Albert Samain "a Lamartine for the upper deck of buses." But we know by way of Henri de Régnier that Mallarmé respected him.[11] Charles Morice became ecstatic when speaking of him. Emmanuel Signoret, in *Le Mercure* (January 1896), proclaimed Lamartine "the best-endowed man for poetry ever born." He added that he had often wasted his gifts. Many of the hazy affirmations surrounding poetry as aspiration, language of the soul, exaltation of the imagination, could have come from Lamartine's very beautiful text of 1834, "The Destinies of Poetry." Again, in January 1902, as we mentioned above, when *L'Ermitage* published the results of an inquiry directed to more than a hundred poets, "Who is the greatest poet of the nineteenth century?", several chose Lamartine, nearly as many as chose Baudelaire. Hugo came in ahead, however, and it is in this issue of the review that Gide answered with three words about which, somewhat ridiculously, a great case has been made: "Victor Hugo, alas."

The currents of sensibility and ideas that animated various French and Belgian circles during the symbolist period equally penetrated estheticians and thinkers.

A many-sided reaction had attacked narrowly conceived positivism, its stoicism, and its perhaps inhuman desire not to venture beyond the tangible and to banish from metaphysics certain ambitious notions: the absolute, the infinite, the super-sensate world, mysterious correspondences, and even the marvels of magic. If the philosophy of Comte, Emile Littré, Taine, and a few German materialists re-nounced exploration of that unknown and preferred to declare it unknowable, poetry arrogated to itself the privilege of translating it into correspondences and symbols. Everywhere else, except in science and philology, the young Renan had written (in a youthful work that he published in 1890), "the vague is the true." At the end of his celebrated *Prayer*, he had inserted the disillusioned statement upon which certain symbolists had seized: "Everything here below is only symbol and dream." Less illustrious philosophers or professors of philoso-phy, returning to Pascal (Jules Lachelier—to whom Bergson dedicated his first book—and Émile Boutroux) or attracted by art (Félix Ravaisson, Gabriel Séail-les), or considering that all philosophy that does not confront the enigma of art is incomplete or timorous, speculated at the time (1890–1908) on the imagination. Théodule Ribot, in his work *L'Imagination* (1900), distinguished two types: plastic imagination (formal, precise, in a word, Parnassian); and diffluent imagi-nation. Ribot's preference was for the latter type, which is fond of indistinct images, vague contours, fantasy and the fantastic, dreams, and which inspires music and symbolist art in general. Later, in 1907, in *Le Mensonge de l'art*, Frédéric Paulhan provided some keen and wise insights on music as the ideal of the other arts and on symbols. He warned the successors of symbolism against the artificiality and bloodless incorporeality that lay in wait upon those who are fanatics about symbols. Among the first (though Mallarmé had not been un-aware of it), he noted that "more than an accurate observer . . ., Zola was . . . an epic poet and, as has not been sufficiently seen, a symbolist poet" (p. 64).

None of these philosophers, however, inspired the practices of the poets of symbolism. Rémy de Gourmont himself, whom Gide had declared (in his *New Pretexts*) to be the one who alone had "concerned himself with giving a philosophical significance to symbolism," proposed scarcely more than a single principle that might have served as a base or a link to the promoters of the movement: "The principle of the ideality of the world." In truth, what various philosophers and psychoanalysts have since written about the symbol lies on quite another plane (C. G. Jung, Alfred North Whitehead,[12] or the orthodox Freudian Ernest Jones in his essay *The Theory of Symbolism*). Jones reveals himself to be quite unrestrictive when he states: "If one takes the word 'sym-bolism' in its broad sense, the subject embraces the entire development of civili-zation," which has consisted in unmasking at each stage earlier, worn-out sym-bols and replacing them with new ones.

If all this seems negative and seems to diminish the accomplishment of sym-bolism instead of exalting it through an ambitious world system, it is because, even more than other movements, it was through what they rejected and fought against that the symbolists defined themselves. Their profound instinct, then, opposed them to positivism, to naturalism in literature and, less clearly, to what was too rigid, too sculptural, too impassive in Parnassianism. Still more generally, they rose up against prose and the prosaic, and their movement attempted nothing less than an invasion of literature (the novel, the theatre, the essay) by poetry, and even an invasion of the other arts (painting, music especially) by poetry. That said, each of these poets or theoreticians sought his own way and found it only rarely, for originality is not so easily conquered—and especially not by a barrage of manifestoes. Robert de Souza, striving to take his bearings in "Où nous en sommes," while launching *La Revue Blanche* (in March 1905), recognized that each poet "had chosen the moral or philosophical armature that suited him." Francis Viélé-Griffin, in the same issue, was not any more specific:

> The generation of 1885 . . . dreamed, willed; it will have posed, like a flight of birds, at the summit of the delicate and vast cathedral rooted for seven centuries in the plain of France, that necessary and symbolic steeple: Lyricism.

Philosophical idealism and subjectivism, then, pushed very far: such is the formula under which one can retrospectively group the poets of that period. The demand for freedom also, and, as a result, the liberation of poetry from the constraints of regularized verse. This watchword had served many other literary revolutions and that of romanticism to begin with. But prosodical experimentations and the anarchy and exhibitionism as well of certain mystagogic and antibourgeois decadents went much further than in the time of *Hernani* or the representatives of "La Jeune-France" of 1835. In 1890 one made more liberal use of the terms *mystery* and *strangeness* than the French romantics had done; those in England and Germany had had a greater appetite for them and had undoubtedly penetrated further into the subconscious sources of the shudder they sought to provoke. "The poem is the celebration of mystery," stated Gustave Kahn. The poet must straight off uproot the reader and precipitate him into a less tangible world, haunted by dreams: Coleridge, Schiller, Novalis, Shelley, doubtless, had already said so, and the Russian symbolists were to say so again.[13] There again, taking up once more the grandiose ambition of the English and German romantics, the poet will aspire to abolishing the separation between the self and the nonself, to dissolve himself into things. Charles Morice, in his imperious and inflated style, had written: "The symbol is the fusion of our soul with objects which have awakened our sentiments, in a fiction that transports us out of time and space."[14] Very few among them had invoked Spinoza (whom Goethe and Shelley had so much admired); they nonetheless sometimes pronounced the word *pantheism* and suspected that there, without doubt, was the true direction of their religiosity. Tancrède de Visan, in 1911, expressed this notion but not without awkwardness; these poets did not want to observe or describe a forest, he wrote, but "to *live* it, . . . [to] intermingle themselves with its breath, [to] commune through a kind of immanent pantheism with its ardor, [to] *become* the forest while identifying oneself with its soul state."[15] With more simplicity,

Bergson had said how much he admired Rousseau and especially his celebrated fifth *Reverie*, which Marcel Raymond was to place at the origin of the contemporary poetic movement.

Novalis, the only one of the German romantics to whom the symbolists might have been able to connect themselves, warned in an often-cited sentence that it is toward the interior that the mysterious path leads, and that this descent into oneself, if it is profound, becomes also an ascension. The French poets of 1885–95 frequently spoke of ascending toward the land of the dream, toward the "taciturn stars" from which Stuart Merrill awaits "blue embraces" toward some celestial and radiant light. The flight of Icarus tempted them. But their weakness is to have dared too rarely to go to the depths of themselves. There is an unwritten law of literature in France, that country where the great authors who go from Montaigne to Rousseau, and those of the seventeenth century, especially, form the base of education in such a way that, sooner or later, every innovative movement is judged in relation to these classic figures. Have they gone, in the exploration of the inner life of the human being, as far as La Rochefoucauld, Pascal, Racine, Diderot? With Stendhal, Balzac, Vigny, Baudelaire, what one called romanticism could reply affirmatively with pride. Can the generation of Moréas, Henri de Régnier, Viélé-Griffin, Huysmans, Barrès, do the same? Marcel Proust, in a curious article in the symbolist-leaning publication *La Revue blanche* of July 15, 1896 (reproduced in his posthumous volume *Chroniques*), replied without posing the question in that way:

> Purely symbolic works therefore run the risk of lacking life and, thereby, depth. If, furthermore, instead of touching the mind, their "princesses" and their "knights" proposed an imprecise and difficult meaning, the poems, which ought to be living symbols, are no longer anything but cold allegories.

It is not always easy to distinguish between *symbol* and *allegory*. Baudelaire, as we have seen, used the second of these terms quite as often as the first. The symbol should be less intellectual, but consciously willed; it should surge up from the subconscious. It ought to throw out its roots into reality as does the symbolism of Dante, Goethe, and Hugo in their great moments. It expands quite naturally into myth if the author is endowed with a powerful enough imagination to be as mythopoeic as Blake, Hölderlin, Shelley, or Rimbaud were. We must admit that such was rarely the case for the symbolists who followed Rimbaud and Mallarmé. It would be vain and cruel to pass their works in review. One encounters a few gracious pieces in the first collections of Moréas such as "Et j'irai le long de la mer éternelle," from *Les Cantilènes*. But one is bewildered in face of the number of people who, from Barrès to Paul Souday, were able to find the gnomic poems from *Stances* admirable. Thibaudet saw more clearly when, in 1912 (Moréas had died in 1910), with respect to the book of A. Barre, he wrote: "One travels into these thin quatrains as though on a slope of dried asphodels, and their mechanical unfurling engenders no song."[16] Samain was a languid and pleasantly decorative sentimentalist, but what is symbolist in the neo-Parnassian description of *Aux flancs du vase?* Viélé-Griffin must have been a man full of charm—generous, combative—and Gide has said how much he was attracted by him. This American had more freshness and vitality than the greater part of his brother poets. Alone, or nearly so, Gide notes in his *Journal of The Counterfeiters*, he escaped the symbolists' gravest fault, "their scant curiosity... in the face of life." He dared be optimistic and robust among so many languid souls "weary of the dreary hospital." His Belgian friends, who had elected him to their Royal Academy, dealt with him more fairly than the French: Fontainas, Mockel. His verses, however, celebrating Greece and her myths, his *Cygnes*, his *Chevauchée d'Yeldis*, his Nordic legends (*Wieland le forgeron*), are hardly read any longer except once every ten years by the producers of university dissertations.

A similar fate struck his countrywoman Renée Vivien, a lesbian, several of whose pieces (Colette praised her) might find a place in an anthology of Sapphic poetry. (The greater number of truly successful pieces therein would, however, be poems written on this theme by men, curious and jealous as they are.) "Psyché, ma soeur, écoute immobile et frissonne" would be one of the most touching of these poems, and even one of the great love poems of symbolism, to be placed near another successful one by Pierre Louÿs: "Celui-ci qui ne fut ni prêtre ni guerrier," a noble piece singing the praises of pleasure and joy, composed in memory of the sixteenth-century neo-Latin poet Jean Second. The "Pervigilium Veneris" of the same Louÿs is also marked by a tragic eloquence in its avidity for carnal joy. For a time at least, Louÿs deserved the esteem that Gide and Valéry felt for him (he had helped them both in the discovery of their vocations). Gustave Kahn, an interesting and restless spirit, was tempted by prosodical innovation and was one of the first champions of free verse; and he was tempted also by socially conscious art. He understood better than the others what the new generation was obscurely seeking. But no one thinks of extracting more than a few lines from *Palais nomades* or from *Le Livre d'images*. In 1912 he declared, in a speech to a group of students: "Poetry must sing under pain of not being poetry.... A poem is only a series of metaphors." His own is quite far from having possessed the gift of either song or metaphor. An enormous English work, written with infinite piety by John Clifford Ireson, has said everything about him.[17] May his verse of patient goodwill (he composed odes to Diderot and to Tolstoi and an entire volume of *Odes de la raison*, 1902) rest in the peace of oblivion.

Henri de Régnier and Verhaeren are (if one does not rank Laforgue among the authentic symbolists) the two poets who, the one being twenty-six in 1890 and the other thirty-four, composed twenty or so pieces that, among a good thirty or more volumes of verse and prose by each of them, one might wish to save from oblivion. Régnier was, between the cenacles of the noisy Bohemian world of symbolism and the salons-antechambers of the Academy, the most effective of intermediaries. He also had recourse to facile clichés: centaurs, satyrs, male goats "like unto some god" symbolizing the appeals within him of pagan eroticism and ideal women, refined companions, and, finally, the vague desire for the heroic life. His Hellenism is rather like that of many other symbolists, an elegant, decorative Alexandrianism. His slight, disdainful, and easily consoled melancholy parades itself in a monotonous setting of vague dreams amid birches and ashes, later on among fountains, ponds, garden basins in which swans slip by at the foot of statues of Leda and Diana. Heredia, his father-in-law, granted him some genius, reserving for himself only talent. Time quickly wore his work thin and one is surprised to read that in 1903 young men at the Lycée Lakanal (Rivière and Fournier) could still feel themselves transported by listening to their professor read verses from *Tel qu'en songe* (1892). The symbols with which he played for a time lack the power of evocation; they amount often to prosaic and banal comparisons: "The fountain that weeps is a soul that suffers," from Ode III of *Jeux rustiques et divins* (1897). There is a superabundance of thyrses, clepsydres, hourglasses, golden seaweed, ochre leaves, pink and mauve skies, and too much marble and stucco. The rare adjectives today seem pretentious: encoraled, inebriant, Medusean. All contact with life and the present seems to have been banished from this poetry, which is satisfied to dream dreams once dreamt by others, from Bion or Moschus to André Chénier. The poet is an obstinate nostalgist and his dream is satisfied amid this decor of Sylvans and Pegasuses. "Old things are engendered by dreams; they filter time in reverie, and time exudes, drop by drop, from them as from mysterious clepsydres," he wrote in *Figures et caractères* (1901). The figures that he evokes are indeed pale and never does his melancholy rise to even a sob. We would like it to be more tragic, less easily consoled. The setting, the too pliant rhythms, the allegories, raise a wall between the stated grave banalities and his reader:

> Le Bonheur est un dieu qui marche les mains vides
> Et regarde la vie avec des yeux baissés. . . .

> Happiness is a god who goes forth with empty hands
> And looks at life with lowered eyes. . . .

or again,

> Prenez garde. L'Amour est vain et n'est qu'un songe.

> Take care. Love is vain and is but a dream.

A few more simple little odes like "J'ai feint que les dieux m'aient parlé," "Un petit roseau m'a suffi," alone deserve to survive in the anthologies designed to make symbolism's posterity feel what was the outmoded charm of his poetry. It would be a waste of time to seek to find in these agreeable garlands poetic symbols capable of enchanting us after three-quarters of a century. Paul Valéry, who came close to lingering over this sort of exercise,[18] later avenged himself by noting, for example, in his *Cahiers* (X, 81): "Symbolism is the ensemble of people who thought the word symbol had a meaning."

The morbid pessimism that seems sometimes to be the attribute of northern lands was not lacking in Belgian painting (James Ensor) nor, from Georges Rodenbach and the young Maurice Maeterlinck to Michel de Ghelderode, in Belgian theatre and poetry. Maeterlinck had, in 1889, in his *Hothouses*, published certain of his languid poems (with numerous tears, faded lips, "desires, ill from hunger," "desires weakened by perspiration," hospitals "with a menagerie in the midst of lilies"), the most characteristic of the period. He spoke in elegies in the mode of Lamartine, but more affected, of the torment of his soul "sad from being weary," and "weary from being sad." He would give proof of more vigor and vitality in his dramas, and in his later meditations as a mystical *moraliste* would show him cured and courageous in the face of life. With their vague musicality, his verses are perhaps the most representative of symbolism from 1885 to 1890.

His fellow countryman Emile Verhaeren also passed through a crisis of dark desolation from which he emerged triumphant and ready to acclaim life. He had known almost a Baudelairian anguish and had spoken forcefully of his inclination toward nothingness. Recovered, he was to cry out his vitality and his exuberance. Like Rimbaud, he perceived the futility for poets of "slandering life." He went beyond these hallucinations and looked about him: the countryside taken over by tentacular cities, the invasion of industry, social suffering. He saw all that and sought nonetheless through a Nietzschean bound of energy to say "yes" to the modern world. He sang the poetry of the city. Baudelaire before him, T. S. Eliot after him, and various Americans have no doubt succeeded in doing this with happier results. The modern mythology that Verhaeren wanted to forge is doubtless a relief after that of Régnier and Viélé-Griffin. But the poet's imagination is not powerful enough to impose itself upon us. More especially, his form betrays him. It is rough and jolting; the free verse that he used in the middle of his poetic career delivered him from all constraint and did not serve him well. The oratorical tone and too facile repetition set too many traps for him. How much dross, how many platitudes in his long poems! What verbosity! "I love man and the world and I adore strength," he cries. One would prefer that he not merely announce it, but would make us feel it. Verhaeren had at least the merit of bringing to symbolism (with which he associated himself) a few new themes, but the Parisian symbolists had seemed to engage themselves in reducing as much as possible the field open to poetry. However, he renounced the ellipses, the unusual, ambiguous, and suggestive conciseness, and, still more serious, the musicality of verse. The last quatrain of a piece on the statue of an apostle, placed in some tentacular city, is typical with the awkwardness of its adjectives and the repetition of its substantives:

Son image d'airain sacra le carrefour,
D'où l'on voyait briller, agrandi de mystère,
Son front suprême et clair et large et comme austère
Dans le tumulte et la rage des jours.

His bronze image blessed the intersection,
From which one saw shining, enlarged with mystery,
His forehead, supreme and clear and broad and as though austere,
In the tumult and rage of the days.

It would be useless to insist further. The second generation of symbolists, born between 1850 and 1865, coming to adulthood around 1885, did not produce a single great writer. Is there at work there, as we have suggested elsewhere,[19] a law of alternation of the generations that says the literary offspring of a great lineage feel themselves overwhelmed by the accomplishments of men fifteen or twenty years older who have opened new paths? This process, we believe we have shown, took place with the second generation of romantics in France (born around 1810) and for a great number of others in France and elsewhere. It will be necessary to await the writers and artists born around 1870 (Gide, Claudel, André Suarès, Proust, Valéry, Péguy) to take up the task with more brilliance, and certain of these will infuse the symbolist heritage with new blood. The message of Rimbaud, Mallarmé, and even Verlaine will require thirty or so years before being finally assimilated and revealing itself fecund. Even that of Baudelaire who died in 1867, after having assisted Verlaine's and Mallarmé's early efforts up to that time, after having impressed Maurice Rollinat and a few decadents, had remained nearly without effect on the symbolists of 1890.

The mannerisms of that twilight-lit, flaccid poetry, seeking to be fluid and vaporous, are only too evident: there is a plethora of grey-green and bronze tones, of silvered lillies, and "lilylike" women (Robert de Montesquiou), of crystal moons, dawns, and evening languidness, of "wild fleeces" and "incarnadine lips" (Stuart Merrill), too many pretentious clichés and false refinements. When a study is undertaken of the symbolist poets' language, and another of the language of the manifestoes and professions of faith, one will see that ridiculousness was more prodigally lavished and that the mortality of their innovations was greater than was the case with Préciosité, the Pléiade, and even the Grands Rhétoriqueurs. The symbolists' imagery counted too many sylphides and swans, too many adornments and jewels that could have been left to the Parnassians. There is too much bad Parnassianism in these poets who, it is true, did not yet know either the *Lettre du Voyant* or Mallarmé's declarations in which that poetry is condemned. The symbol itself became an artificial guessing game, a false mystery, and an intellectual game much more often than an internal, affective, and perhaps half-conscious necessity. Neither the pretentious Ecole Romane, which literary historians have made the mistake of taking seriously, nor, even less, the "Naturism" of around 1900, nor the feminine romanticism of Mme. de Noailles, nor Charles Maurras, one of the most execrable versifiers France has ever numbered among her poets, put an end to the symbolist skirmish or crusade. The movement had not rested on a firm enough philosophical or esthetic base of thought. It had not renewed either the theatre or the novel, or history, or criticism, as romanticism had formerly done. Yet another generation, born around 1885, whose spokesman on this occasion would be Jacques Rivière, was to prove cruelly severe towards symbolism's failures. Certain minds, inclined towards irritability (that of Vladimir Nabokov, for example, writing in the *New York Review of Books* for October 7, 1971) were to declare themselves unable to tolerate the word *symbol* any longer, a word that numbed all capacity to enjoy art with amusement and enchantment, and that attracted only schoolish types with little computer minds who amused themselves deciphering riddles.

Despite so many insufficiencies and failures, however, an atmosphere propitious to poetry had been created in France by the symbolist movement. The proliferation of little reviews read by a handful of readers, the great number of thin books of verse appearing at the time, had made of France a country of poets. Symbolism's prestige among the Germans, the Italians, the Russians, even among certain English and North Americans, had become considerable by the end of the century. Without doubt, some did not rigorously distinguish symbolists from Parnassians, Mallarmé from Théophile Gautier, Verlaine from Heredia. But greater foreign poets than those of 1890 in France (W. B. Yeats, Ezra Pound, James Joyce, Stefan George, Rubén Darío, Antonio Machado, several Russians) were to interpret and spread beyond France's borders the best or the most enduring part of that symbolism.

7

IN SEARCH OF THE MORBID AND THE STRANGE:
THE DECADENTS AND LAFORGUE

Never before, no doubt, had one spoken so much of illness, boredom with life, and universal decadence than in the last quarter of the nineteenth century in France. The small group (poorly defined, moreover) of those who, around 1885–90, are called decadents (and whom others mocked as "deliquescents") had in itself little importance. Associated with them, however, was a poet who died young in 1887, Jules Laforgue, who promised to be the most original talent of the generation that followed that of the great poets of symbolism. Born in 1860, he came twenty or so years after Mallarmé, Verlaine, and the impressionist painters. But there is a good bit more to Laforgue than decadence. Historians of poetry readily argue whether they ought to associate the decadents with the symbolists or present the latter as being opposed to the decadents and, relying on the voice of Moréas in his famous manifesto of 1886, as discovering their identity and donning their label so as not to be confused with the decadents, of whom the Parisian press made such light.

We think such an argument quite futile. Cenacles, very ephemeral in any case, and small reviews have sought to oppose the ones to the others. But even when they repudiated the term (as Mallarmé did) the writers of those years that, historically, go from the French defeat of 1870–71 to the Dreyfus Affair, have felt, thought, and written in a spiritual climate of doubt, narcissicism, dilettantism, the cult of art, and sometimes the seeking out of occult worlds and rare sensations. It is then that one encounters on all sides the word and the notion of *decadence*. More than the symbol, the synthesis of the arts, synesthetic effects, and even the marriage (rarely satisfying) of music and poetry, it is the attraction of a certain decadent estheticism that is, at the time, the factor common to poets and theoreticians of the beautiful in France, Great Britain, Germany, Russia, and Latin America.

Once again, with the passage of years, their continuity appears to us more notable than revolutionary innovations among the men of 1885–90. Still again, the symbolists are found to have been very near the romantics of 1820–40 and even to the "preromantics" who had, around 1760–80, been devoured by boredom, attracted by all that touched upon death, and fascinated by the contemplation of the self. If it is Parisians who boastingly glorified themselves as being decadent, and if a few foreigners (Tolstoi and the Austrian Max Nordau) thought to see in Paris a Babylon whose ideas and esthetics were contaminating Europe, it happens that decadence was elsewhere even more marked. Even youthful peoples, supposedly newer and more robust (the Anglo-Saxons, the Irish, the Hispano-Americans, and the Russians, sometimes a few Scandinavians), embraced with the greatest fervor the ideas called decadent and were the most inspired by this movement: Walter Pater and Oscar Wilde, W. B. Yeats and John Synge, Stefan George and his very narcissistic *"Kreis"* or circle, Gabriele D'Annunzio, Valeri Bryusov, Vyacheslav Ivanov, and the Egyptian-Greek Konstantin Kavafis eclipse the greater number of French decadents who might have been an inspiration to them. The milieux in which they had to write, when they did not expatriate themselves, were less hospitable than that of France, a country for centuries accustomed to hearing itself qualified as decadent and which could not have cared less; their originality was therefore to be magnified. Still today, it is foreigners who have most often attempted to follow and analyze in their studies the decadent movement and the concept of decadence. (The titles of some works on the subject are listed in the bibliographical note at the end of this volume.)

The eighteenth century had introduced into the philosophy of history, with Montesquieu and Gibbon, the notion of the decadence of civilization, and Rousseau had tied that degenerescence to the arts and letters. But neither the Marquis de Sade nor the numbers of men of letters who battened at the time on funereal poetry and meditations over graves had formulated any esthetic of evil. One is always decadent for someone. The romantics were compared by the very academic Désiré Nisard to the Latin poets of the late empire. There were among them, in France, some alcoholics and some candidates for suicide and still more consumptives over whom death hovered. But most of them, even those who introduced Satan into their writings or who cultivated some eccentricity to shock the bourgeoisie were of vigorous temperament. Quite early in their careers they threw themselves into action, politics, business on occasion (even if it were, as in the case of Balzac, thereby to collect bankruptcies). Théophile Gautier engaged actively in travels, newspaper serials, and consoled his sadness with his adoration of formal beauty. His Parnassian friends did likewise. The lycanthrope Petrus Borel finished his career in 1859 as a minor civil servant in Algeria. Flaubert must soon have come to smile at his most intemperate declamations in *Novembre*. With the Bohemian world of 1835 (that of Nerval, Gautier, and their friends), then with Baudelaire, the clear awareness of the artistic possibilities of a decadent art penetrates into literature. The first tercet of "The Enemy" on the "new flowers" that the poet dreams of and that will sprout in the earth of a cemetery, his declarations on the strange charm of Latin poetry of the later periods, his remark on the new and the piquant, or even the voluptuous and the rare, that the "poetic spirits will find in the play of this agonizing sun," gave the theme respectability in esthetics. The key text is the celebrated preface by Gautier, in 1868, to the posthumous edition of *Les Fleurs du Mal*.

One has ridiculously and with pathetic seriousness overdone "explanations" of the *mal du siècle*, of art for art's sake, of decadence, by way of questions of production and exchange in the economy, of social classes in Europe, and by way of the triumph followed by the insecurity of the bourgeoisie. The application of economic and social theories, elaborated by Friedrich Engels and Georgi Plekhanov nearly a hundred years ago, to literary and artistic history has until now thrown little light on individual creations or even on the appearance of certain currents of sensibility. The failure of revolutionary hopes in 1848 could have contributed to the pessimism of the period of the second empire, and the prosperity, until that time unequaled in France, of the reign of Napoleon III could have channeled intellectuals (often the last to enjoy the benefits of that kind of prosperity) towards a systematic antibourgeois feeling. But there was much more than mere bravado in Baudelaire's anguish or in the haughty denunciations of the moderns and their appetite for gain by Leconte de Lisle and Renan. One might suggest that the lugubrious decadence of the poets of 1885 came in part from what these young men who had been, like Laforgue, Samain, or Kahn, ten or twelve years of age in 1870, felt and thought as a generation humiliated by defeat. But Belgians like Ivan Gilkin or Max Elskamp, still more lugubrious than the French, did not have the same reason to react as defeated people. Besides, the financial and political renaissance of France after 1872 astonished the world by its vigor and its rapidity. More than ever, Paris seemed to have become the intellectual capital of Europe. The notion, or the mystique of the "end of the century," could have played a role in the widespread conviction in the last decade of the century that the era needed a rejuvenation, were it to consist of welcoming barbarism or in acclaiming the colonial expeditions and the war against the Boers. But the century had not yet come to feel itself moribund at the time of Baudelaire, of the Goncourts attracted and horrified at the same time by the "melancholy rachitis" of suburban areas, and when Laforgue, shortly after his twentieth year, dreamed of an epic lamentation on "the Earth's Sob." Thibaudet has remarked somewhere that it is easy, after the fact, for the historian to enumerate the excellent reasons why that which has occurred in the arts and letters "had" to occur. But the people of the time, who were all the same not in a bad place to judge, were not aware of it. Historians would find no less good reasons for explaining exactly the opposite if it had been the opposite that had occurred.

There was some exhibitionism in what is called by a somewhat pretentious term, the decadent "movement," and a juvenile need to create for oneself an original place among the groups that swarmed in Paris at that time. Quite mediocre poets and some artists, but astonishingly few, joined together thus in Paris between 1880 and 1885, before symbolism had asserted itself. The anecdotal and entirely external history of the movement has been produced in recent years by Noël Richard in A l'aube du symbolisme: Hydropathes, Fumistes, et Décadents[1] and in Le Mouvement décadent: Dandys, Esthètes, et Quintessents.[2] The names of the promoters of these groups scarcely evoke any memory today, and their work is buried, even that of Jean Richepin, who knew his moment of glory and who could appear to be the ancestor of our "hippies"; or that of the one who passed for having been the most fertile of French poets and who certainly devoted the greatest number of poems to wine, if one may call them thus, Raoul Ponchon. The most gifted and most pathetic of these poets who met together on occasion to say "zut" to life, the Zutistes (different from those who had, as in the case of Rimbaud, contributed earlier to the Album Zutique), was Charles Cros.

But he was tired and sad in the 1880s, after having wasted his too rich and, especially, too varied gifts (he was to die in 1888); Louis Forestier has devoted an exhaustive work to him. A review that one might consider decadent, *La Nouvelle Rive Gauche*, launched in 1882, lasted a little longer than many others, three years, and merged with *Lutèce*, in which Verlaine wrote and to which Laforgue gave a few poems. A caricatural and quite amusing mystification organized by two writers (Gabriel Vicaire and Henri Beauclair), almost forgotten today, diverted the Parisian public at the expense of the decadents: *Les Déliquescences d'Adoré Floupette* (1884). A newspaper, *Le Décadent*, appeared in 1886, and soon there was also a review bearing the same name. Verlaine, who jeered at all these groups and their Byzantine discussions and who was beyond the period of his own experimentations, proved amiable toward his younger brethren. He hailed "le décadisme" as "a word of genius. . . . This barbarism is a miraculous sign." He was, after all, the author of a striking sonnet whose first line did much to launch the movement and perhaps even conferred its name on the movement (if it is true that it was orginally a matter of founding a review to be called *Décade*):

Je suis l'Empire à la fin de la décadence,
Qui regarde passer les grands Barbares blancs
En composant des acrostiches indolents. . . .[3]

I am the empire at the end of its decadence
Who watches the passage of the tall, white Barbarians
While composing indolent acrostics. . . .

Mallarmé consented to publish four pieces in *Le Décadent*, founded by Anatole Baju, an obscure elementary school teacher come to Paris from Bellac, but he did not like the word and the label *decadence* and advised one of those activists of the literary life, Léo d'Orfer, to "renounce everything that resembles it." That publication obtained what it sought: publicity. It set forth neither any new idea nor a program, except that which was "to destroy the outmoded," rather than to found something. Dada, thirty-five years later, was to say the same thing. Huysmans' *A Rebours* (*Against the Grain*), in 1884, attracted even greater attention. It is the only truly considerable book in French that the literature of decadence produced. Paul Valéry was to say that he had read it five times. Proust was very much marked by Huysmans. Oscar Wilde in his *Dorian Gray* (1890), D'Annunzio in his novel *Il Piacere* (1889), where the evocation of Rome is that of a consummate artist, Stefan George in the poem *Algabal* (1892), in which he describes the Neronian tastes of a strange Roman emperor originally from the Orient, all bear the traces of *A Rebours*. The man who had been the model for Des Esseintes, Robert de Montesquiou, by his monstrous vanity, the studied effect and affectation of his verses, the hollowness of his inspiration, could represent, as opposed to the Bohemians of Montmartre, the aristocratic side of the decadent movement.

The English writer G. K. Chesterton made the remark that for an author obstinately to seek ways to shock his public by astonishing it is as sure a way of becoming subservient to it as doing one's utmost to please the public would be. There was much of that kind of reverse conformity in the decadence of the years 1880–86. There was also as much a lack of critical intelligence as there was imaginative impotence. The best of what was contained in symbolism was not contaminated by it and gained, on the contrary, in seeing itself liberated from these somewhat charlatanesque, mediocre men of letters. The links between certain symbolists and a rather mysterious current of occultism were closer. The French, it is well known, while proclaiming themselves the friends of rationalism, have numbered as many (if not more) occultists, superstitious people, and practitioners of spells and black magic as any other people: at the court of Catherine de Médicis, in the circle of Mme. de Montespan, in the time of Saint Martin and Fabre d'Olivet, in the period of Pierre Ballanche and that of Eliphas Lévi. But to determine with precision what Balzac and Nerval might owe to Swedenborgianism, Hugo to talking tables, Rimbaud to certain esoteric books that he might have borrowed from his friend Arthur Bretagne, is an impossible task, or almost so. The nature of these esoteric beliefs is to hide themselves and especially to reject any logical systematization. It is rare, moreover, that such a belief is accepted so completely that the esoteric artist takes his place in a group or a sect—in France at least. Baudelaire might have addressed litanies and perhaps prayers to Satan (and to Edgar Allan Poe as well, and to his childhood servant). Louis Ménard called himself a "pagan mystic," others, mystical pantheists, and even Rosicrucians, without there being any question of anything more than momentary inclinations on their part. Nothing of what people have been pleased to state concerning Rimbaud as an oriental voyant, "magus or angel," reader of Eliphas Lévi or of the Kabbala is convincing or helps us to understand him better. Mallarmé used the words *wizard's book, spell, alchemy*; he probably thought by analogy as much as he did according to some logical system. But he replied only with courtly detachment to the invitations of Victor-Emile Michelet, Schuré, and even those of Villiers to take a more direct interest in esoterica.[4] Villiers was much more strongly attracted to occultism, as was Germain Nouveau, at moments, by "the folly of the cross," and especially by that of humility. Sar Péladan published certain of his books in the same period as the symbolists: *Vice suprême* in 1885, *La Décadence esthétique* in 1890. But he made little impression. If there flowed a subterranean trickle of esoteric and purportedly suprarational *philosophia quaedam perennis* behind symbolism, if certain ones like the friend of the young Barrès, Stanislas de Guaita, even lost themselves in it (drugs abetting), none of the symbolists who truly count were touched by it to the point, for example, that Yeats was to be in Great Britain.

The noise made for a time in the literary life of Paris by these little groups of decadents and the exaggeration they brought to their provocations illuminate certain traits of symbolism—weariness first of all. After a half-century of considerable poetic accomplishment, sometimes inspired, and of novelistic creation

hitherto unequaled in France, it was natural for the young coming to literature to
have the impression that everything had been said and that they had to venture
into the byways and thorny paths, bordered with poisonous flowers, to find new
inspiration. They took up again, therefore, the notion on which Gautier and
Baudelaire had already conferred a certain prestige: that art, at certain moments,
must turn its back on nature and cultivate the artificial. D'Albert, in
Mademoiselle de Maupin, had already advanced the facile paradox that "the
correction of form is virtue." The partisans of art for art's sake had maintained
that religion, morality, politics, social preaching, must in no way contaminate
the inviolable purity of art. In the face of the naturalists' prose, which claimed to
capture all of reality (the worlds of business, workers, and peasants) and to reveal
its laws, poetry then sought to diminish its domain, to limit itself to a very small
number of themes. One of these themes, which Nerval had already treated with
nostalgia and grace in *Sylvie* (1854), was the weariness born of having been too
well aware of history and of the long procession of our ancestors (Egypt, Greece,
and Asia Minor, religious syncretism in Rome when the beliefs of the Orient
abounded there). Mallarmé himself, if he disapproved of the word *decadence* as a
label or as a banner, said in the fine prose of his "Autumn Lament" how much
he loved "everything that is summed up in this word: fall." He appreciated the
reading of the decadent poetry of Rome's last days when outside the walls there
grated the clashing sounds of barbarism. The title of Verlaine's celebrated sonnet
"Langor" fully tells the preference of these Lamartinian souls, weary for what
the poet of "The Vine and the House" had loved in the coming of evening:

. . . ces langueurs sereines
Que la fin donne à tout, aux plaisirs comme aux peines.

. . . those serene langors
That the end gives everything, to pleasures as well as to sorrows.

But where the romantics had looked for renewal of their inspiration through
contact with the people, political life, travel, and either the heroic epic (Hugo) or
the intimate and familiar one (*Jocelyn*), symbolism was to prefer to depict abandonment to weariness and to await the coming of the barbarians. Verlaine's
sonnet evokes them; Gauguin's letters were to repeat this need for "the barbarism
that is a rejuvenation" and for a return to the primitivism of childhood. Yeats,
later, in two poems that are among his best, was to invoke Byzantium and the
myth of its slow decay (Edward Gibbon said it lingered for a thousand years), a
Byzantium that took delight in its own fall without entirely succeeding in dying.
Stefan George was to be equally attracted to the barbarians who were to bring to
the totally disillusioned West a brutally new vigor. The Greek Kavafis, who died
in 1933, is the author of a strange dialogue in verse whose refrain—replying to
the inaction of the consuls, the rhetors, the senators, completely paralyzed by
their conviction of the vanity of everything—is: "On this day will come the

Barbarians." In 1905, awaiting a cataclysm in the land of the tsars, Bryusov had predicted that inevitable assault, feared but desired, of the Huns descending from the plains of Pamir, in a poem entitled: "The Coming of the Huns." Baudelaire had already noted in the work of Delacroix this taste among many artists for violence and had spoken in this respect of "the eternal and incorrigible barbarism of man."[5]

Baudelaire is at once the almost mystical, exaggeratedly respectful singer of women in many of his love poems, and the one also who more than any other denounced woman as vampire, witch, too natural to please the dandy, and unworthy of entering into conversation with God in a church. That duality towards the feminine is discernible again in Flaubert, who died a bachelor, in Maupassant, the great seducer, and in those other misogynistic bachelors the Goncourts, who presented, nonetheless, in *Manette Salomon* (1867), some of the most delicate descriptions of the skin, the face, the grace of the young Jewess who is a painters' model. It is true that here it is only a matter of the flesh. There is no longer any more question of the person thus admired having any soul or inner life or knowing how to dream than there is for Renoir's copious beauties or Degas's laundresses. The decadents were also to toy with the hardly flattering conception of woman as a vampire, a never-appeased Messalina, a cold devouress, an indifferent Salome; Gustave Moreau was to be their painter. Their systematic disfigurement of woman (often by way of much drapery, jewels, and serpentine headdresses) was to attract various foreign poets who, in the last decade of the century (the English call that period "The Yellow" or "The Mauve Decade"), were to see themselves as the continuers at the same time of the Parisian decadents and the symbolists. The one in England who did the most at the time to extol the French symbolist movement, Arthur Symons, amused himself by insulting woman, the better to tell her to let herself be loved in and for her body alone, in the mediocre verses of his *London Nights* (1895):

> I know that woman has no soul. I know
> That woman has no possibilities
> Of soul or mind or heart, but merely is.

There was, by contrast, obstinate idealization of woman among the symbolists: Maeterlinck, Viélé-Griffin, Samain. She appeared to them as though disincarnate, pale like a spectral creature from one of Poe's tales, sickly and made for Beatrice's paradise rather than for this brutal earth. It was necessary, Nerval had already written (in *Sylvie*) on this angelization of woman, "that she appear as queen or goddess, especially that she be unapproachable." Like Mélisande or Ophelia, whom the English Pre-Raphaelites loved to paint, she was a creature marked for death, too ethereal for the world here below. This served as an easy pretext for poets not to analyze or to fathom their female companions (who were sublimated like untouchable goddesses or monotonous replicas of a legendary Isolde)—thus better to contemplate themselves.

Narcissus is in fact the figure most typical of these poets. In him, symbolists and decadents cherished a contemplation of themselves. By comparison, the romantics' individualism and Stendhalian egotism had been anodyne. The poets of 1885 fled the brutality of daily life and the too demanding depiction of feminine flesh that risked distracting them from their dream world. Blonde princesses, infantas in white veils and court dresses, a few chaste nymphs, blessed damosels leaning over some celestial balcony, traversed their vision. But all that was no more than evocations brought to life by their "creative" self, since the entire world was only the representation that they made of it. Women or men, they were, like Herodias and her creator, haunted by the theme of the mirror. One ought some day to analyze these evocations in verse, in prose, and on canvas of this Narcissus (an extensive Swedish dissertation by Louise Vinge, in 1967, has done so in English, at Lund, for the centuries before the nineteenth) among Mallarmé, Joachim Gasquet, Jean Royère, the very fine *Treatise on Narcissus* from Gide's youth (1892), published by a house specializing in symbolist works, and Valéry's verses of which certain ones, before *The Young Fate*, so narcissistic in itself, were by his own admission those that pleased him the most from all his work.

It is hardly surprising that the theatre and the novel should not know a glorious fortune in the decadent and symbolist atmosphere of the years 1885–95. For the theatre at least, there were equally important economic and material reasons. It is less costly to gather together seven or eight people in a café, to found a group, and to launch a little review with a provocative title than it is to find a hall, a director, actors, and a public. It was not only, moreover, Mallarmé, Villiers, Verhaeren himself, who dreamed of a stage where Herodias, the Faun, Axel, and Helen of Sparta might be able to acquire power and life. A French scholar, Jacques Robichez, has retraced and analyzed several theatrical attempts by the symbolists, and a no less well-informed American scholar, Haskell Block, has studied sympathetically and with close attention to detail the temptation of the theatre that obssessed Mallarmé all his life.[6]

Maeterlinck must be considered apart. His theatre from the ten or twelve final years of the century, too lightly treated today and probably impossible to stage after three-quarters of a century, maintains a place in the history of the poetic theatre in France. *Axel* is written to be read. Henrik Ibsen, Strindberg, and, in a certain sense, *Ubu Roi* were the only dramatic successes between 1885 and 1900 that one can associate with symbolism—and, retrospectively, *Tête d'Or* (1890), for even though the play was praised at the time by Maeterlinck, it was not played until after Claudel's death in 1955. It was doubtless inevitable that the prosaic sense of reality returned first to the theatre, with the efforts of André Antoine, and that the inclination for moral and philosophical predication should replace on the stage the well-made and empty play (François de Curel and Eugène Brieux); only later were small houses (the Théâtre d'Art, the Théâtre de l'Oeuvre) able to offer to a very limited public works in which other-worldliness and dreams dominated.

It is somewhat difficult today to conceive how very little the decadent and symbolist "movements" counted in the literary life of France and even of Paris and Brussels. Led astray by the classifications of manuals and the labels of the so-called schools and cenacles, we also tend not to recognize that the naturalists and the symbolists, and also the impressionists and postimpressionists, were very far from being enclaves inimical to one another. The public and the best-informed critics, like Jules Lemaître, mingled them all together as the "avant-garde" or the "Bohemians" breaking away from the clarity and restraint of the classics. Then as today, and in France more than in any other country, the most influential critics (Francisque Sarcey, Jules Lemaître, Émile Faguet, Ferdinand Brunetière) were all academic figures or refugees from the university. They hoped that the new would conform to the ancient and be submissive to the values they taught in their classes. The truth is that the same men in many cases advocated indifferently or alternately naturalism and decadence, or even naturalism and symbolism: Huysmans, for example, or Paul Adam, whose first, very naturalistic novel (*Chair molle*) created a scandal and who founded (with a friend) *Le Symbolisme*. Barrès at the start of his career was neither one nor the other; but he respected Taine as much as Baudelaire, and he was to go, without much difficulty, from very solipsistic novels to somewhat heavy novels with a purpose and to realism in his *Les Déracinés*.

The symbolists, if one does not include among them the author of *A Rebours*, were hardly successful in the novel. They were not even open to the ambition of conquering it. Barrès was above all an amiable moralist and ironist, as narcissistic at the beginning as Gide, who quickly came to envy him and then replaced him in the admiration of the young, was capable of being. He also made allusions to barbarians, thought himself the offshoot of an exhausted race, and invoked Schopenhauer and Eduard von Hartmann. He even claimed, in his *Jardin de Bérénice*, to have "put Hartmann into action," and he summed up the meaning of that tale by way of the formula then in vogue among the symbolists: "It is we who have created the universe." Rémy de Gourmont had more inclination for the flesh and even a rather unhealthy eroticism, and Jean Lorrain was inclined toward a certain overly refined sadism and jewels loaded with symbolic meanings. But none of their novels was worthy of survival.[7] *Les Lauriers sont coupés*, by the Wagnerian symbolist Edouard Dujardin (1887), is a very thin work (despite the skill of its technique) and did not deserve the honor that Joyce and, after him, Valéry Larbaud, paid Dujardin for having launched the interior monologue. This technique, whose effect and value were at one moment overestimated, had already been encountered in Russia and was already embryonic in Browning's dramatic monologues. Dujardin lacked the power of invention; his thin novel, only a little symbolistic besides, gives evidence especially of some stylistic skill. In this entire novel, contemporaneous with the first successes of Anatole France and Pierre Loti, which are barely less solipsistic, the quest for form and the artificiality of a too self-conscious prose overshadows the invention, which is weak, and the movement, which is almost nonexistent. The English novels of the same period that derive from them (Walter Pater's *Marius the Epicurean*, for instance, or those of George Moore or Oscar Wilde) have the same weaknesses. The space of yet ten to fifteen years would be needed and the genius of Thomas Mann and Proust for the symbolist novel, still solipsistic and at the same time attracted by estheticism, finally to take form and count master-pieces. The "symbolist era," if it is limited to the last fifteen years of the century, had all but buried the genre of the novel.[8]

But so it is with generations in the arts and letters in which genius abounds and all sorts of innovations are attempted, sometimes too hastily and impetuously, but from which no genius is forthcoming who might assure them of an eminent place in the eyes of history. Neither French mannerism nor French baroque, between 1580 and 1640, nor the rococo later, had the good fortune to produce incontestable masterpieces that today would deserve the admiration of others than scholars and curiosity seekers. The decadent atmosphere, if one insists on so designating it, and then the symbolist atmosphere, which many, along with Paul Bourget in his *Essais de psychologie contemporaine* (1884–86), depict as pessimis-tic and fascinated with nothingness, did not have the luck to encounter in France its philosopher, its critic who might have modified its orientation, its novelist, or its dramatist. Perhaps it needed to engage several of the young writers who were then experimenting with new forms in ways that did not prove fruitful so that, later, profiting from these partial failures, greater writers, taking from symbolism what was seminal in it, would accomplish lasting works. Solipsism, the prefer-ence given to art over life, the contemplation of the self, the fondness for what is outside the rules, eroticism: all that will reappear in differing degrees in Valéry, Gide, and Proust, in Cocteau, Julien Green, and even in André Malraux and several of the surrealists. Their debt to the poetry and the art of 1885–95 will be considerable. Drieu la Rochelle and Marcel Arland are not, in their *mal du siècle* of 1920–25, without echoes of the analogous malady of 1890 and of the characters from those years who are without will, unable to break out of them-selves. But the greatness of that relatively disinherited generation of symbolists of around 1890 remains in their having disinterestedly fled the conventional and the banal and in their having, above all, cherished poetry in their writing and in their lives.

Jules Laforgue is often associated with the decadents, in part because it was in a "decadent" group, Les Hydropathes, where this poet—aged nineteen, paralyzed with timidity and still a child in his candor—met Gustave Kahn. Laforgue, in his memoirs as in his literary innovations at the time, did not distinguish between the decadents and the symbolists. Also, because he was residing in Germany as reader to the aged empress and was cut down by tuber-culosis in 1887, Laforgue was unable to have heard of the symbolist movement, which became aware of him only later. Moreover, he did not have a great deal in common with Mallarmé, whose metallic brilliance and purified beauty he did not appreciate. He was equally far from Verlaine, despite his fondness for popu-lar commonplaces and bantering songs. He recognized the genius of Rimbaud at a moment when very few dared do so, and he hailed in this "enormous, spontaneous someone," the only poet to be set beside Baudelaire. On Baudelaire, with indeed some severe reservations, he has left a few perspicacious pages, the only ones perhaps that give evidence of an original appreciation of the quality of Baudelaire's poetry before twentieth-century criticism. But he was more struck by the intimate quality of *Les Fleurs du Mal* than by their symbolism or the "correspondences." Laforgue himself is too direct in his verse to have recourse to symbols, and he would have been the first to smile at the clichés and the settings of the symbolist poetry of 1888–93. He had sketched the same vague dreams, experienced the same inclination towards idealization of woman. His letters from his twenty-first year, palpitating with romanticism, express it, as in a letter of December 1881 to Charles Henry, for example:

> I contemplate a poetry that would be psychology in a dream form, with flowers, wind, odors, inextricable symphonies with a melodic phrase whose design reappears from time to time.

Ten years later—several years after his death, but before publication of posthumous writings, certain of which gave proof of a remarkable penetration, still unknown—Laforgue would be very frequently cited in Jules Huret's *Enquête*. The symbolists (Gustave Kahn, Robert de Souza) realized he had been perhaps the most original sensibility of his generation, that which had been born around 1860. It was clearly seen that certain of his innovations would have to be taken up one day. He was unclassifiable, and so much the better. Moreover, he knew at the age of twenty-five that he had not yet found himself. We can only speculate on what he might have become in 1895 or in 1910 if he had had before him the seventy or more years that were granted Claudel, Valéry, or his protector and friend Paul Bourget. Wisely, this young man, who had attended Taine's lectures at the Ecole des Beaux-Arts, had declared in an essay on impressionism (collected in his *Mélanges posthumes*):

> Each man is, according to his moment in time, his racial milieu, his social condition, his moment of individual evolution, a certain keyboard on which the external world plays in a certain way. My keyboard is perpetually changing, and there is not another identical to mine. All keyboards are legitimate.

One element of Laforgue's originality was his critical lucidity with regard to his predecessors, his contemporaries, and himself. If he had survived, he could have been the least logomachic of the group's spokesmen, and also its most original innovator. Huysmans, replying to Huret in 1891, declared Laforgue the most gifted of the symbolists. Laforgue had read and reflected more than others; the distance from the Parisian groups, maintained because of his functions in Berlin, Baden-Baden, or Coblenz, allowed his judgment more independence. He was nourished on Schopenhauer and especially on the philosophy of the unconscious of Hartmann, whose profundity he exaggerated a great deal. But that led him at least to expand his melancholy into a less egocentric pessimism and to echo, in verses that seem to seek an epic breadth, "the Earth's sob." The metaphysical unconscious, of which genius makes itself the interpreter, filled for Laforgue the role that the absolute plays in Mallarmé. But this admirer of Hartmann possessed as well the intuition of a psychological and internal unconscious, of virgin forests in each of us, which his poetry already—and much later that of the surrealists—was seeking to lay hold of. In a curious and fine article, published in *Les Entretiens politiques et littéraires* (February 1892), five years after his death, Laforgue speaks of "the internal Africa, domain of our unconscious," where he imagines "rich mines, lodes, underwater worlds that ferment unknown. Ah! It is there that I would like to live, it is there that I would like to die!"[9]

Laforgue's originality derives in great part from a strange mixture of affectation and sincerity. T. S. Eliot, who was fascinated by him at the time of his debut in American poetry, praised "the disassociation of the sensibility" that he appreciated equally among the English Metaphysical poets and in Laforgue. All the most ethereal dreams of the romantics (and of the symbolists), Laforgue, at the end of his adolescence, had dreamed. "Ah! to live only with one's soul!" He had affected with respect to women a cynicism quite as amusing as it was anodyne. "These creatures are adorable," concluded one of his best *Complaintes*. Then, beginning to realize that "these angels have pants and genital organs," he saw in that "the great sadness of his life." He was twenty-two years old and, in those distant times, such naïveté was pardonable. Schopenhauer and (long before him) grim or morbid Christians had denounced woman for similar reasons. Of course, at the age of twenty-six, this disillusioned man of the world, this brattish "little hypertrophic," as he called himself, fell modestly, respectfully in love with the gentlest of British young ladies, Leah Lee, whom he met in Berlin, one of sixteen children of a cloth merchant from Devonshire. She, also tubercular, followed him by a few months in death.

Laforgue had had the courage to perceive that the only way of rendering bearable in literature a sensibility that bordered on sentimentality was to put on masks and play the clown. Behind his verbal clowning and his mischievous insolences, the sincerity of the young man haunted by death quickly appears for anyone who knows how to read. Outcries similar to those that the romantic and Parnassian pessimists had uttered a hundred times would become tolerable and almost tragic. "Stars! I do not want to die! I have genius," or "Ah! to become once again irrevocably nothing." A playful tone would interrupt the movement towards declamation of what he calls (in "Curiosités déplacées") his philosophy pupil's questions: "But who then drew the Universe out of the night?" To the poetry of the symbolist era, which was singularly lacking in it, Laforgue brought a new note: irony—disillusioned irony, but never mean; a generous irony that rather resembles humor, for it is at himself that the poet laughs above all. He is fully aware of the distance that always separates expression from the sentiment as it was experienced, of the internal contradiction that the work strives in vain to resolve. Extremely vulnerable and knowing it, even more timid, he defends himself against the wounds that he might receive from others by laughing at himself first. His sentimental reveries on the eternal feminine and his appeals to the ideal woman would sound less foolish if he made pleasantries as Lord Pierrot does in his lament:

> Celle qui doit me mettre au courant de la Femme
> Nous lui dirons d'abord, de mon air le moins froid:
> "La somme des angles d'un triangle, chère âme,
>   Est égale à deux droits."

> She who would bring me up to date on Woman
> We shall say to her at first, with my least chill air:
> "The sum of the angles of a triangle, beloved soul,
>   Is equal to two rights."

His pretensions to metaphysics and his postures as a thinker are the more easily forgiven him because he began by smiling at his secondhand knowledge:

> Et je vais m'arlequinant des défroques
> Des plus grands penseurs de chaque époque.

> And I go along, Harlequin-suited, in the castoffs
> Of the greatest thinkers of each epoch.

Laforgue's prescience led him, even before those whom we call the minor symbolists had abused rarefied sentiments and a pretentious vocabulary, to caricature their mannerisms:

> Oui, c'est l'automne incantatoire et permanent
> Sans thermomètre, embaumant mers et continents,
> Etangs aveugles, lacs ophtalmiques, fontaines
> De Léthé, cendres d'air, déserts de porcelaine.

> Yes, it is the permanent and incantatory autumn
> Without thermometer, embalming seas and continents,
> Blind pools, opthalmic lakes, fountains
> Of Lethe, airy cinders, porcelain deserts.

Ezra Pound has praised the Laforguian irony which, Pound says, invites one to think. At a certain moment in its evolution and, as it began to feel itself weary of its own poetic tradition, Anglo-American poetry found in Laforgue the one who would lead it pitilessly to examine itself and to join together lyricism and intellectualism. It turned to him as France had once turned toward Edgar Allan Poe. As in the case of Poe, understood, praised, but not imitated by Baudelaire, Mallarmé, and Valéry, Laforgue's influence in English-speaking countries was salutary. He helped those greater than he to mature more surely than they would have done without him—he who took delight in the impish tricks of a very gifted and very young artist while he knew that he was marked by death.

If he has nothing of the visionary and world-restructuring symbolist in the mode of Rimbaud, nothing either of the impressionistic and musical Verlaine,[10] or of Mallarmé who led poetry to its most refined essence, Laforgue had the merit of trying once again (after Baudelaire and a few others) to extract a kind of poetry from the urban and familiar setting, at the risk of accepting the banal and of overusing the pun. Insolent daring was needed for this in those years around 1880, before Walt Whitman and Verhaeren. Here again, T. S. Eliot's Prufrock will be his direct descendant:

Ses grandes angoisses métaphysiques
Sont passées à l'état de chagrins domestiques.

His great metaphysical anguishes
Have changed into domestic annoyances.

While symbolism tended to reduce the domain of the poet to a very small number of themes and to rarefy more and more his atmosphere, at the same time being fascinated with technical games, Laforgue attempted what one line slipped into a project for a preface to Les Fleurs du Mal had ambitiously defined (the poet addressing himself to the great city and advocating, like Constantin Guys, Degas, Monet, modernity and even passing picturesque fads): "You gave me your slime and from it I have made gold." That gold is rarely pure; the music of the verses is sometimes sharp (at least this Pierrot addressing himself to "the chlorotic moon" has inspired some great musicians). The French have not been generous with him, either in his own time or later when the young Rivière judged him guilty of immaturity and refused to let himself be led to Laforguism by his friend Fournier.[11] But alongside the academic critics who have, up to our time, been grudging toward him, Apollinaire, Jean Giraudoux, Jules Supervielle, and, in a different key, Jacques Prévert and Raymond Queneau attest to the fecundity of the example of Laforgue who, out of bitterness or through juvenile boasting, had sometimes called himself a decadent.[12]

8

SYMBOLISM, PAINTING, AND MUSIC

Every critic and professor with any sense has warned readers and students twenty times over against the temptation of proposing analogies between literature, painting, and music. Pitfalls open up, yawning, at every step on this very slippery terrain. Even more than writers who themselves make use of words and concepts, artists become annoyed with critics who translate their works into words and, even when they mean to be kind, resent them. "Artists have new eyes, art critics have spectacles," Paul Eluard mocked. Much earlier, the peevish Degas (who, however, tried his hand at poetry and had friends among men of letters) had declared: "Letters explain the Arts without understanding them. The Arts understand Letters without explaining them." The second term of this epigram is, in any case, contestable.

The fact, however, is that, solicited by questioners, chatting in cafés or in their studios with journalists and others, artists are human enough to launch a few declarations on their art that are as peremptory as they are poorly defined in the terms they use. "One is always sorry for having spoken on the subject of painting," noted Braque, who nonetheless did so, even in writing, in his *Carnets*. They need writers of prefaces for the catalogues of their exhibitions, intermediaries between their work and the visitors to salons and galleries. Despite what they may say, they live on the same planet and often in the same quarter of a major city; they glance through the same reviews; they are subject to the same philosophical or social influences. The anarchists themselves, and the symbolist era had a certain number of them, are fond of meeting other individuals, enemies of the laws. Rarely in France have the ties between painters, music lovers, and men of letters been closer than at the period we call symbolist and that includes many others than symbolists: Zola, Huysmans, Octave Mirbeau, Emile Verhaeren, Félix Fénéon, were art critics and not among the least lucid of them. The fact that neither one nor the other among them rigorously defined the terms that proliferated at the time (*symbol, synthesis, unity, unconscious, idealism*) has little real importance. The history of the arts and that of letters would be dull indeed if the members of a given group (Parnassians, impressionists, symbolists, Nabis, and, later, the Fauves) had professed exactly the same point of view and had ranked themselves under the rule of a single ideological master. Surrealism alone thought itself able to demand such orthodoxy, and it could not avoid desertions, excommunications, and implacable enmities.

Writers from other periods had sometimes addressed poems to their painter friends, as Ronsard had to Janet (the royal painter François Clouet), Molière to Pierre Mignard, Victor Hugo to Louis Boulanger. Painters had kept their distance from men of letters, if one judges on the basis of Nicolas Poussin's, Claude Lorrain's, or Delacroix's reserve in that direction. The most literary of the great painters of the nineteenth century, curiously enough, was Van Gogh, nourished on George Eliot, Alphonse Daudet, Jules Michelet, Hugo, and social literature by which he hoped to replace his lost faith as a son of a Dutch minister. Gauguin was vexed by such romantic and populist inebriation and complained of it to Emile Bernard in 1889. But Van Gogh did not express his metaphysical anguish by abstract or allegorical means in his painting. His art is, as Rouault was to say of his own, "an ardent confession." Let one call it expressionistic before its time, if a label is needed, but Van Gogh was too tormented, too drawn (like Verlaine) into a tragic eddy of tortured forms and strident colors for one to associate him with symbolism. Besides, he died too soon, in 1890.

It was noted in an earlier chapter that it is permissible to delimit (in Verlaine and sometimes in Rimbaud or Mallarmé) a certain literary impressionism, parallel but not identical to pictorial impressionism that received its name in 1874. Beginning around 1880–90, this group of painters was dispersed or lost its cohesion. A still-restricted public took an interest in their paintings. They had imitators and this later movement of heretics and rebels ran the risk of becoming, among the avant-garde milieux, a new orthodoxy—an academism, Gauguin was cruelly to say. Certain painters, innovators in their own way, like Gustave Moreau, the best master of the century if one judges on the basis of the quality of the disciples he formed and whose originality he did not repress, had remained marginal. His celebrated *Oedipus and the Sphinx* (1864) dates almost from the same period as the Salon des Refusés. Huysmans, later, would easily associate him with the decadents. He had a fondness for women who were more than *fatales* (Salome, Messalina, Dalilah, Leda, Pasiphaë) or for strange androgynous creatures: he lived with Orpheus, Narcissus, and the dead gods on whom, as Degas joked, he hung watch chains as visible as the jewels with which he burdened his feminine nudes. While the impressionists took upon themselves to render the ephemeral quality of modernity (horse races, women at their toilets, boaters, beaches, the Saint-Lazare station), he turned his back on his epoch. There was much belated romanticism in his satanic allegories, his ecstatic women, his taste for blood; there was also a worshipful adoration of his own self. His declarations were peremptory:

> I believe neither in what I touch nor in what I see. I believe only in what I do not see and uniquely in what I feel. My brain, my reason seem to me ephemeral and possessed of a doubtful reality. My internal feeling alone seems to me eternal and incontestably certain.[1]

Gauguin and several of his friends (Pierre Puvis de Chavannes, Eugène Carrière, Odilon Redon, and later Maurice Denis) are recognized names that come to mind when one thinks of pictorial symbolism. To the extent that his unstable character allowed it, Gauguin was the leader of this group or the most staunchly affirmative about its tendencies. He was around forty (having been born in 1848) when, at Pont-Aven, he became an enthusiast of "la Synthèse." He reproached his impressionist predecessors for their superficiality: "A surface art, nothing but coquetry, pure material. Thought does not reside in it." They had been wrong in "seeking round about the eye and not in the mysterious center of thought." In Degas, he wrote in September 1889 to Emile Bernard, "something is lacking: a heart that beats." Far from seeking luminous symphonies like the impressionists, he looked for monochromatic effects. Rather than render on canvas the evanescent nuances of misty or radiant nature, he wanted to go beyond and pronounce words dear to the theoreticians of literary symbolism: "The unfathomable mystery remains unfathomable."

In his occasional staccato, mordant, bitter declarations, when he wanted to define his originality by contrasting it to that of those who had preceded him, there reoccur the terms *suggestion*, *abstraction*, and, eventually, *synthesis*:

> Do not paint too closely after nature. Art is an abstraction. Draw from nature while dreaming before it. . . . Seek the suggestion more than the description indeed as music does. . . . Art, instead of being the copy, becomes the subjective deformation of nature.[2]

He even affected the expression *soul states* to which phenomena, the signs the world offers us, direct us; and he confides his dream of "creating diverse harmonies corresponding to the state of our soul."

To the extent that the painter's often peremptory declarations, exacerbated by the incomprehension of a contemporary or by the frightful loneliness of his existence, express what his hand colored on his canvas, Gauguin can doubtless pass for a symbolist. The center from which everything must proceed, he repeated, is the creator's brain. At the time of his first letter to his friend Emile Schuffenecker, on January 14, 1885, he did not hesitate to declare: "For me the great artist is the form of the greatest intelligence; to him come the feelings, the most delicate and thus the most invisible translations of the mind." It is from his emotions, from his dreams, from what his memory provides him that the artist must depart. His successor Maurice Denis, who was to be the theoretician of a certain symbolism in painting and who was to interpret Gauguin after his death in 1903 (perhaps betraying him), praised him for having adopted a new position in art: it consisted "in reproducing our visions and our dreams while representing them by way of harmonious forms and colors."[3]

The danger of such statements (and of declarations by the painter himself) is in their making Gauguin appear to be a literary and quasi-philosophical painter in the manner of the "nazarenes" of the beginning of the nineteenth century in Germany, of a few Swiss painters, or even of his friend Pierre Puvis de Chavannes, from whom he was as insistent upon differentiating himself as he was from Van Gogh. At the end of his life, when a timid success finally came to Gauguin and Maurice Denis wanted to include his paintings in a Parisian exhibition of "symbolist" painting, Gauguin declined the proposal. From Tahiti, in June 1899, he replied that "his Papuan art would have no reason for being beside the ideistic symbolists." To the poet André Fontainas, a friend of Mallarmé and an art critic for *Le Mercure*, Gauguin, in a very beautiful and grave letter of March 1899, defended himself against any literary intention in his large canvas *D'où venons-nous? Que sommes-nous? Où allons-nous?*. As he explained with a rare lucidity, these questions, by their actual inclusion on the canvas, are a signature, not a title. He laid them on only after the work was finished. "I have tried in a suggestive setting to translate my dream without any recourse to literary means, with all the simplicity possible to the craft." In another letter to the same correspondent, in August 1899, he asserted again never having departed a priori from an abstract idea. He even compared his creative process to that of the Bible; like Christ, he infused his parables with a double meaning: the one literal but mysterious, materialized the pure idea; the other was figurative. The mode of expression is sometimes gauche and confused in these letters from a solitary man at the gates of death, refusing all compromise after having been scoffed at for so long. But Gauguin's position is firm. Like certain symbolists in literature, he had sought the One behind the multiple and had attempted synthetic forms; he had wanted to suggest and not describe, to simplify colors. But the vocabulary, often full of pretentious jargon, of the symbolist theoretician who became his collaborator in *Noa Noa*, Charles Morice, hardly attracted Gauguin. The esthetic pursuits of Mallarmé urged the poet more and more toward the unreal and the negation of nature. Gauguin was proud of having formerly known the poet, but he knew that his own way led elsewhere, "far from all allegory." In that same first letter to Fontainas of March 1899, he cited with pride the very limpid phrase that Mallarmé had pronounced with regard to his canvases: "It is extraordinary that one should be able to put so much mystery into so much brightness."

What the painters who followed impressionism have in common was this need to go beyond what the impressionists had, in their eyes, incorporated of naturalism in their work. They proclaimed their right to their dreams and their need to impregnate their pictures with thought and to provoke in those who contemplated them certain "soul states," as Maurice Denis calls them. The word *symbolism* was useful; literature had taken it over, as a challenge at first and then with pride. Was it not equally suitable for painters? Puvis de Chavannes, whom Gauguin respected while feeling very different from him, explained that he hoped to extract the thought enclosed within the confused emotions excited by a spectacle, a reading, a reverie. He turned it about in his mind to bring it to light and then sought a spectacle that might translate it faithfully.[4] Odilon Redon, the greatest of these painters after Gauguin, was the most severe with regard to impressionism and declared to Paul Sérusier that he could not embark on their boat with its "too low ceiling." He wanted a more mysterious art, more shot through with inquietude, resorting to thought and deforming the real. His art often reveals this need for mysticism that obsessed him and that he derived perhaps from his origins: a father who had gone to seek his fortune in America and who had there married a Creole from New Orleans. He had much admired the visionary painter Rodolphe Bresdin; he was annoyed with the followers of the impressionists, among whom he counted Paul Signac. He admired Mallarmé, whose death overwhelmed him; he appreciated, long before many literary figures, at the beginning of the twentieth century, Claudel's *Tête d'Or* and Gide's *Nourritures terrestres*. But he did not confuse painting and literature and hoped the former would never forget that it works on palpable matter.[5] He believed a great deal in subconscious urgings and, paraphrasing without realizing it a remark of the Goncourts in which "books" takes the place of "art," he repeated that "one does not produce the art that one wishes to." But in him there is no disorder and no unleashing of the instincts whatever. His goal was, by his own avowal, "to give visual logic to imaginative elements," a very felicitous definition. There is something of Shelley's Ariel in him, and something of Milton's Lucifer, but also a luminous and melancholy serenity. Those in France who hail periodically the dawn of a classic renascence have claimed him as their own: Charles Morice and Maurice Denis among others, and, later, Robert Rey. Pictorial symbolism, which dates from the last decade of the century was, however, soon going to be succeeded by other artistic revolutions, fauvism and cubism, which were inspired by Van Gogh, Cézanne, and Seurat.

The fate of all innovators, after having struggled to affirm their originality with respect to their immediate predecessors, is to see themselves one day merged with them. Albert Aurier, the combative art critic who had done the most on *Le Mercure* to formulate the symbolist esthetic (ideistic, synthetic, subjectivist), had died in 1892, at the age of twenty-seven. In the same review, on August 1 and 15, 1905, Charles Morice opened an "investigation into the current tendencies in the plastic arts" and admitted that everything coexisted in a state of generalized confusion and that the future was dark. The refrain was not a new one. Three years earlier a new review, *L'Occident*, had been launched; it was to welcome Claudel and Jacques Rivière and to pursue symbolist ideas with Robert de Souza and Viélé-Griffin, but balanced all that with much paler and more pseudoclassic articles. *L'Ermitage*, which had sought at its beginning in 1890 (the same year as *Le Mercure*) to support symbolist innovations, had also become eclectic, contradictory; Charles Maurras had advocated in it *L'Ecole Romane* in 1892, Hugues Rebell had reminded a France fascinated by Northern literatures and dreams of its Latin traditions (September 1893), and Gide had sometimes mocked therein the symbolists' solipsism in his "Billets à Angèle." Maurice Denis published in 1922, in his *Nouvelles Théories*, the preface of a catalogue for an exhibition in Zurich in 1917, "Impressionism and France," and confused or brought together under that term the most diverse of painters, from Monet to Gauguin and even Toulouse-Lautrec, Pierre Bonnard, and Edouard Vuillard. He professed to see in them all "something of Mallarmé's and Verlaine's poetry, of Laforgue's and Rimbaud's fantasy" (p. 60).

In an essay on Giorgione that dates from 1877, Walter Pater had already advanced the proposition, which long impressed French estheticans (including the Abbé Bremond at the time of the debates over pure poetry in 1925), that "it is to the law or the condition of music that all art aspires." The very role of musical instruments in the Italian painter's pictures was one of the signs of this. Mallarmé in poems like "Sainte" had also liked to evoke the "mandora" or other archaic musical instruments. He had been fascinated by the attraction of hieroglyphics that the musical score written on the page assumes for the nonmusician. There is, however, an enormous gulf from there to immolating literature, and especially poetry, to music. None of the great poets of symbolism (or later) wanted to be swallowed up in music. The question of relations between musicians and poets at the end of the last century has caused much ink to flow and brought forth some very imprudent generalizations. Examined closely, it leads the investigator to a skepticism that casts doubt on the authenticity or the fecundity of the relationships between the two arts. In fact, labels of "Wagnerianism" were too quickly brandished with regard to the fortuitous repetitions of "motifs" or themes in novelistic works, and certain of Debussy's pieces were too easily confused with French or even foreign literary works (D. G. Rossetti, G. D'Annunzio) that had served them as points of departure. Recent more precise and impartial studies permit us now to take our bearings more wisely. Apart from rare moments (the sharp debates over Italian and French music in the eighteenth century, for example), French writers had in general taken only a moderate interest in music. Rossini, Meyerbeer had impressed Balzac after he had given himself a bit of musical education, and Beethoven, he said, was the only genius of his century toward whom he felt jealous. George Sand is the writer of that time for whom music mattered the most. But Berlioz's genius, strangely enough (for he was also a writer of talent and had been inspired by Shakespeare and Vergil), had scarcely any influence on the French romantics. Claudel, much later, was to express his admiration for him. But it is abroad, and recently in England, that he has found his most enthusiastic posterity. Liszt, Richard Strauss, and also a number of orchestra conductors and music critics have ranked him highly. In similar fashion, it has been in France less than in his native Germany, Thomas Mann excepted, that literature has spoken the most highly, often the most hermetically and most pretentiously, of Wagner. Sonnets were devoted to him by Verlaine, Mallarmé, René Ghil. Reviews were founded to advocate, sometimes to comment upon, his work. What symbolism entailed that was tender, melancholy, softly dreamy, and, certain people would say, effeminate, was, paradoxically, attracted by the robustness, the often excessively heavy-handed sound effects, the trumpets and cymbals of Wagner's music. For many Frenchmen who had especially appreciated Weber's *Die Freischutz*, then Meyerbeer's *Robert the Devil*, Mendelssohn, Offenbach, Auber, and Massenet, Wagnerianism opened wide the gates of a new and otherwise ambitious musical world.

Here again, Parnassians, symbolists, and even naturalists are not clearly distinguishable and do not line up as friends and enemies in the way the manuals like to present them. Gautier had attended a performance of *Tannhaüser* in Germany, in 1857, but his true admiration for Wagner was suggested to him much later by his daughter Judith. Banville, in 1869, subscribed to Wagner's theoretical views on the joining of lyric drama to music and poetry. For him, and for a few others, the sublime role of the magus, almost that of a mystagogue, reserved by Wagner for the artist, carried forward the most grandiose declarations of the romantics on the glorification of the poet. Baudelaire wrote a warm letter to Wagner in 1860 and also the celebrated article on him that appeared in *La Revue europééne* the following year. But the most convinced realist, and the most prosaic, Jules Champfleury, had, in 1860–61, equally supported without reservations "the hyperromantic German musician" in whom he praised "the Courbet of music."[6] Villiers de l'Isle-Adam was the only first-rate French writer to have known Wagner quite well in Paris in 1865, and then in the course of his visits to Germany in 1868 and 1870, and finally in Bayreuth in 1876. But it was not he who led several writers called symbolists to the cult or simply to hearing Wagner. He was to die, moreover, in 1889. This role belongs rather to the fiery and unmethodical Catulle Mendès, to the French-naturalized Pole Théodore de Wyzéva, and to Edouard Dujardin. Mendès, bustling and clever rather than gifted, but then respected by the most serious men of letters, wrote two articles on Wagner rather late, in 1894 and 1895, in *La Revue de Paris*, which had just been revised under a new format and which addressed itself to a rather wide public. Wyzéva and Dujardin had received solid musical educations and judged Wagner's music and even his theoretical ideas knowledgeably. They were the organizers of *La Revue wagnérienne* in 1885–86 (it lasted until 1888).

Another enlightened and enthusiastic Wagnerian was the Alsatian Edouard Schuré, born in 1842 (therefore the exact contemporary of Mallarmé and Verlaine). In 1866 he had written a very competent history of the German *lied*. In 1876 he published his *Histoire du drame musical* whose very well-deserved success has been lasting. Therein he renders justice to Gluck as the true initiator of this kind of drama among the moderns. His turn of mind attracted him towards mystics of all traditions, from ancient India, the Hellenic mysteries, Orpheus, Plato, Jesus, to a few moderns. His book *Les Grands Initiés*, published in a review in 1886 and often reprinted since, is one of the most enlightened while at the same time one of the most fervent of works devoted to esoteric thought. He rose up "against the iron yoke of positivistic science," as did a number of the symbolists, but he did so without affectation or bombast and with no display of Rosicrucian rituals. To be sure, and according to the perspective of his era, he mixed Arthur de Gobineau (Wagner, it is true, admired him and dedicated his prose works to him), Ibsen, Ada Negri, Moreau, Shelley (whom he read and truly understood), and even Nietzsche in his studies on the precursors and rebels whom he gave as ancestors of the new faith. But he would deserve the sustained attention of a historian of ideas and sensibility. The symbolist movement numbers few apostles so well informed and so little touched by narcissistic egocentrism.

Wyzéva's role is more difficult to specify. He wrote much, on a number of foreign writers and often with the overview of a cultivated journalist. His most lasting work, later, was devoted to Mozart, whom he came to prefer to the author of *Parsifal*. In Wagnerian opera, he had, in 1885–88, hailed the marriage of three art forms: plastic, literary, and musical. He received from it "a psychologi-cal revelation," he proclaimed, and in the obscure style of the time, he saw in this an incitement "for souls to create life." The task devolved upon the self is to create, and alone the creative self will survive. But this talented Jack-of-all-trades had the lucidity to come quickly to mistrust fashionable formulas. He perceived the emptiness of many symbolist declarations and the ridiculousness of René Ghil and of several others. Léon Guichard cites and approves of several frank declarations that Wyzéva gave to *La Revue wagnérienne*, accusing the symbolists of not understanding a great deal about symbols, of not seeking in them profound correspondences or "the means of recreating instantly through a few suggestive images, all of life" (p. 66). He even contested their right to bear the title of "symbolists." In the Wagnerianism for which he and Dujardin had contributed to setting a vogue, he did not hesitate to denounce a certain char-latanism.

Dujardin translated some of Wagner's poetic and theoretical texts. He knew that *La Revue wagnérienne* could not hope to be technical and truly musical in a country where few people are connoisseurs of music. From Wagnerianism he wanted especially to extract a pessimistic, vaguely Schopenhauerian philosophy, and support the group of poets around Mallarmé with a body of doctrine ex-tracted from the works of the German composer. But even when the most competent Germanists sought to synthesize him (such as Henri Lichtenberger in *Richard Wagner, poète et penseur*, in 1911, published by Alcan), Wagner's thought remained disorganized and incoherent. It vacillates according to the readings he was engaging in, from Schopenhauer, Feuerbach, Gobineau, to the influence of Liszt or of a mistress, to his outburst of anger against the Jews. He was not often clear-sightedly faithful to the title of one of his own texts from 1881, "Erkenne dich selbst." Moreover, very few of Wagner's indigestible vol-umes were accessible in French to symbolist writers. Guichard concluded rightly that these French Wagnerians of 1885–92 "were searching less for Wagner than for themselves. Wagner helped them find themselves" (p. 66).

One is permitted not to linger over poets who thought of themselves as Wagner-ian with the greatest conviction, but whose work has not survived: Emmanuel Signoret, hardly a symbolist anyway, and René Ghil whose sonnet "Hymen" (the Wagnerian marriage of music and drama) is ambiguous and whose Wag-nerianism was stamped with defiance toward the imperialist musician from across the Rhine (such was also Mallarmé's feeling on the matter). Stuart Mer-rill, the best informed among them, strove to convert his American compatriots to his interpretation of Wagner at a moment when Wagner was being performed much more in New York than in Paris. The sonnet "Parsifal" that Verlaine gave to *La Revue wagnérienne* in 1886 reveals a fine and unprejudiced comprehen-sion of Wagnerian opera and counts among the poet's fine accomplishments, once again prey to carnal weakness, but recalling his dream of triumphing over the flesh. Verlaine celebrates this hero who has conquered prostitutes (and light-hearted lust), Woman "of the shrewd heart," Hell, the king himself, and redeemed men as the priest does in the symbolism of the mass. The final line, inspired by a phrase of Judith Gautier, takes on a mysterious allure:

Et, ô ces voix d'enfants chantant dans la coupole!
And, O those children's voices singing in the cupola!

Parsifal in this case reflects certain inclinations of the poet, liberated, as he stated elsewhere, "from the last of prejudices," but without betraying too far the meaning of the master's opera.

The issue of *La Revue wagnérienne* (January 8, 1886) in which Verlaine's sonnet appeared contained seven others honoring Wagner, including that of Mallarmé. It is one of the most hermetic and most discussed of homages or "tombs" by Mallarmé, and it seems that the poet himself made light of the arguments in which his friends (Wyzéva, George Moore) and a few enemies (Adolphe Retté) were engaged either to interpret them or to make fun of them. It is possible in fact to find either entertaining or out of place the eighth line that cuts mockingly through the rest: "Rather hide it in a wardrobe for me." Recently, subtle exegeses have been proposed seeing therein (Lloyd Austin) an allusion (one that would in no way enlarge the beauty or the profundity of the sonnet) to the death of Hugo on May 22, 1885, coming two years after that of the musician who, it happens, had been born on May 22, 1813. More generally, with the allusion, dear to the poet, to the sibylline appearance of written music ("wizard's book," "hieroglyphics," "parchments"), Mallarmé seems to have quite simply been honoring Wagner for having, through his comprehensive drama, displaced the light opera in which, up to that time, the French had found such satisfaction.

Mallarmé as we know—he did not hide it—had neither a competence in nor an inclination for music, and he was similar in this respect to many other poets, particularly those whose musical quality in verse is the most praised. In his earliest writings, he subordinated music to poetry and envied music hardly anything except its manner of transcription, which for him was hieroglyphic. He was, again like other poets, to sense in music not a sister, but a rival. One of the best students of symbolism, J.-H. Bornecque, discovered a very typical remark made earlier by Alexandre Dumas in "Un Dîner chez Rossini":

Poetry as Victor Hugo writes it, as Lamartine does, has its own music within it. It is not a sister of music, it is a rival; it is not an ally, it is an adversary.[7]

It was only in 1885 that Mallarmé allowed himself to be taken to the Sunday concerts where Wagner was played. There he dreamed more than he listened, it seems, and scratched down notes or sketches. He contemplated there everything to which he was the most opposed: the assembled crowd, sound that sometimes seemed like noises that were assaults upon silence and dreaming, and "too powerful Music," as Valéry calls it in this regard, that filled him with "a sublime jealousy." Arduously, he composed for Dujardin's review, to which he had promised it, an article, "Richard Wagner, Reverie of a French poet," which was included in *Divagations*. The article appeared in the review on August 8, 1885.

In sybilline but firm terms, while recognizing Wagner's genius, then so highly celebrated by the youth of Paris, and without dissembling his incompetence in musical matters, Mallarmé picked up Wagner's challenge:

> Singular challenge that upon poets, whose duty he usurps with the most candid and splendid bravura, is inflicted by Richard Wagner!

He is struck by the quest for an artistic structure in this musical drama and—this was to be the aspect that would most lastingly impress French writers until Proust—by the return of leitmotifs. He saw in them a search for underlying unity behind phenomena. He admired in them also that independence with regard to the material world that is the privilege of music when it is not descriptive or seminarrative. Intellectually oriented as he so deeply was, he feared in this art the invasion of the unconscious that certain music enthusiasts were to celebrate, in opposition, moreover, to Wagner himself.[8] But he also pronounced the words *magus* and even *minstrel* ("jongleur"). He insinuated that the dance, to which he was more sensitive than to music and which was a more satisfying art form for one as visually inclined as he, was missing in that ambitious drama that sought to be total—especially that element of the dance that would not be disturbed by such loud accompaniment and that would allow one to dream. He was to praise in 1893, in the *National Observer*, Loie Fuller's ballets.[9] Above all, he wanted to maintain his dream of The Book, in which the words would be *seen* on the page and would have a meaning as well as sonorities. "Nothing will remain without being proffered," he stated firmly in 1896, in "Crise de vers," while affirming the poet's duty "quite simply to take back our heritage." He describes there the brasses, the strings, the woodwinds, of musicians as "elementary sonorities." It is "the intellectual word at its apogee" that will be true music. Already, in the article on Wagner and in face of the sometimes delirious arguments over terminology of the French Wagnerians, Mallarmé had opposed a formal denial of the Wagnerian claim:

> If the French mind, strictly imaginative and abstract, casts a light, it will not be thus; it finds distasteful, being in that in agreement with Art in its integrity, which is inventive, the Legend.

He ends with an apostrophe to the recently deceased German composer while isolating him from his admirers, who hailed in Wagnerian drama the sublime temple in which everything was to converge in fanatical adoration, people "bored with everything so that they find definitive salvation."[10]

The rather melancholy conclusion to which the critic must come who dreams of seeing the arts lend new force to one another, as Baudelaire had desired, and of seeing the nations of the West communicate in a single universal, artistic language—music, is that the efforts attempted by symbolism only came to failure. Baudelaire had also written, in recounting what voluptuousness subsequently transformed into knowledge, what Wagnerian music had caused him to experience: "First of all, it seemed to me that this music was mine." Doubtless, in fact, what the French found or rediscovered in Wagner was what they were looking for themselves. Doubtless also, it is quite difficult for creators to separate themselves from the traditions and the tastes of their nation. All comparatism, even that most free from chauvinistic narrowness, that most attracted by the strange and the foreign (as Gide's was, for example), ends by affirming the heterogeneity of various national forms of literature, painting, music. The enthusiasm for Wagner of the French of 1885–90, sometimes delirious in its verbosity, was to be followed by a wave of admiration for the one who was to call himself "a French musician," Debussy, and then by a movement in the direction of pure music. After his first colorful and ardent works, Stravinsky was to strive to repeat to his contemporaries that a sound is not a symbol and does not express religious mysteries or esoteric enigmas, but that it is quite simply a sound. Gide, very soon, exclaimed his horror of Wagnerianism. Valéry was to follow Mallarmé in his revulsion toward this same Wagnerianism and his struggle for poetry against the enemy, music. Claudel would recover from the exaltation in which, for some twenty years, *Parsifal* had plunged him. He was to treat *Tristan und Isolde* with sharp irony along with the leitmotifs, which the master had abused "to the point of nausea." Proust himself would move from Wagner to Debussy, and it is known that he appreciated musicians who were hardly Wagnerian and certainly could have encountered among them, rather than in Wagner, the inspiration for his "little musical phrase." Debussy understood quite early the danger of finding among his predecessors so imperious a genius and knew that he had to exorcise his influence and turn against him.

Debussy had numerous friendships among the poets of symbolism and among the too eloquent heralds of Wagnerianism.[11] At the age of thirty-one, in 1893, he had been persuaded by Catulle Mendès to participate in a partial presentation of *Das Rhiengold* and had come out of that exhausted and perhaps envious and overwhelmed. He went twice to Bayreuth, in 1888 and 1889. He quickly broke away. His nearest friends among the poets were Henri de Régnier, after 1890, and soon thereafter Pierre Louÿs, to whom he was very close for a short time. Louÿs did not overcome his friend's anti-Wagnerianism, despite the intelligent effort that he made in a long letter of October 29, 1896. But he sensed Debussy's originality when few did, in 1896–98, and he supported him materially and morally. The reports, or the hearsay, that have suggested that Mallarmé appreciated only a little the *Prélude à l'Après-midi d'un Faune* are not in agreement. It is far from certain that he replied to the musician who informed him that he was composing a musical work on the Faun: "I thought I had done that myself." But it seems indeed that Mallarmé did not manifest much enthusiasm for his young admirer. After the poet's death, when *Le Mercure*, rather fatuously, presented Debussy as aspiring to take up Mallarmé's heritage (in 1905), Debussy set about putting to music three short pieces by Mallarmé, "Soupir," "Placet futile," and "Eventail," and dedicated them to Geneviève, the master's daughter.

On May 17, 1893, the drama *Pelléas et Mélisande* had been acclaimed in Paris. Mallarmé and Debussy had been equally impressed by the mysterious atmosphere and the appeal of death. For both, there was in it a kind of re-creation of the nuptials of love and death in Poe's tales. Maeterlinck, who confessed to being entirely "blind" in matters of sound and music, permitted his drama to be set to music. The task was a laborious one and was finished only in 1901. The opera was then performed at the Opéra-Comique on April 30, but Maeterlinck did not attend and did not agree to hear it until 1920, two years after the composer's death. A quarrel had driven them apart. Debussy had confided the role of Mélisande to Mary Garden and not to Georgette Leblanc, the Belgian poet's mistress. The rumor ran about that Maeterlinck was practicing at pistol shooting with a mind to challenging Debussy to a duel. In 1925, nearly a quarter century later, he admitted to having been wrong in showing himself to be so easily offended. "Tantaene animis caelestibus irae!" But one likes to learn that the most ethereal poets of symbolism did not love only ideally blessed damosels and Princess Maleines.

No group of poets or theoreticians has ever spoken so much of "musical poetry" and of the marriage between the two arts as that of 1888–95, and even later among the survivors who liked to recount their memories of that era, which seemed to them heroic. "Every impassioned language really becomes of itself musical," suggested one of them, Edmond Barthélemy, writing on Carlyle in *Le Mercure* of 1895. Later, in *La Phalange* of September 15, 1908, Francis Viélé-Griffin, evoking the orchestra conductor Charles Lamoureux, and Mallarmé in top hat, very solemn, resenting this triumph of music, concluded nevertheless that "music made symbolist expression possible." Wyzéva had gone so far as to maintain that suggestion, the very essence of the new poetry according to its high priests, was a musical process.

But nothing is more deceiving than that use of terms that seem to have been borrowed from another art, which no one takes care to define, and under which each places the meaning that suits him. *Harmony, melody, modulation, counterpoint, musical fluidity*: poets and critics play with these terms and set forth grandiose declarations on the musical purity of any poem whatever, or almost any. Schiller, Coleridge, Walter Pater, and many others today have thus legislated in a haze, calling musical what appeared to them vague, dreamy, very often sentimental and delicately sensual. But what contemporaries had declared to be cacophonous in Browning or in Hugo or in Claudel often seems to us, fifty years later, musical and euphonic. This is even more true with the musicality of prose, which is no less real and is treated just as vaguely by the critics. It was not very long ago that Proust, with his impossible sentences, was scorned by many (and notably by music lovers) as totally devoid of harmony. The danger today is that these same sentences (on Albertine asleep or on the hearing of the "little musical phrase" at the salon of Mme. de Sainte-Euverte) could have so easily joined company with Chateaubriand's or Renan's cadences. The wisest of theoreticians, of that young branch of literary studies that is comparison of letters and the arts, advise against this borrowing from music of a terminology that is in no way suited to literature; they also advise against separating, when it is a matter of poetry, the sound and the meaning. But such self-imposed restraints at all levels are scarcely possible for commentators on literature. Confounding the two is too tempting and the practice stands a good chance of reigning forever.[12] It remains for perceptive critics to know how to analyze with precision the musicality of poems like Lamartine's "Ischia," Baudelaire's "Le Jet d'eau," Mallarmé's "Apparition" or Verlaine's "Votre âme est un paysage choisi," without separating it from the poem's images, its suggestions of feeling, of sensuousness, or of the senses themselves. Sonorities, alliterations, assonances, rhymes, refrains, conceal only up to a certain point a poem's musicality. Further, one must remember that composers have very rarely chosen the most profound or the most powerful works of Goethe, Shelley, Hugo, or Baudelaire to set to music, and that many poets we praise for the musical quality of their verse were indifferent to music or liked a musical performance only in that it permitted them to dream and for the extra-musical suggestions it awakened in them. Valéry stated very plainly in his *Choses tues*:[13]

> Music bores me after a short time, and that time is all the shorter as music has had more of an effect upon me. . . . I conclude from this that the true connoisseur of that art is necessarily he to whom it suggests nothing.

It was this possibility of dreaming under the influence of music, sometimes to seek out in their verse the softness and the vagueness, the fluidity of sounds, and the least possible of sculptural clarity of contours that certain symbolist poets loved in music. But opposed to this, there was Mallarmé's hostility for that rival that Valéry evoked in his very subtle homage to Lamoureux.[14] It was also the attitude of several of his admirers. Claudel, who later became, however, an intelligent admirer of Beethoven and Berlioz, wrote on May 25, 1895, of his slight inclination for "the proximity of that mad creature [music] that knows not what she is saying." Valéry, at the very moment when he was finishing *La Jeune Parque* with its almost Wagnerian invocation to spring, and to death, was writing to Pierre Louÿs on June 10 and June 13, 1917: "Do not forget that we are *against* music, Apollo against Dionysos." "Cave musicam," Nietzsche used to say. Still elsewhere: "Music intimidates me, and the art of the musician confounds me. He has at his disposition all the powers that I envy."[15] With more determination than his master, he took unto himself Mallarmé's declaration of war: "Take back from music our heritage." In *Analecta*, he even calls it a form of massage and laughs at Wagner who made of it "the great means to unleashing nonexistent tempests and of opening empty abysses."[16] There would be an entire book to be written on "French Symbolism Against Music."

The synthesis of the arts, of which people spoke more than they attempted to furnish examples of it, was no doubt designed to annoy every mind desirous of purity and noting ironically that "stupidity is not his strong point." For Mallarmé, that synthesis would have been the deed, not of music, but of an ideal poetry that would have encompassed all the arts. For Gauguin and a few of his friends, who knew how to smile also at their pretensions and who, as a joke, spelled the French word *synthèse* as "sintaise," the object was to achieve a so-called philosophical unity through their individual, fragmentary efforts to translate their vision of things into an art form. These efforts and those of René Ghil in literature, which parallel them, have something of the willful and the calculated that render that quest for symbols quite laborious. The Swiss thinker C. G. Jung decreed later that such symbols were, from the outset, deprived of magical power and that only those symbols are true that critical intelligence is powerless to explain. Gauguin sensed this when he wrote in a celebrated letter to Strindberg, a painter of talent and a dramatic genius, that he wanted to return to his childhood hobby horse and rejuvenate himself through "barbarism." But painters and musicians, during the symbolist period, were contaminated with the vogue for amphigorical language, which partially concealed in many of them a total lack of intellectual rigor.

Less ambitious than the hope of bringing together several art forms in one supreme art was the affirmation of the correspondences between the arts that the symbolists owed to Gautier and Baudelaire; even that had had more distant ancestors. People have, since forming the desire to extract an entire mystique from the sonnet "Correspondences," been given to much hair-splitting over the synesthetic effects that the tercets seemed to suggest or illustrate. For Baudelaire, and despite the "dark and profound unity," the various arts are parallel rather than identical to one another. They aspire with their very diverse means to a single world that surpasses them.

But Swedenborg was almost never invoked in symbolist milieux and even quite rarely the grave sonnet from *Les Fleurs du Mal*. Rimbaud's sonnet "Voyelles" was more often mentioned, if not taken seriously. The remark from the "Lettre du Voyant" requiring a language "of the soul, for the soul, incorporating everything, sounds, odors, colors" was not known to the symbolists. The decadents and Huysmans, with much fanfare, played with these synesthetic effects. René Ghil made himself the apostle of synesthesia and thought he was able to provide the phenomenon with a scientific and evolutionary basis. He also ridiculed it for a long time. "Les Phares" and a few others of Baudelaire's poems offered some very fine examples of these translations of one art by another and sometimes even synesthetic effects of sensations simultaneously perceived and corresponding to one another. The poets who followed took almost no advantage of these models. A *Rebours* had played with them too cleverly, which caused the book to be branded as decadent by Max Nordau and other scoffers or social therapists who sought to be moralists and professors of moral hygiene. At times a humorous element enters into these colored sounds or into those musical bever-ages. The poet Saint-Pol-Roux, traveling toward his native Midi by train, spoke of "the cup-of-coffee tunnels followed by the abrupt cognac of the bright sunlight suddenly reappeared" ("La Rose et les épines du chemin"). He announced that art was going to become synthetic and symphonic and therefore complete. Others claimed to have arrived by this means at the realization of a program formulated by Charles Morice in a remark worthy of Hugo on his less felicitous days: "Express all mankind by the entirety of art." To be sure, the synesthetic effects of which Father Castel had dreamed in the eighteenth century are not a trick of the mind; psychologists have demonstrated the incontestable reality, among certain highly sensitive natures, of colored hearing and other correspondences of sensations. But the result for the arts and especially for poetry remain modest indeed. This is not itself one of the great or permanent achievements of symbolism.[17]

The solemn and surprising revelation brought by Mallarmé in 1894 to the students of Oxford and Cambridge has remained celebrated:

J'apporte en effet des nouvelles. Les plus surprenantes.
Même cas ne se vit encore.
On a touché au vers.

I bring in fact some news. The most astonishing.
Such a thing has never yet been seen.
Someone has laid a hand upon verse.

The most difficult of all revolutions for the least revolutionary of countries in matters of language and prosody had taken place. The prose poem, the poet confided to his English listeners, was flowering. He even named as a happy discovery "free verse, individual modulation . . . because every soul is a rhythmic node." He hailed that new fluidity of verse while he himself held to somewhat traditional metrics. In another text, whose disjointed paragraphs were written at three different times (in 1886, 1892, and 1896), "Crise de vers," Mallarmé paid homage to Hugo and Verlaine, who had prepared the way for the great rhythmic revolution, and to the bold strokes (entirely relative to our modern ears) of the young such as Régnier, Viélé-Griffin, and Kahn. His adherence was, moreover, reticent. He remained convinced that "on ample occasions, the solemn tradition, whose preponderance derives from classic genius, will always be obeyed." Others, born twenty years after him, already accustomed to Verlainian innovations, went much further. "Verse is free," cried Viélé-Griffin in 1889. He did reassure the proponents of earlier forms of poetic expression by taking shelter behind the "broken verse" that Hugo, in 1843, had recommended, and to which free verse constituted only a logical continuation. Hugo had insolently slandered "that great simpleton of an alexandrine" and claimed to bite into its long sacrosanct caesura. It was only a matter of pursuing the natural evolution and of letting "the song bird" escape from the "rigid case of the alexandrine" (Viélé-Griffin in 1898, cited in the volume of *Documents* by Guy Michaud). Viélé-Griffin had been encouraged very early by his compatriot Stuart Merrill, who had spoken to him in 1887 of his joy at not being "the only American who is trying to introduce into the French alexandrine a little of the spell-binding music of English verse."

The precedent of foreign poetry doubtless played a role. Several of these poets had praised Shelley, Swinburne, Poe (of course), and Walt Whitman. Others, more rare (de Wyzéva, Marie Krysinska), could have been familiar with German or Polish poetry. The first example of free verse in French, that of Rimbaud in "Marine" and "Mouvement," impressed only a very small number of informed readers; and besides, these poems have perhaps been overrated because of their novelty. Otherwise powerful works in hardly regular verse, like "Mémoire" and indeed the *Illuminations* in prose, could have served to liberate traditional verse. Much vanity and some animosity entered into the debates over the prior claim of this or that one as the initiator of free verse: Gustave Kahn, Marie Krysinska, and Jules Laforgue, who had already disappeared from the scene but who had launched many original views taken up by his friend Verhaeren. The question has only a historical and an academic value. Like many innovations, that of free verse was an almost simultaneous polygenesis.

The technical study of the use of free verse can only be carried out fruitfully in specialized works with numerous calculations or graphs and, occasionally, musical transcriptions. That has been accomplished for three symbolist poets (Verhaeren, Régnier, Viélé-Griffin) by a Swiss scholar in 1943–44, Henri Morier, in *Le Rythme du vers libre symboliste*.[18] Too often, to reassure themselves, French university critics have recalled the precedent of La Fontaine's "free" verse, which used in its own way a number of variable syllables but observed all the other metric conventions: rhyme, caesura, elision, prohibition of the hiatus. People have since preferred to make use of the terms *liberated verse* or *polymorphous verse*. This symbolist verse constituted the first concrete attempt to free French verse from syllabic count and to base rhythm on tonic stresses: no more imposed alternation of feminine and masculine rhymes, no more fixed stanzas. Every form of rigidity was the enemy of this verse. Some great poets have preferred to stay with traditional meter, with stanzas of six or ten lines and with the decasyllabic or alexandrine meters. Valéry was one who affected constraint; recent poets (Eluard, Louis Aragon) have combined these with free assonances. Among others (P.-J. Jouve, Yves Bonnefoy, André Du Boucher, Claude Roy) free verse finds its own rhythm according to the poet and his own psychic state. With Claudel, the *verset*, based on the biblical verse, would produce its most varied effect, and the poet was to formulate his physiological theory of rhythm. Certain poets of this symbolist group, often so intellectual and self-conscious, nonetheless returned, thanks to that freedom of verse, to the song poem and to a popular and sentimental lyricism, as one of them (Robert de Souza) called it. The enrichment brought to French poetry by this symbolist liberation has been incalculable. To undertake this task much courage was needed, not only to take by assault the old fortress of traditional verse, but to run the risks of facility, of lack of rigor and form, of clumsiness disagreeable to the ear, inherent in the polymorphous and autonomous verse that is, henceforth, French verse.

9

THE HERITAGE OF SYMBOLISM IN FRANCE
AND OUTSIDE FRANCE

The almost inevitable and disillusioned conclusion of every investigation undertaken after the event on any collection of literary talents that have been casually
called either classicism, impressionism, or symbolism is that there was neither a
common doctrine nor a clearly perceived goal nor even any technique around
which agreement might have been achieved. It is thus too easy for a mind trained
in analysis and desirous of upsetting the too facile categories of traditional literary
history to poke fun at these poorly defined great words. "Symbolism," Valéry
noted in his *Cahiers* (X, 81), "is the ensemble of people who thought that the
word symbol had a meaning."

There were those who did, and they found not just one meaning (which would
indeed have had an impoverishing effect), but several. And those who did believe
in the word deserve more than our mocking disdain. Very few great poets, we
have already said, were revealed among the generation that came to literary life
around 1885–90, and novelists and dramatists were even scarcer. Never has there
been so much verbosity in manifestoes and so much pretentiousness in the
vocabulary through which they tried to enrich the French language: "uncon-
taminated vocables," "the divine numerator of our apotheosis," "the overwhelm-
ing affirmation of the Absolute," and so on. But it was a question, after all, of setting
out on new paths, and neither the language of Boileau nor that of the *Préface de
Cromwell*, nor even less that of Jules Lemaître or Brunetière was appropriate to
what they were trying to express. That generation, coming after masters who had
left brilliant works and who were not yet fully understood, was no doubt to play
the role of a sacrificed generation. The forward march of literature (and of any
art) is never rectilinear; the end is never envisioned with clarity. What one finds
in the final reckoning is, as in the sciences and political history, something else
than what one had in mind. It was probably necessary to attempt often naïve,
sometimes foolish experiments, to explore (with the various decadents, or René
Ghil, or seers enamored of esoterica) avenues that were found to be barred or
unproductive so other talents could, fifteen years later, profit from these wander-
ings and fully realize themselves. The proverb of the English poet who ought to
have been proclaimed one of the ancestors of French symbolism, but who was all
but unknown at the time, William Blake, holds for literary figures as well as for
moralists: "If others had not been foolish, we should not be wise." There survives
from each generation, and even from each century, but a small number of
unquestioned geniuses, and that is fortunate; otherwise, what would be left for
future groups to aspire to and to attempt? But a collective mystique can be
created by these cenacles and congregations of devout followers of an art form
that they seek to spiritualize. The whole is frequently quite another thing than

the sum of its parts. The most lucid (and often the most dissenting) among the minds who were to pick up the heritage of symbolism, Paul Valéry, is also the one who found accents deeply touched with gratitude and almost piety in order to treat of this Parisian movement that had plunged him, a young provincial of eighteen years, into wonderment.[1]

Symbolism's *virtues*, for that word is the most suitable, were ethical more than esthetic. Valéry confirms this, and they were virtues, in fact, that the youth of the time, decadents or not,[2] perceived and praised and that struck the visitors who flocked to Paris from Belgium, Germany, England. If the symbolists played a little too lightly with the great words of ideality of the world and pursuit of the incorruptible Idea, they at least affirmed their faith in spiritual realities. They repudiated that naturalism whose minor representatives, around Zola, demonstrated themselves, moreover, to be as inferior to *their* great man in imaginative and poetic power as the symbolists were to Mallarmé and Rimbaud. They repudiated positivism as well, along with the pretenses of the half-learned scientists of the time and of a few science-struck philosophers to expel all mystery from the human spirit. They thought to perceive in beings and in things appeals, signs, and to decipher hieroglyphs that spoke of other realities than the overly commonplace ones that surrounded them. Continuators in that respect of men they scarcely knew (the German romantics, Nerval, even Hugo whose encumbering official personality at that time concealed his strange daring in esoteric matters), these symbolists professed to reintegrate mystery into everyday reality.

In so doing, they doubtless revived certain hopes that romantics have always nourished. But there was not among them (even among those whose proclamations contained some charlatanism, such as Moréas or Ghil, even among those like Régnier who quickly acceded to the Academy and knew worldly success) any of that *arrivisme* that had precipitated certain French romantics towards honors, money (or for Lamartine and Balzac, debts), politics. The enthusiasm of these groups for the "beautiful" and the "dream" was a religious enthusiasm and was accompanied by fanaticism and vituperations against those whom it was thought suitable to excommunicate. They generously or timorously founded reviews without a guarantee of any tomorrow. Literary prizes, state subsidies, buyers for the paintings of Van Gogh, Gauguin, Seurat, humiliated by the direst poverty, official patronage for a poor and imprudent Debussy, lectures in the provinces, cultural missions abroad: nothing of this sort came to the aid of the artist of that time. Belgium alone proved to be generous toward them.

Doubtless these poets aspired to too much purity and, as one of Montaigne's chapter titles (II, XX) says, "We never partake of anything pure." They rejected all compromises with the earth and the mob. They disincarnated poetry, emasculated the novel, cursed reality. Reality took its revenge. Too proudly, Mallarmé never ceased saying, they raised hedgerows of thorny signs between the masses and the expression of their dreams. Poor themselves, they sought to be aristocrats of the spirit and did not lose hope of creating little by little the public that would understand them, but would come more than halfway to reach them.

They well knew that the majority of them would be crushed or forgotten, and that only two or three would achieve some glory in their old age or after their death. There was some estheticism and artificiality in their declarations and in their accomplishments. Posterity has avenged itself, since it has condemned most of them to oblivion. But it is through them that poetry, painting, and music were renewed in Europe, thanks often to younger successors who were greater than they.

It was inevitable in the face of that great tidal rush of poetry, disdainful of the concrete and the human, "striking out the real, because it is vile," that less ethereal minds proclaimed their impatience and their hunger for a more substantial nourishment. The Dreyfus Affair, in the final years of the century, catapulted politics into the foreground and literature joined in the fray. Claudel, Valéry, and the more ambitious who had stayed only for a time within the bounds of esthetic individualism, like Barrès, did not prove very lucid in their initial reactions. Gide took a long time before evincing an interest in what he then called, with a certain haughtiness, the people. But from all sides the combat reverberated against the doors of the ancient cenacles. One feels a certain embarrassment even today in noting that—the volatile Péguy excepted and, very timidly, the Proust of *Jean Santeuil*—men of letters were hesitant and lacking in critical lucidity in the face of this unfurling of hatred and this derision of all justice.

Out of that, nevertheless, came the attempt of several writers to participate in popular universities, to write for the Théâtre du Peuple, and to remind Parisian listeners of the great deeds of the Revolution. There grew out of it also a thrust of intransigent nationalism and various neoclassic movements; people began to smile with condescension at the symbolists' audacity in language and versification. One saw in their defense of the rights to dream and to mystery, in their mistrust of rationalism, a form of romanticism, feminine, some hinted, or effeminate, in its preciousness. It is even surprising that one should not have more often charged Rousseau with the responsibility for Rimbaldian mysticism or Verlainian disorderliness. The symbolists were accused at a time when France, humiliated by Germanism, should have fallen back on her Latin traditions, of having betrayed their country by too freely invoking the outside models of Northern literatures.

The history of these groups, in the midst of which the literary edifice of the time crumbled away, has been traced in great detail: the Ecole Romane, naturism that thought itself inspired by Zola, the neoromanticism of Mme. de Noailles and others, the celebration of the machine, the city, speed (Verhaeren, futurism soon to come, Blaise Cendrars), a renaissance calling itself classic and aspiring to a Catholic and occasionally Thomist order (Francis Jammes, Ernest Psichari, Henri Ghéon, Henri Massis, Jacques Maritain).[3] The difficulty with these too detailed literary histories is that they are tempted to grant too much attention to very minor reviews that did not reach five hundred readers, to sensational interviews with writers, with the youth of today or tomorrow, to minute polemics between little subgroups desirous of differentiating themselves from one another. The works themselves disappear. The currents that operated profoundly at the time (the spread of Bergsonism, of Nietzscheism, and, soon, of Dostoevski's influence, the return to the novel with Gide, Rolland, and young writers rich with future potential), more difficult to uncover, are neglected. They pinpoint unanimism whose promotional theses had hardly any consistency or, for that matter, much prestige, and whose poetry is certainly one of the most execrable in the French language over the last hundred years.

In fact, people too quickly thought they had buried symbolism and could move into the vacated space while laughing at Mallarmé or Villiers and foolishly underestimating the explosive charge buried within Rimbaud's work. *La Phalange*, published by Jean Royère, maintained the enthusiasm for the poetry of the years 1888–92, and Royère himself, while brandishing a banner of his own, "Le musicisme," turned out some slender and languid verses on the theme of the "adolescent and androgynous" Narcissus that one could almost take for poems from Valéry's *Album de vers anciens*. It is in that review that Thibaudet published his first essays on Greece before producing the important work on Mallarmé that suddenly revealed, in 1912, the master's survival. *La Nouvelle Revue française*, taken in hand by André Gide after a false start, was much more than a belated defender of symbolism. Thibaudet contributed literary chronicles to it that Claudel was to praise as the best of the post-World War I years; and with Claudel himself, with the first verse works of St.-John Perse, with other poets still later, it was faithful to the cult of literature that had been the true symbolist religion. The only true fidelity in these matters, moreover, is that which pursues what the preceding esthetic held of value, but contradicting it more than once, correcting it, and (especially) rethinking it. If there is some validity in the Goethean aphorism, "that alone is true which is fruitful" (*fruchtbar*), symbolism, too hastily buried by its successors, was to find itself, between 1900 and 1930, one of the truest and most fruitful movements of artistic and literary life.

The most sympathetic and most reflective frontal attack came, moreover, from a young critic in *La Nouvelle Revue française* who, after 1919, took over direction of the review, Jacques Rivière. During his student years he had been a fervent supporter of symbolism, of Henri de Régnier, Laforgue at one time, and Jammes. Letters he exchanged with Alain Fournier were obsessed with the then young and contemporaneous literature (around 1905) grown out of symbolism. Everything in these letters is bookish. The discovery of Claudel's genius had tamed his attraction to what had been stammering and porous in the poetry of the minor symbolists and also in his own delightful hesitations. He had shuddered with all his being upon reading those dramas of possession of the earth and of passion, *Tête d'Or* and *Partage de midi*. Then Gide had drawn him toward the concrete and placed him on his guard against the insidious facility that the prose poem and liberated verse held out to the literary debutant. He had admired the attachment to the soil, to his native land, to his childhood memories of the one who was to become his brother-in-law and write an adventure novel (without exoticism and without action), *Le Grand Meaulnes*. People were talking at the time, in the wake of Robert Louis Stevenson and Joseph Conrad and, especially, Marcel Schwob in France, of the adventure novel, and the term itself or the genre greatly tempted Gide who was then working on *Les Caves du Vatican*.

That great article, published in *La Nouvelle Revue française* in May-July 1913 and included today in *Nouvelles Etudes* (Gallimard, 1947), describes in broad strokes the novel of the future that the young critic prayed for and that would be the opposite of the symbolist novel. The novelist would be neither too self-conscious nor too intelligent. He would turn his back on the cramped and dreary French psychological novel (the very form that Rivière was to attempt twice after the war) and be inspired by Emily Brontë or Dostoevski. The critic set himself up as a prophet or even as a midwife seeking to bring to being from his contemporaries the work that they perhaps carried within them without knowing it.

But first the terrain needed to be cleared, and Rivière, in the first part of his article, took the symbolist movement to task:

> It is an art of extreme self-consciousness, the art of people who are terribly conscious of what they think, what they want, what they do. . . .Everything in the symbolist work bears the mark of a too self-conscious creator.

Rivière does not, however, cite any title, any text. It is with the symbolist novel in general that he is concerned. But what are the examples of this novel? Is it fair to judge the whole of symbolism by precisely the genre that it neglected the most, while leaving aside poetry and investigations into matters of poetics? The symbolist work, he maintains, does not seek and does not encounter any resistance in the concrete. It occurs above all in the mind of its author. It has for a subject only emotions and lacks any internal armature. A single example is mentioned, "L'Après-midi d'un Faune." The words are carefully chosen, but

> The entire poem is made up only of the sparse blossoming, yet everywhere so full, of all those bubbles that escape from the rustic pipes and dissolve in the warm atmosphere.

All that literature, then, is an elite literature, condemning itself from the start to unpopularity. Making a complete reversal of himself, the arrogant critic, twenty-eight years old, admits that, for those very people who had, like himself, loved that literature, rereading it amounted to a disenchantment:

> That verse is like pebbles come from the water in which they shone; one no longer even sees their color in the mind. Something has flown away from between the lines, and precisely because it was something that was only between the lines.

In this sense, Rivière decreed, symbolism is dead.

The verdict was juvenile and severe. But it was time, in 1910 or 1915, to turn toward something else. Rivière's article denotes at least the awareness that the young literary generation of circa 1909–13 had of its own message, which it had to deliver. A splendid renewal of the arts and letters was being produced in Austria, France, England, and the fruitful influence of symbolism still operated on it, but belatedly. In any case, it would not be a matter of imitation, in France at least (Verlaine was imitated in Spanish and Laforgue in English), but of a broadening spiritual influence and a poetic vision of the world to be shared.

"I, too, am a symbolist," the young Gide confided to Valéry, then in Montpellier, on January 26, 1891. Gide adored Mallarmé as much as, from afar, did his friend, who was later to declare to the master that he would have his head cut off for his sake. Gide frequented the circles where one met Régnier, Viélé-Griffin, Louis Hérold. He was preparing to publish, through a publisher that accepted esoteric booklets and symbolist poems, his *Traité du Narcisse*, while his friend, in Montpellier was writing a poem on the same mythological character so dear to the symbolists. *Les Poésies d'André Walter*, published the following year, certainly count among the vaguest and most languid of poems from those years; they do not yet give any indication of what the true Gide was to be, once freed from the clichés of the day and from the unavoidably insincere effusions of a too sincere young man. "My body gets in my way and carnal possession frightens me," the author confides in the *Cahiers* of the same André Walter, his double. Therein one dreams only of ever more chaste caresses. One defers all consummation of desire, all contact with a body, or with the real; and happiness is dishonored as crude and perilous for the soul that it puts to sleep.

In *Si le grain ne meurt*, Gide recounted his schoolboy's enthusiasm for Schopenhauer and how it was good form, among young symbolists, to believe only in the ideality of the world and "to represent" here below, in accordance with the French translation of the title of *Vorstellung*. It was only later that he discovered Leibniz, Spinoza, and then Nietzsche, whom he then preferred over the pessimist to whom he had owed his philosophical initiation. He met Gauguin and James Whistler; he was one of the youngest to attend Mallermé's Tuesdays. He scornfully held, he says, in the mode of groups of the time, "as contingent all that is not absolute." But he soon grew tired of that hothouse atmosphere and of this fanatic cult of the book. We know how he rather quickly convinced himself that this existence, in which he cherished letters to forget the appeals of the flesh and transferred into that adoration of the word something of his Protestantism, vitiated his deeper nature. In October 1893 he embarked for Algeria, leaving behind both his Bible and the effusions and quibblings of the Parisian symbolists. Upon his return, he composed his book, full of irony, *Paludes* (1895), and then *Les Nourritures terrestres* (1897), by way of which he separated himself cleanly from the group (or from what survived of it) in Paris. Through litanies and prose poems that retained much of the symbolists' mannerisms, he cried out his need to touch the real, the warm sand of the beaches, the fruits of the orchards; in a lyrical work that, in effect, emanates application and artificiality, he told what an effort it was to make himself interested in life. A little later, with *L'Immoraliste* (1902), he tried to pass (but still not without effort and repudiating solipsism) from the lycrical "I" to the third person pronoun of the novel.

There could be an entire book written on Gide's persistent symbolism: for neither Nietzsche's attraction for him nor Dostoevski's later nor all his adventures and travels overcame what always remained in him of the bookish. He had to have his pockets stuffed with books, and life had to appear to him through culture. From *Saül, Philoctète, Prométhée*, to the somewhat obvious and gauche theme of counterfeit money in his long novel, up to *Thésée*, how many symbols are in his works!—the little garden gate in *La Porte étroite* and the amethyst cross, physical or moral blindness in *La Symphonie pastorale*, etc. But if one ignores certain minor and paler works (*La Tentative amoureuse, Le Voyage d'Urien*), it was into his *Traité du Narcisse*, as he himself confessed when writing to Valéry on November 3, 1891, that Gide poured all his esthetics, his ethics, and his philosophy.

These few pages are written in a mannered prose that bears the mark of the period: the banks of the river where Narcissus contemplates himself are "like a rough frame in which the water is mounted like an unsilvered glass," and one thinks of the Mallarméan mirror. There it is a matter "of colorless ambiance," of tears shed by the androgynous man, of "leaves from the immemorial Book" and of "Forms" behind which "Truth" resides. Capital letters, of course, abound. The precepts to which the contemplation of his own life and the solitude of its unity had led him are formulated by the author as esthetic rules of universal import:

> Every phenomenon is the Symbol of a Truth. Its only duty is that it manifest it. Its only sin: that it prefer itself.
>
> We live to manifest. The rules of morality and esthetics are the same: every work that does not manifest is useless and, for that very reason, bad. . . . Every representation of the Idea tends to prefer itself to the Idea that it manifests. To prefer oneself—there is the fault. The artist, the scientist, must not prefer himself to the Truth that he wants to speak: therein lies his entire moral code; neither the word, nor the sentence preferred to the Idea that they seek to reveal: I would almost say that that is all of esthetics.

Behind this ambitious attempt to furnish to the symbolist movement its philosophy of the symbol—for the *Traité du Narcisse* aimed at nothing less than that—Gide, as one of his most perceptive commentators has indicated,[4] wished to resolve his personal problem, to leave off the monotonous contemplation of self of his André Walter, repudiate narcissism and "manifest himself" by engaging in esthetic creation, by discovering "the Other" and a truth more general than his small obsession with himself. From symbolism, he was passing already to a kind of classicism. Not to prefer oneself to one's work, to make the sacrifice of oneself, eventually to achieve (this would take Gide some years) a sobriety of style that would approach the natural while at the same time preserving a secret and quasi-sensual vibration, "to become banal," Gide was to say later—the irony directed against himself was going to assist him in that. Gide was to continue to revere Mallarmé and was to give a lecture full of piety on him at Beirut (Lebanon) at the end of World War II. He said how much the *Illuminations* had consoled and guided him at the time of his "convalescence" during his twenty-fifth year. But he quickly understood that one cannot be faithful to an influence except by going beyond it and by setting free the will for innovation and adventure that earlier had urged the great symbolists to scale their slope, moving upward and disdaining immediate popularity to be judged "on appeal."

It would be ridiculous to present Claudel as a symbolist, or to fix any other label on him.[5] The reading of the *Illuminations* was, however, very much for personal reasons, the most powerful upheaval of his life. He spoke on various occasions of his admiration for Verlaine with discernment and praised certain of the least banalized and most tragic of Verlainian pieces: "Bournemouth," "Kaleidoscope." His poem on Verlaine is charged with emotion as much as with humor. Finally, while still a young man and still timid, he attended Mallarmé's Tuesdays, sent a few poems to the master, and corresponded with him (even from faraway China). His first visits must have taken place in 1887. But quickly he admitted to his friends that Mallarméan metaphysics and esthetics found no echo at all in him. He especially admired the poet's form, and also the proverbial graciousness of the master towards the young. He wrote to Mallarmé his gratitude at the time of his return from America to France and congratulated him after the publication of *La Musique et les lettres* (1895) for having distantiated the cumbersome proximity of "that mad creature, music." He added, however, something that is scarcely in the Mallarméan line: "The poet affirms and explains where the other one (the musician) goes like someone who seeks, crying out." The oddity of the Mallarméan sentence with its fragile equilibrium among the absolute ablatives and parenthetical clauses, and what he called on July 26, 1897, "the supreme vault of (the poet's) thought," enchanted him. But he was too earthy to be tempted to imitate that prose in any way. Everything that was ethereal, languid, "vaporous" in symbolism, he was to say on occasion, was antipathetic to him. "One is in creation in order to conquer it," he liked to state, and critics as subtle as Maurice Blanchot had described him (over his protests) as Nietzschean. The only lasting lesson he retained from Mallarmé, visible in *Connaissance de l'Est* and loudly proclaimed in *Les Mémoires improvisés* and his old age, is the question that the poet had taught him to ask: to place oneself before the object and to ask oneself: "Qu'est-ce que cela veut dire?" ("What does that mean?"). Claudel underlined the verb *veut* in that expression. For him (and here he distorted Mallarmé), everything has a meaning and strives to signify and to express something, thus to play its role in the immense harmony of creation.

This is to say that, very quickly, Claudel inflected the Mallarméan message in the direction of his religious faith. Later, when he read *Igitur*, he was frightened at the attraction of the void for the poet and, in general, of the religion of art and the beautiful as the only truth, which so many symbolists had professed. Among the master's poems, he set little value on those that followed "Le Toast funèbre."

Claudel's theatre, praised at the very outset by Maeterlinck, moved away quickly from the disembodied plays of the Belgian dramatist. Maeterlinck's mysticism in his other works would not have been any more appealing to him. He certainly was fond of those he called the poets of the night, Baudelaire and Euripides, "the Greek Baudelaire," but still more he was fond of Aeschylus, Vergil, Dante, and, much later, Racine. Guy Michaud at the end of his long study on symbolism has attempted a kind of apotheosis of Claudel, seeing in him the final achievement of the entire movement. That view of things might be found to be far too partial. From symbolism Claudel had inherited a poetic vision of the world and a sense of freedom with regard to traditional poetic forms, even though he took very little interest in the rather futile controversies over free verse. But, more than Valéry or Suarès (more than Victor Ségalen, among younger writers), much more even than Gide, he had felt himself unhappy "in that special atmosphere of suffocation and stagnation . . . breathed from 1885 to 1890."[6] Much later, on November 7, 1905, and when he was hoping to snatch Gide away from the cult of letters and to bring him to the Catholic faith, he wrote to him:

> Let what one calls "Art" and "Beauty" perish a thousand times if we must prefer creatures to their Creator and the vain constructions of our imagination to our substantial and delectable difference beyond ourselves![7]

Allusion has been made to Valéry's various texts on symbolism with respect to Mallarmé and music. Of all those who, barely twenty years old in 1891–92 (it was in the autumn of 1891 that the young native of Montpellier, at the age of twenty, made his first visit to Paris, to Huysmans and Mallarmé), frequented symbolist circles, Valéry is the one who preserved the most lasting nostalgia for them. Certainly he smiled at the confusion that reigned among these devotees of letters, each of whom affirmed his individualism and often gorged himself on quite empty words. Their sacralization of literature touched him at first, if it was later to cure him for a number of years of that malady of "literaturitis" and turn him towards a fondness for precision and the skillful dismounting of the mechanisms of intellectual creation. The symbolists' aristocratic attitudes, culling the common fold from their readership, amusing themselves sometimes by mystifying the masses, was long for him a favorite attitude, or a pose. There are among his truest admirers those who regret that he should have deviated from his haughty attitude toward the masses and governments after popularity and honors had come more generously to him—or more perilously—than to any other poet since Victor Hugo (or Jacques Delille). One likes to imagine the inscription that Mallarmé might have composed for the Palais de Chaillot of his day, in place of the platitudes devised by the official poet of the Republic. Among his first poems, "Féerie" (with its "silken swans," its "snowy rose," the "sacred light of the moon," his outcry, "Is this to live?"), "Baignée" (with its "young fountain basin," "the mirror," "the golden tresses"), "Le Bois dormant" (and the princess' rings of gold, the "melted wind of the flutes"), and still many others appear to come straight out of a symbolist anthology. "Hélène," "César," could almost have been signed by Heredia or at least by his son-in-law when Régnier had passed beyond his "Odelettes" and free verse to his *Médailles d'argile*. "Le Bois amical," in lines of nine syllables, could be by a Verlaine less ironic and more Vergilian than the poet of "Ingénues":

> Nous marchions comme des fiancés
> Seuls, dans la nuit verte des prairies,
> Nous partagions ce fruit de féeries
> La lune amicale aux insensés.

> We were walking like fiancés
> Alone, in the green night of the plain,
> We partook of this fairy-tale fruit
> The moon friendly to those who have lost their senses.

Of the ten or twelve symbolist poets who wove rather monotonous tapestries on the theme of Narcissus (and, at first, in Latin at least, and according to the name the young poet had read on the grave of a young woman in the park at Montpellier, it was Narcissa, a Herodias, or a Fate), Valéry is the one who showed the greatest persistence—he returned to it three times—and genius:

> Le plus beau des mortels ne peut chérir que soi.[8]

> The most beautiful of mortals can cherish only himself.

and

> J'aime... J'aime... Et qui donc peut aimer autre chose
> Que soi-même?...[9]

> I love... I love... And who then can love another thing
> Than himself?...

Already, however, Valéry was slipping into these verses the most charming musical modulations of all his poetic works and a refined sensuality that stands out clearly against the coolness of the pieces by Ivan Gilkin or by Jean Royère on the same theme. In 1922, when he went back to the three fragments devoted to "that miserable adolescent" who thought himself supremely beautiful, and tied them together, Valéry even thought about explaining in a few pages of prose "his metaphysics of this myth" (letter of May 17, 1926). It is regrettable that he gave up this project and, at the same time, did not set down his reservations with regard to a certain saccharine form of symbolism.

But it would be childish to put so great a poet as Valéry in a cage, a symbolist cage or any other kind. At the same time that he was assembling his first verse works for a collective volume, he was also composing the dense and powerfully reasoned pages of the "Introduction à la méthode de Léonard de Vinci" (1895), "La Conquête allemande" (1897), and he produced, in *La Soirée avec M. Teste* (1897), the wittiest of the novels of the so-called symbolist era. Quite as much as Claudel, he wasted no time in becoming completely himself and generously retaining his gratitude for the Parisian groups that had revealed him to himself. He wrote some deeply felt pages on Verlaine. He was shaken by Rimbaud. He left a few acerbic remarks on Baudelaire and certainly did not make a great case for correspondences or for symbols envisaged as grips on the absolute. He pardoned him for little (in his *Cahiers*) except his having discovered Poe and his having "engendered" (thus going a bit far) poets greater than himself. Baudelaire's eloquent panegyric on the modern appeared to Valéry to verge upon what he most disapproved of: the pursuit of the element of surprise, the shocking, the strange. Baudelaire and all other poets paled for Valéry once he discovered, at the age of nineteen, "Hérodiade."

It is Mallarmé, to be sure, who represented for Valéry the best and the purest of symbolism. About the man, Valéry often wrote with tenderness; he wrote rather little, in truth, on his poetry, his syntax, his ideas, and no one has yet entirely encompassed that mysterious subject of the relationship between the two poets. For both, Valéry indicates in his *Cahiers*, "poem is problem." Both, and Poe is their master, sought to banish the arbitrary from the work of art and to "introduce order into chance." But for Valéry, poetry is above all technique, while with Mallarmé it sought to be *all*: metaphysics, religion, music. On different occasions, Valéry admitted that a poet like Mallarmé is not to be imitated, that he could not exercise any influence. Mallarmé had raised poetry to such perfection that after him one could only remain silent, assassinate him through side experiments and courses on poetics, engage in a kind of murder of this Saturn whose sons were threatened with being annihilated, if not devoured. This great mind who deflated so many windbags was a mystic in his own way, daring even in his most celebrated poem to affirm that "the dream is knowledge." After having so mocked love and calling his old friend Gide an old tart because of his passion for a too coquettish sincerity, Valéry confided in his *Cahiers* of 1918–21: "I think as an arch-pure rationalist; I feel as a mystic."

If symbolism had any influence on the poets of a younger generation, who did not participate in the cenacles, discussions, bursts of enthusiasm for Wagnerian music, or free verse of the years 1885–95, that influence was effected only by way of Rimbaud's or Mallarmé's works read by those who reached their twentieth year around 1900. Victor Ségalen was twenty-eight in 1905, Guillaume Apollinaire twenty-five, Max Jacob twenty-nine, Léon-Paul Fargue twenty-seven, St.-John Perse eighteen. Apollinaire was relatively severe towards Baudelaire, and if he mentions any predecessors (as he sometimes did openly), they are rather Nerval, Heine, and Laforgue. All his will as an artist was directed toward the future of which he wanted to be the announcer. He took the part of the cubists in painting, but not of Gauguin or Redon. If Perse and Ségalen looked toward one of their elders, it was toward Claudel; Perse even voluntarily admitted it. His hieratic ritualism is very different from that of Mallarmé, and his cult of poetry was not as exclusive. Of them all, it was Ségalen, spurred during his years as a navy physician by Wagner and Schopenhauer, faithful reader of Gourmont, soon a fervent admirer of Gauguin, whose trail he had followed to Tahiti (and Rimbaud's to Abyssinia), who seemed most to relive some of the symbolists' fervor for synesthetic effects, for Gustave Moreau, and for certain themes dear to the poets of 1890. He wrote a drama on *Orphée-Roi*. He brought together his scientific knowledge and esoteric experiments in original fashion. But his *Stèles* in no way recalls symbolist free verse or prose poems. Like Apollinaire, he pursued certain lines suggested by the inspired "Coup de dés" in poems inspired by Chinese characters and a kind of "calligrammes."

Proust also is too diverse and too powerful to be reduced in his youthful works to a single position with respect to life and literature. Too much a part of the *beau monde* in his eighteenth year to rub shoulders with the bohemians of the left bank or those of Le Chat Noir, more touched at the time by Baudelaire, Leconte de Lisle (and even Sully Prudhomme) than by Rimbaud or Mallarmé, it was toward Whistler and John Ruskin that he first turned. But he shared with the artists of the symbolist circles a feeling of youthful enchantment before the beauty of flowers, seascapes, feminine fashions, and music that led to dreaming. He had also in common with them the religion of art and the Schopenhauerian conviction that the world is explainable, or acceptable, only as an esthetic phenomenon and that art alone may permit us to escape from our solipsism. Perhaps he would have been no different if he had been completely ignorant of the symbolist movement. But he had breathed that air, been drawn to the decadents, and read Huysmans closely. His novelistic summa was to reply splendidly, twelve or twenty years later, to the expectations of a novelist to come that symbolism had not had, and that Bergson had called forth with all his might.

Foreigners smile readily at the tendency of French comparatists to consider quite naturally that Paris is the cultural center of the Western world and that influences are always exercised in one direction only, all radiating from that center. We think we have not underestimated here the appeal to foreign influences (German and English romantics, mystical philosophers, Wagnerianism) that the symbolist movement often sounded, whether it wished to protect its innovations behind great predecessors, or whether it believed sincerely that it had discovered, as in Poe and perhaps in Hegel, rich lodes not yet exhausted. But it is foreigners themselves who have proclaimed, the loudest and the earliest, their admiration for the works, the poetic message, the esthetic, and the philosophical attitude of the French and Belgian symbolists. The French, who had in their great majority paid little attention to these avant-garde cenacles and to the hazy proclamations on the pursuit of the ideal, were the first to be astonished. They readily made light of it, maintaining that Mallarmé became suddenly clear when he was translated into English or that foreigners were perfidiously seeking to encourage France to sink into decadence and Byzantinism.

We must, however, accept what is evident. Although French romanticism had exercised little influence outside France (even with Hugo and Balzac), and although the poetry of French romanticism had appeared to be equal (perhaps) of that of the English and the Germans, but in no way more original or more daring than theirs, it happens that the poetic movements in these two countries underwent a relative weakening towards the middle of the century. Poetic primacy passed into France with Baudelaire, then with the first great symbolists, but also (for the foreigner rarely separates them) with a few Parnassians and with Gautier. The entire question of the enormous prestige that the artist, master of a sober and constricting form, enjoys in Gautier's work (especially—which surprises the French—the Gautier of *Emaux et Camées*) was bound one day to be explored. The South Americans doubtless needed that discipline of form to subdue their flamboyance. But minds as critical as those of Ezra Pound and T. S. Eliot sought lessons, if not models, from Gautier. It is, of course, much less dangerous for a poet's originality to transplant the stanzas, the style, the irony, and the insolence of a writer from another language than to risk imitating too obviously predecessors that he might have in his own country. Byron, Heine, Poe, became original and influential once transposed into French. Gautier, Banville to some extent, Tristan Corbière, Laforgue later on, were able to serve profitably as models for the Anglo-American imagists and for Eliot. In poetry as in philosophy (and as in the novel: recall the homage paid by Joyce to *Les Lauriers sont coupés* and that of very subtle British minds rendered to Rémy de Gourmont the critic, and even to the paltry novelist that he was), it is not always the best who exercise the greatest influence; it takes too much time and patience to spell out their message.

There is no way of making even a summary sketch of what one might call the various European and American symbolisms and to evaluate what they sought from France and thought they had found there. Such a task could only be approached by a constellation of specialists intimately versed in the national languages, and not French by preference, for a certain patriotic vanity slips easily into these subjects. Our conviction remains, moreover, that in every spiritual exchange the influence (and its capacity for assimilation and imaginative transformation) counts infinitely more than the person from whom the influence emanates. If he has the least bit of authenticity in his talent, Gabriele D'Annunzio, Rubén Darío, Stefan George, Rainer M. Rilke, Oscar Wilde himself, and W. B. Yeats, and any given Russian symbolist will quickly affirm his own personality and free himself from those who first set him into motion. In a history of European symbolism, it is the originality of technique, language, prosody, and inspiration that ought to be emphasized for each country. It matters little whether they took up the theme of the swan, of Salome, Narcissus, or Axel, or whether they used synesthetic effects. If they could not shake the prestige of this or that "decadent" or *précieux* model, and, by contradicting him, become themselves, they remain only *minores* in the literatures of their respective countries.

One of the merits of Parisian symbolism is that it was not dominating and exclusive. Never had France been so openly hospitable to foreign writers, even confiding to them (to Moréas) the drafting of the manifestoes of combat and, later, the advocacy of a return to older "French" qualities of sixteenth-century poetry (Viélé-Griffin, an American, and Moréas, who had become the champion of the Ecole Romane). The Belgian contribution, in reviews full of texts of a remarkable quality, was extraordinarily rich during the symbolist era (and has remained so since), infinitely more than that of the Swiss, the Canadians, or the Levantines.[10] D'Annunzio's Italian compatriots, whom one would not have expected to be so moralistic and puritanical, did not easily pardon his too open decadence, his verbalism, his embarrassing personality, which corresponded a bit too well to the caricature of the Italian held by the Ultramontanes and the Nordics. Even so, *Il Piacere, L'Innocente* are beautiful, sometimes delicate poetic novels, even in their morbid aspects superior to those attempted at the time by the French (1889–92). If he often dipped deeply into the works of Verlaine, Huysmans, even Sar Péladan, and played with themes popular at the time with the French poets, D'Annunzio is not any the less, at his soberest moments in prose or in verse, a great poet. He was capable of imposing his mark on what he had shamelessly borrowed.[11]

Relatively few Spaniards and Spanish-Americans were encountered among the symbolist circles, and it is only later, with the new century, that many of them came to France and voiced aloud their admiration for Valéry's poetry or for that of Claudel. Barrès' attitude and certain of his poses, Heredia's flamboyance, the Parnassians' sonorities, and Verlaine's musicality had, around 1890, fascinated the poets of the New World come to Europe such as Rubén Darío, born in 1867, with a temperament that came near to that of poor Lélian. Certainly, French poetry meant much to him, as it did to the very great group of Spanish poets who are called the generation of 1898. Contrary to the popular belief that often suggests that Spanish poetry is declamatory, too colored and excessively sonorous, or too external, these poets, from Antonio Machado to Jorge Guillén, are the least intoxicated with verbalism, the least sumptuously decorative, the most sober and perhaps the most thoroughly imbued with the inner life, of European poets in their time. The facile and sentimental decadence of the minor symbolists had little attraction for them. Nowhere else did the example of French symbolist poetry act with more discretion and, at the same time, in greater depth.

Mallarmé's and his disciples' prestige was much more imperious in the case of Stefan George, a Rhinelander born in 1869. Disappointed by the mediocrity of his country's contemporary poetry, George came to Paris in 1889 and fell under the charm of the then three heroes of letters: "Villiers, proud enough to occupy a throne, Verlaine, a saint and child in the midst of sin and remorse, and Mallarmé, bleeding for his ideal" (*Franken*). He attended Villiers' funeral, reflected seriously on the symbol and the means of translating thereby the profound self in its mobile state of becoming, translated most of *Les Fleurs du Mal,* and upon returning to his country, launched the review *Blätter für die Kunst* (1892–1900), which did the most in Germany to naturalize symbolism. Curiously, neither he nor any other German esthete made reference at the time to the German romantics that certain symbolists had wanted to hail as their predecessors. George and his group realized that, rather than what had been dreamy, vaguely mystical, and perhaps flaccid in Novalis, Schlegel, and Brentano, they needed form, clarity, and practiced technique. Contrary to his French and Belgian friends, George maintained that German poetry had no reason at all to reject the Parnassians, as Mallarmé might have had reason to do. For us, he wrote to Albert Mockel, one of those who introduced him into the Parisian symbolist milieu:

> Parnassianism is a necessary beginning....We must first develop the plastic possibility of language; we have to create our tools, teach our poets their artisans' craft. [12]

"Hérodiade" served that purpose and it was recited. But so was Banville. The technical revolution to be accomplished in Germany was at the opposite pole from the liberation of verse over which the French were rejoicing. George never appreciated free verse. He worked to form a poetic language set apart from "the words of the tribe," a language sometimes erudite and ritualistic, as that of St.-John Perse was to be. Very impressed by *Axel* and *A Rebours* but led also by his own temperament, George enjoyed donning the decadent and mysteriously hermetic drapery of certain of the French poets. He celebrated the strange and sickly Roman emperor (Syrian in origin), Algabal (Heliogabal) in 1892, and later he grouped his intimates and admirers around the cult of an adolescent boy of extraordinary beauty who, it is said, was marked with the stamp of genius and who died of meningitis at the age of sixteen. This Maximin became a symbol incarnate and remained for the initiates of this cult the piously revered example of a divinized Narcissus.

At the same time, a young Austrian poet of astonishing precocity, Hugo von Hofmannsthal, full of Victor Hugo and Banville (he wrote his first youthful essay on the former and an article on the latter in 1891), and intoxicated on Baudelaire and his poisonous flowers, oriented himself toward the profusion of sensations and colors (rather than nuances) and toward a certain passion for the morbid and the rare, which he had appreciated in French writers. [13] In Bismarck's Germany, so proud of its military power and imbued with a materialism within which (around 1885) a kind of naturalism had been loudly affirmed, advocating the themes of industrial and social life for the novel and poetry, the symbolism inspired by Paris, if it was to find an audience, had to make itself rarefied, esoteric, and had to pose as the claimant for the most haughty artistic purity. This Germanic symbolism lacked somewhat Laforgue's humor and even Mallarmé's irony. Perhaps its truest representative, making his literary debut a little before Proust, more marked by Rodin and (later) by Valéry than by Mallarmé and his circle, was Rilke—and not in his *New Poems* of 1907, still a vague and somewhat pretty work, too preoccupied with objets d'art, but in his great *Elegies* of 1923. The seventh of the grave, serene *Duino Elegies* achieves a fullness of thought and emotion exempt from all mannerism of form that is one of the summits of European symbolism.

Can one speak of a "symbolist movement" in Great Britain, a country where cenacles, schools, groups of writers (the Pre-Raphaelite confraternity excepted) have never played a major role in literary creation? Certainly it is easy to extend the term to include some estheticians and poets of the romantic period: Coleridge, Shelley, Keats, and even De Quincey. Plato, Bishop Berkeley, Schelling, were at the time its philosophical or mystical sources of inspiration. But it happens that this current of speculative thought dried up around the middle of the century. When the English (among whom various Irishmen are included) experienced the need for a renewal of their poetic inspiration, near the end of the century, it was quite naturally toward France that they directed their attention. For them, as for the Germans and the Spanish-Americans, the distinction between Parnassians and symbolists made little difference, and neither did that between Gautier and Henri de Régnier or Laforgue, orthodox symbolists, or decadents. Across the Channel, there was a rich source of fresh ideas on poetry, of themes that seemed new, and a whole lode of lessons in technique to be taken over.

It is never easy for a foreigner to acquire an accurate perspective when he is confronted by a disorganized fermentation of groups, talents, doctrinaire spokesmen, of whom none (neither Morice, nor Wyzéva, nor even Gourmont) took any care truly to clear up the Parisian confusion. England owed its initiation to French symbolism to an inquisitive, adventurous, and also superficial spirit, Arthur Symons, whose book long remained the only one in English from which one could acquire some enlightenment on the subject: *The Symbolist Movement in Literature* (1899). The work was dedicated to Yeats who, having little expertise in French, learned a great deal from it. Symons was to declare later, near the end of his life, that he had detested logic and had always imagined more than he had thought. This was not a negative attribute for studying sympathetically these poets who were still poorly understood in their own country. Symons, the son of a minister from Cornwall, rebelled against religion. He went to Paris in 1889 in the company of Havelock Ellis and returned there the following year, when he showed up at Mallarmé's Tuesdays. Decadence in literature and art, of which one was talking a great deal, fascinated him. It was not designed to repel a compatriot of Swinburne or George Moore. His book having appeared and gained some repute, Symons had some unhappy love affairs and some financial difficulties. In Italy in 1908, he was struck with a serious spell of insanity. Finally cured, he survived a bit like Edouard Dujardin, half forgotten, until World War II. He died in 1945.

The eight chapters in Symons's book (on Nerval, Villiers, Rimbaud, Verlaine, Laforgue, Mallarmé, Huysmans, and Maeterlinck) do not contain any original critical or precise analysis of texts. The author does not hide his preference for a certain mysticism; he praised very highly not vagueness, but mystery. He defined symbols according to Carlyle and maintained that without symbolism there was no literature or even any language. But the novelty of France was in making it so "the unseen world is no longer a dream." Literature in Paris,

... in speaking to us so intimately, so solemnly, as only religion had hitherto
spoken to us, becomes a kind of religion, with all the duties and responsibilities of
the sacred ritual.

The poetry that Symons himself wrote has little value, but his various books of
criticism (on romanticism and other subjects) are not without merit. His compatriots have been hard on this Methodist minister's son become the traveling
salesman of literary Bohemia. Like other artists in his country, he felt himself
pushed either toward solitude (which had been the lot of his master Walter Pater,
and was later to be that of Alfred Housman and E. M. Forster) or toward the
cultivation of his idiosyncrasies. He himself said of Blake, and the avowal is
touching: "He was abnormal, but what was abnormal about him was his health."

There were also the English symbolists who then looked with the greatest
admiration towards France: Richard Le Gallienne, born one year after Symons
in 1866, and Ernest Dowson (1867–1900). Oscar Wilde, ten years older than they
(born in 1856), died as well in 1900. Doubtless, the writers of this British *fin de
siècle* and its artists (like Aubrey Beardsley, 1872–98) exhibited a decadent dan-
dyism and an obstinacy to live like adolescents hurling a challenge at all the
conventions and at death that made them go considerably beyond the pretensions
of their French predecessors. Perhaps it is true of symbolism, as Heine claims it
had been of romanticism in France, that there always remains a stratum of
reason at the base of any French folly, while the Germans or the British throw
reason to the four winds.[14] These English decadents did not have among them a
man of genius or a master capable of teaching them any artistic discipline. In
Oscar Wilde, sometimes at least, and in a no less tragic but more touching way,
and with less pose, in Dowson there were aspects of a great poet. He was nearer
Verlaine than any of Verlaine's fellow countrymen, even in his taste for absinthe
and for the young (in Dowson's case, for not-yet-nubile virgins like those with
whom Ruskin was taken, rather than young males). Like Verlaine also, at certain
moments Dowson thought to find in Catholicism a haven and the voluptuousness
of repentance. Familiar with French from his youth, he did some very good
English versions of the least translatable of Verlaine's poems; and certain of his
own melancholy poems, like the celebrated "Cynara," are the most Baudelairian
in the English language.

There can be no question of "influence," strictly speaking, once it is a matter
of dealing with poets as great as Yeats and Eliot, who quickly affirmed their
originality. They would not have discovered it, however, and they have so
proclaimed with an almost excessive generosity, if they had not first turned away
from their national traditions (judged by them to be arid) and found momentary
inspiration in the poets and theoreticians of French poetry.

Yeats had behind him Blake and Shelley, whom he did not cease to revere and
whose literary fortunes and influence on English poets have never been studied
in detail, which is regrettable. In 1894, at twenty-nine years of age, Yeats hap-

pened to be in Paris in the company of Maud Gonne, whom he later loved long and in vain. With Arthur Symons, he paid a visit to Verlaine. He never frequented, whatever may have been said, the home of Mallarmé with whom, besides, he would not have been able to converse in French. Yeats never came to know that language at all well, although he tried to learn it in Dublin, at the age of fifty, through the Berlitz method, and although he did translate "La Chair est triste, hélas. . . ." It was in France, in January 1939, that he died. It was in France also that, in 1896, he had met, at the Hôtel Corneille, his fellow Irishman the dramatist Synge. Villiers' *Axel* impressed Yeats all the more for his having poorly understood it; he thought he found in this work "the sacred Book to which I am aspiring." He revered Mallarmé, but also the bizarre minds that were interested in magic, Rosicrucians, Péladan, Strindberg. It seemed to him that everything had just been written and painted by the French and he wonders (*Autobiography*), "What more is possible? After us, the savage God!"

Villiers, the man and the writer, impressed him, especially *Élen* and *Axel*. These plays left their imprint on Yeats' dramatic works, if one dares call dramatic the symbolist essays from *The Shadowy Waters* or *Where There is Nothing*. Yeats said he owed to Mallarmé the refined form of his book of verse *The Wind Among the Reeds* (1899), a work very different, however, from the French poet. Yeats continued, even late in his life, to take an interest in those among the younger French poets (Jammes, Claudel, and even Péguy) who appeared to him to pursue the parareligious mystical experiments of certain symbolists.[15] A few images glimpsed through his reading of the French poets stayed with him: "Herodias dancing apparently alone in her narrow and moving luminous circle" (*Autobiography*), the Salome of Moreau, the symbols of the solitary and aloof tower, and especially the swans—Leda's swan in a celebrated sonnet, and the thirty-six wild swans of Coole—all, it seems, the issue of a single couple of placid winged creatures returned to the wild state and capable of flying. After Poe's raven, which enchanted French schoolboys, the swan became the totem of European symbolism and Byzantium, its imaginary pilgrimage site, celebrated in two beautiful poems by Yeats.

It was in 1914, on March 1, while he was in the United States, that Yeats pronounced at a banquet given by the review *Poetry* (edited by Harriet Monroe), the speech in which he praised French symbolism most highly. He began by regretting that too many remnants of a past already repudiated in Europe (sentimentality, rhetoric, moral intent) still subsisted in American poetry. He continued:

> That is not because you are too far from England, but because you are too far from Paris.
> It is from Paris that nearly all the great influences in art and literature have come, from the time of Chaucer until now. Today the metrical experiments of French poets are overwhelming in their variety and delicacy. The best English writing is dominated by French criticism; in France is the great critical mind.[16]

Yeats repudiated above all the tendency toward predication in Victorian literature and its lack of simplicity. At the same time, he put the Americans on guard
against free verse, much more difficult than rhymed verse, and which he never
appreciated. Like so many other poets praised, and with good reason, for the
musicality of their verses, Yeats was himself totally insensitive to music. The son
and brother of painters, he was, on the other hand, quite sensitive to pictorial art.

On various occasions, much earlier, and without being caught up in the
communicative warmth of American banquets before Prohibition, Yeats had
already expressed himself on the same subject. He had rejected the didacticism of
nineteenth-century English poetry, but excepted Shelley from this reproach. In
1898 Yeats had proclaimed that:

> ... All art that is not mere story-telling, or mere portraiture, is symbolic. . . ,for
> it entangles in complex colours and forms, a part of the Divine Essence. (*Sym-
> bolism in Painting*)

In 1900, citing the French symbolists and Symons (*The Symbolism of Poetry*),
Yeats distinguished between intellectual symbols and those—the only true
ones—that are charged with emotion: "Metaphors are not profound enough to be
moving, when they are not symbols. . . . Poetry moves us because of its symbolism." Similar views are scattered through his essay of 1900 on "The Philosophy of Shelley's Poetry," collected in *Ideas of Good and Evil* (1913). Blake is
praised in the same book as the first in the modern period to have "preached the
indissoluable union of all great art and of the symbol." The allegory is condemned as deriving from fancy (according to the celebrated distinction of Coleridge) and as constituting only a decorative entertainment, and the symbol, the
creation of august imagination, is "the only expression possible of some unseen
essence, a diaphonous lamp around a spiritual flame." Yeats rejected, however,
the temptation in some of his contemporaries to have recourse to those immediate or traditional symbols offered by Catholicism or by the return to Hellenic paganism. Quickly, it was toward old Ireland that he turned to revive living
symbols, and then toward occultism. English-language writers have done their
utmost to associate themselves with an international confraternity inspired by the
French symbolists and, thus, have detached themselves from their national
traditions, at least from that called "Anglo-Saxon."[17] Doubtless, like Synge,
George Moore, Lady Gregory, Joyce later on, and so many other Irishmen,
Yeats took great care to separate himself from English literature. But he became
quickly convinced that his work ought to be rooted in Celtic folklore and
mythology, and in an esoteric faith at which those around him played, for he was
readily credulous. He stood, in the eyes of his English-language admirers, at the
crossroads of European symbolism, which, like the phoenix, began to revive
outside France after having passed for dead in Paris.

Yeats barely appreciated the young Eliot, who was too puritanical for him, too
austere, too inclined towards a language without luxuriance, without musicality.

He accorded Eliot a modest place in the very capricious anthology of the poetry of his time that he assembled for the Oxford University Press shortly before his death; but he had characterized Eliot as "an Alexander Pope working without apparent imagination." Suspicion accompanied by quiet scorn had been mutual, moreover. Yeats expected from poetry and from his occultist experiments the revelation of another world; he loved to think of himself as inspired by the spirits to bring together through some Jungian process the feelings and the myths of all time. It is in an entirely different sense that Eliot asked of the artist that he sacrifice the self and refuse to translate his personality directly. He wanted a more biting irony, a less imagistic and less ornate language; he was unconcerned with musicality in the manner of Swinburne or Verlaine, and he made no secret of the degree to which (as translator of Baudelaire and interpreter of French symbolism) Symons had seemed antipathetic to him (the same was true, moreover, of Walter Pater and his estheticism and even of Matthew Arnold). However, Eliot did recognize that it was to Symons that he owed his discovery of Laforgue and Verlaine.[18] It is in an article on Yeats in *Purpose* in 1940 that Eliot declared how he had learned to orient himself in his young years, not toward English predecessors or masters, but toward France and the symbolist period:

> A very young man who is himself stirred to write . . . is looking for masters who will elicit his consciousness of what he wants to say himself, of the kind of poetry that is in him to write . . . the kind of poetry that I needed, to teach me the use of my own voice, did not exist in English at all; it was only to be found in French.

Among these French poets, Baudelaire, as a Christian (in his own way) and a classicist, was later to touch him; Rimbaud in no way, Verlaine very little, Mallarmé less still, at least at the beginning (he came to appreciate him, but only later). Eliot was not often to speculate on the symbol in general or to deify poetry or the book as a means of ascension toward the absolute. He would align himself more and more with Anglican orthodoxy. Born in 1888, he reached his twenty-fifth year only on the eve of World War I. The influence of symbolism in Paris was very weak by then. Eliot, besides, had various enthusiasms among French writers, whose language he spoke (and wrote on several occasions). Through his professors at Harvard, he had been oriented toward Gourmont's dissociation of ideas—excellent no doubt for an Anglo-Saxon mind desirous of seeing clearly, but not too favorable to poetic enthusiasm for reveries and symbols—toward Julien Benda and, stubbornly for a time, toward Charles Maurras. Later, he greatly admired *Anabase* and certain of *Les Charmes* of Valéry.

The poets who were being discussed in Paris around 1888–90, and whom Eliot discovered there twenty years later (thanks in part to his French teacher Alain Fournier), numbered Gautier especially (Eliot's "The Hippopotamous," collected in anthologies like that of Yeats, is a rather humorous and moreover successful adaptation of three stanzas by Gautier of the same title, and of which Ezra Pound was very fond), Laurent Tailhade, whom the French have (regrettably) half forgotten, and Jules Laforgue.[19] Laforgue's ascendancy (and, through him and to a lesser degree, Corbière's) was for Eliot a veritable phenomenon of one artist's possession by another; he himself called it that. By a strange turn of events, Laforgue led Eliot to the late Elizabethans (Webster, Tourneur, Middleton) and to the Metaphysical poets, especially Donne, that he was to restore to popularity as being strangely modern in their "dissociation of sensibility."

Eliot sought at the time instinctively and confusedly what he found in Laforgue: an antisymbolism, one might say, at the very first. Far from castles engulfed in fog, and from ethereal princesses, unicorns, and swans, far also from the narcissism and the pretensions to an orphism that would explain the universe by singing of it, he wanted a concrete, objective evocation of the world of today, of the city, and of what it concealed of the mysterious beneath its sordid external appearances. He believed he detected all that in the poet of *Complaintes*, on the subject of boring Sundays, with a more modern note and one closer to himself (Eliot) than that of his fellow countryman Walt Whitman or of the "Tableaux parisiens" of Baudelaire. Furthermore, Laforgue's slightly bantering insolence, compensating for his timidity (or betraying it), and the conventionality of his life at the German court, taught the young American, distant and a bit stiff, to unburden himself of his awkward sensibility that is typical of youth, to cure himself of individual feelings, and to see himself as one among many others, adrift and tediously melancholy. He confessed to having seen in Laforgue "the inventor of an attitude, of a system of feelings or of ethics," and also the one who introduced into a poetic form, at the time too sumptuous and too distant in its dreams, a resolutely modern language. Finally, Eliot—one of the rare ones among the non-French—appreciated the flexibility of Laforgue's verse. Without boasting at all, but to state the factual truth, Eliot declared in a preface to some selected poems of Ezra Pound that he considered Laforgue's verse, more than that of Pound or Whitman, closer to "the original meaning of free verse."

A rather unusual symbolist, this poet come from America, while Apollinaire, Claudel, Valéry elaborated an entirely different poetry, neglecting Mallarmé, struck only by one or two very youthful verse pieces of Rimbaud (like "Vénus anadyomène"), discovering in Laforgue the master who liberated him and who revealed to him his own originality—as he expressed it much later (in *Purpose*, 1940, speaking of Yeats), "retaining all the particularity of his experience to make of it a general symbol."

American poetry of the twentieth century, especially since the "imagists" and the founding of the magazine *Poetry* (Chicago, 1912), has, more than any other, looked towards France, neglecting the English tradition. But the intersections of influences are very subtle. In some regards, the poetics discovered in Baudelaire and Mallarmé could seem to the Americans to restore to them the Edgar Allan Poe they had misunderstood. Other elements, mystical in a very broad sense, present in France in 1890, were similar to what Emerson, Hawthorne, and Melville had already expressed around 1850–60. It is too easy to affirm influences, and even imitation, while there were at most affinities, and it is a bit unfair to take advantage of this or that overly generous declaration by American poets, taken with France or preferring its literature to their own, long less polished, to enlarge their "debt" to the France of symbolism. This is somewhat what has been done by René Taupin's intelligent but too hasty book on the subject, which today needs to be rendered more precise and better balanced.[20] A contrastingly prudent and very perceptive essay by Haskell Block in a collective volume, *The Shaken Realist*,[21] entitled "The Impact of French Symbolism on Modern American Poetry," indicates the spirit in which these evaluations of subtle relationships between literatures ought to be conducted.

After Walt Whitman, American poetry, toward the end of the century, had known a rather dull period. When its renascence burst forth, it asked of France, as Eliot had done, lessons in sober, concrete technique, almost objective in tone, to escape both moral predication and sentimentality and even the somewhat exaggerated effects adhered to by the singers of modernity and the city. But the imagists were very far from Mallarmé and from the idealist aspirations of the Parisian symbolists; at most, they borrowed from Verlaine a few of his more facile effects. Amy Lowell had more enthusiasm for French poetry than she had original talent; F. S. Flint also, and he was modest enough to say so aloud. Walter Arensberg was a gifted translator (of "L'Après-midi d'un faune," for example) but not a poet of original inspiration and diction. Ezra Pound often expressed himself on the subject of his readings in French and on his trenchant, very arbitrary, and peremptory tastes, notably in a 1928 letter to Taupin, in French, published in 1965 in the second of two large *Cahiers de l'Herne* on Pound. He said there to have learned from Gautier, Rimbaud, somewhat from Laforgue and Corbière, but that, for the essential, he "was oriented before knowing the modern French poets." If there were a lesson to learn there, it was not that of the symbol, but that of form, and not vague, musical, suggestive form, but cleanness of contours. He added: "Nearly *all* the technical experimentation in poetry from 1830—until me—was done in France. . . .The *technique* of the French poets was certainly of a kind to serve as an *education* for poets of my tongue—from Gautier's time to 1912."

With more discretion, such also was the response given on several occasions to those who questioned him by the great American poet of 1920-40 Wallace Stevens. Certainly, he read the French poets, had recourse to titles, to allusions that came from them. He said he was little attracted by the obscurity and a certain esthetic mysticism in Mallarmé, and we ought to believe him. He had read more in Verlaine and liked him better. But an author often is fond of that which differs the most from his own work and which offers him a respite from his more arduous explorations. Stevens is being neither coquettish nor a liar when he refuses to recognize any influences consciously undergone. But the fact that his architectural, powerfully thought poetry, philosophical it its sensibility, but neither cerebral nor the translation of a system, can be compared to Mallarmé's work with which it shows some affinities, seems to us incontestable. It is only the more original for that, as was Hart Crane for having realized the greatness of Rimbaud, or later, Robert Lowell for having appreciated and occasionally translated (and unabashedly betrayed) Racine and Baudelaire.

The echoes of French symbolist poetry are discernible in nearly all twentieth-century American poets of any eminence, but none of them was merely an imitator. None has been attracted by the pursuit of the dream world or the absolute, concerned with mystical correspondences, or tormented by an obsession with purity in art. The distance in time (there is, after all, more than a quarter century between 1890 and the great flowering of American poetry after 1920) and in space, some profound need for vitality and concrete strength in the national character, led that American poetry, as admiring as it may have been of France, into other paths. Eliot, Pound, and the survivors of the ephemeral imagist movement quickly took the decision to liberate themselves from that French influence, only to remain faithful to its spirit.[22] What could be more American than the fact that e e cummings and Robert Lowell, both of whom, while at Harvard (like Stevens and his college friend Arensberg), had been imbued at first with French models? An exception among the poets of the New World, who very quickly installed himself on a Californian promontory and returned to the long dramatic and narrative poem, often through allusion to the most tragic of Greek myths, Robinson Jeffers, deliberately turned his back on the heritage of symbolism. The will chemically or mystically to refine poetry, which Poe and his French successors had placed at the center of their preoccupations, seemed to him, he said, defeatist. Poetry had conceived such a terror of prose that it strove to save its soul at the price of abandoning its body:

> . . . It was becoming slight and fantastic, abstract, unreal, eccentric; and was not even saving its soul, for these are generally anti-poetic qualities. It must reclaim substance and sense and physical and psychological reality.

Boldly and with greatness, Jeffers dared to return to narrative poetry and to themes of contemporary life (stylized and enlarged by his tragic conception of life) and to philosophical and scientific ideas transposed into verse, reclaiming thereby, he maintained, a freedom that poetry had too easily renounced.

If indeed there resided, fifty years later, some virtue in the legacy of French symbolism, it could only become fruitful in four or five other literatures and be appreciated in its essence and in its spirit by undergoing various metamorphoses and by ridding itself of what had been mere accessory ornamentation.

APPENDIX

It is up to those who have the good fortune to be able to read Russian and to respond directly to the texts of Russian poetry to treat it knowledgeably. The Russian symbolist poets are not included in these remarks on the spread of symbolism and the prestige of the French symbolists in the Slavic countries. This is certainly regrettable in many respects for these poets are the most authentic of all the European symbolists and, along with those of the great symbolist generation in France (Verlaine, Mallarmé, Rimbaud), perhaps the greatest.

None of them frequented, in Paris, the decadent or symbolist circles of 1885–90. Among them, decadence and symbolism were inseparable. The earliest of them, Fëdor Sologub, born in 1863, was obsessed with the demoniacal. Konstantin Balmont (born in 1867) espoused decadence and narcissism to a point that would have made the Parisian avant-garde turn pale with envy. Valeri Bryusov, somewhat younger (1873–1924), took several "voyages into Hell" and emphasized his affinity for Verlaine before turning like others to Gautier to learn from him a more sober and formalistic art. Aleksandr Blok (1880–1921) is the most morbid, but also the most profound and most accomplished of these poets, perhaps the greatest in Russia after Pushkin and Lermontov, both of whom died in duels. Bely brought forth, in verse and in some of the finest prose written by a symbolist, a world of apocalyptic phantasmagoria. V. I. Ivanov (1866–1949) blended Hellenico-Asiatic Dionysism with a strange form of Christianity. Among all of them, a romantic *frisson*, a will to go to the very end of the esthetic mysticism inspired in part by Paris, and an almost desperate effort to erect a philosophy defying reason and logic on the base of their artistic faith, gave a wild originality to these Slavic poets. Their symbolism (often touched with Parnassian flamboyance and sumptuousness of form, far more inclined than that of the French to consider music and poetry identical) quickly led them far from their French predecessors. It can be admired only on its own terms and in its Russian context with its fluctuations between Messianism that led several among them to acclaim the Russian Revolution, and despair that shook their reason. The greatest of them, Aleksandr Blok, early turned against the influence of the French (and thus differed with Bryusov and Balmont), while Ivanov preferred to look back to the tragic poets of Greece, and Andrei Bely (Boris Bugaev, 1880–1934) looked through and beyond the French toward German romanticism.

There has scarcely been any question in this work of two of the most original and, doubtless, most "symbolist" of European forms of poetic expression whose affinities with French poetry of the years 1880–1900 are great: those of Spain and Latin America and that of Poland. Those who read the Polish poets in their language place very highly Cyprjan Norwid (1821–83), that Polish "poet of the intellect," as Jean Fabre called him, and several poets of the European literary center that was Cracow: Miriam (Zenon Przesmycki), Rimbaud's translator, the "decadent" Stanisław Przybyszewski, and the powerful symbolist dramatist Stanisław Wyspianski. We unfortunately lack the competence to respond to and judge these poets, seldom translated into French.

NOTES

Chapter 3

1. With André Parinaud (Paris: Le Point du Jour, 1952).
2. "Flagrant Délit," in *La Clé des Champs* (Paris: Sagittaire, 1953).

Chapter 5

1. Robert Goffin, "Retrospections [devoted to Mallarmé]," *Syntheses* 258-59 (December 1967/January 1968):67.
2. *Correspondance*, I, p. 53.
3. *Correspondance*, I, p. 156.
4. J. Cohen, "L'obscurité de Mallarmé," *Revue d'Esthétique* 15 (1962): 64-72. The subtle but sometimes as heavily dogmatic book by Charles Mauron, *Mallarme l'obscur* (Paris: Denoël, 1941), has not avoided the faults indicated here. The work he published in English with Roger Fry, where the poems are translated into awkward foreign prose, is still more disappointing (New York: New Directions, 1951).
5. "The part played by the intentional and the conscious is very much exaggerated; no poet whatever more than Mallarmé is led, tryrannized by words, images, the most accidental and unforeseen associations; as a poet, he is nearer the romantics and Verlaine than the classics and Baudelaire." Such is Thibaudet's judgment in his *Réflexions*, p. 10.
6. *Correspondance*, I, p. 245.
7. Jacques Scherer, *Le Livre de Mallarmé* (Paris: Gallimard, 1957).
8. *Correspondance*, II, p. 266.
9. *Oeuvres* (Paris: Editions de la Pléiade, 1945), pp. 390–95.
10. *Correspondance*, I, p. 104.
11. The most accurate remarks on this theme of Mallarmé's philosophy seem to have been formulated by Antoine Adam in an article, "Premières étapes d'un itinéraire," published in a special issue of *Lettres* devoted to Mallarmé: 3 (1948):125–34.
12. *Oeuvres*, p. 869.
13. *Correspondance*, I, p. 241.
14. Gustave Kahn, *Origines du symbolisme* (Paris: Messein, 1936).
15. Letter from Besançon of May 14, 1867 (*Correspondance*, I, p. 243). It is in the same letter that Mallarmé prided himself on having struck down "the old and wicked plumage, God," and proclaims as a lie all that is not poetry. Curiously, Paul Eluard's beautiful declaration in *Donner à voir* (Paris: Gallimard, 1939) could recall this of Mallarmé: "They are somber truths that appeared in the work of true poets; but they are truths, and almost all the rest is lies."
16. Camille Mauclair, *Idées vivantes* (Paris: Librairie de l'Art Ancien et Moderne, 1904).
17. See chapter XII, "Le Vaisseau fantôme," in Léon Cellier's book, *Mallarmé et la morte qui parle* (Paris: Presses Universitaires de France, 1959).
18. *Correspondance*, II, p. 155.

19. March 1865 letter to Cazalis, *Correspondance*, I, p. 161.
20. Letter to Cazalis, *Correspondance*, I, p. 137.
21. There are certain lines on the interpretation of which one may still differ, in the first section of the poem especially, but the worst kind of betrayal is to seek too far and to subtilize to excess. Charles Mauron, among Mallarmé's exegetes, especially in his English commentary in conjunction with Roger Fry's translation, has fallen into this trap. Other explications are those of Emilie Noulet (*Dix Poémes de Mallarmé*), Robert Cohn (*Toward the Poems of Mallarmé*), and Henri Peyre, in *The Poem Itself*, ed. Stanley Burnshaw (New York: Holt, Rinehart, & Winston, 1960).

Chapter 6

1. Saint-Pol-Roux, "Poesia," *Vers et prose* (June-August 1907): pp. 68–71.
2. Charles Morice, *La Littérature de tout à l'heure* (Paris: Perrin, 1889).
3. *La Revue indépendante* 2 (June 1889): 487–96.
4. Charles Morice, *Du sens religieux de la poésie* (Paris: Vanier, 1893).
5. Tancrède de Visan, *L'Attitude du lyrisme contemporain* (Paris: Le Mercure, 1911).
6. The most considerable of these studies is the dissertation of a Canadian priest, Roméo Arbour, *Bergson et les lettres françaises* (Paris: Corti, 1955). Pierre Moreau has added a few indications to the subject and pointed out the perils of these studies in two *comptes-rendus: Revue d'Histoire littéraire de la France* (April-June 1958), and *Revue de Littérature comparée* (September-December 1963).
7. Henri Bergson, *La Philosophie française* (Paris: Alcan, 1915).
8. One of the symbolist poets, and not one of the most lucid, Saint-Pol-Roux (his actual given name was Pol, but he was born in Saint-Henri in the Midi), writing on "The Miracle of 1886," in the issue of *Les Nouvelles littéraires* dated June 20, 1936, devoted to the fiftieth anniversary of symbolism, declared proudly: "The memory is others; the imagination is ourselves. . . . Minds always meet in the field of memory, never in the infinity of the imagination." The entire article is quite delirious.
9. Henri Bergson, *La Pensée et le mouvant* (Paris: Alcan, 1934), p. 266.
10. Eméric Fiser has several pages on the subject of the symbol according to Bergson in his book, *Le Symbole littéraire* (Paris: Corti, 1942). Marcel Raymond presents some subtle remarks in "Bergson et la poésie recente," *Cahiers du Rhône* 4 (1942): 218–32.
11. Henri Mondor in his *Vie de Mallarmé*, II, p. 532, tells how, in 1888, the poet one day took Henri de Régnier to the Avenue Henri-Martin to visit the abandoned chalet where Lamartine had died. Régnier adds: "Then, Mallarmé spoke to me of Lamartine as he knew how to talk of poets, with the best critical finesse and ingenious sympathy that he applied to all his literary judgments." Mondor refers the reader to Régnier's *Proses datées* (Paris: Le Mercure, 1925), p. 104.
Charles Morice, in *La Littérature de tout à l'heure* (Paris: Perrin, 1889), p. 145, writes: "Lamartine remains our only Poet, the only one whose name evokes a whole world of enchantment, aristocracy, dreams, Beauty. . . .Alone of French poets, he escapes the didactic."
12. Alfred North Whitehead, *Symbolism, Its Meaning and Effect* (Cambridge: Cambridge University Press, 1925).
13. An American book, which is very superficial, has touched on this subject, which

needs to be taken up again in depth: James L. Kugel, *The Techniques of Strangeness in Symbolist Poetry* (New Haven: Yale University Press, 1971).

14. Morice, *Du Sens religieux de la poésie*, p. 47.

15. de Visan, *L'Attitude du lyrisme contemporain*, p. 453.

16. Albert Thibaudet, *Reflexions sur la littérature*, I (Paris: Gallimard, 1932).

17. John Clifford Ireson, *Gustave Kahn* (Paris: Nizet, 1962).

18. "We have thought pure things / Side by side along the paths, / We held each other's hand / Without saying. . . ." ("The Friendly Wood"), or again "The Bath" ("La Baignée"), in Adolphe Van Bever and Paul Léautaud's anthology, in which one finds trembling gardens, pools, pendants, lilies, and so on.

19. In our book on *Les Générations littéraires* (Paris: Boivin, 1947).

Chapter 7

1. Noël Richard, *A l'aube du symbolisme: Hydropathes, Fumistes, et Décadents* (Paris: Nizet, 1961).

2. Noël Richard, *Le Mouvement decadent: Dandys, Esthètes, et Quintessents* (Paris: Nizet, 1968).

3. Paul Verlaine, "Langueur," *Le Chat noir*, May 26, 1883.

4. Such seems to be the considered opinion of the author who has recently and rather competently (confusedly also) treated this subject: Alain Mercier, *Les Sources ésotériques et occultes de la poésie symboliste* (Paris: Nizet, 1969).

5. Renato Poggioli has associated this modern Greek poet and this Russian poet with the decadents of France in an essay first published in English and then in French in *Diogene* 38 (April-June 1962): 77–90. The title, "L'automne des idées" comes from Baudelaire's "L'Ennemi."

6. Jacques Robichez, *Le Symbolisme au théâtre: Lugné-Poe* (Paris: L'Arche, 1957); Haskell Block, *Mallarmé and the Symbolist Drama* (Detroit: Wayne State University Press, 1963).

7. An American scholar, Karl Uitti, has written a very good book on the little-explored subject of the symbolist novel: *The Concept of the Self in the Symbolist Novel* (The Hague: Mouton, 1961). He gives a large place therein to Rémy de Gourmont, on whom he has also published a large work: *La Passion littéraire de Gourmont* (Paris: Presses Universitaires de France, 1962).

8. Théodore de Wyzéva, the Wagnerian, the well-informed connoisseur of Mozart and of several foreign literatures, is also the author of a novel, *Valbert ou les récits d'un jeune homme* (Paris: Perrin, 1893). The narration is sober, thin, and often awkward. The pale hero, smitten with music, loves—he says—only love; he wants to love, but he suffers from the inability to give of himself. He pities himself to the point of satiety: "I am alone, frightfully alone, and everyday I feel the void enlarge itself around me." This Hamletlike attitude recalls the early novels of Paul Bourget, but here it is more dreary and more static.

9. On Laforgue's thought, his readings, and especially his prestige among Anglo-Saxon poets the best work is that of Warren Ramsey, *Jules Laforgue and the Ironic Inheritance* (New York: Oxford University Press, 1953). The best studies in French are those of Marie-Jeanne Durry (Paris: Seghers, 1952) and Pierre Reboul (Paris: Hatier, 1961).

10. A curious thing, and one that reveals Laforgue's flair: he was among the very few among the symbolists who understood and praised the impressionist painters. In a letter from Coblenz on December 1, 1881, he waxes ardent over the memory of the pictures he had liked best among those that his friend Charles Ephrussi possessed: Pissarro, Sisley, Renoir, Berthe Morisot, Degas, Monet. Laforgue justified his fondness for impressionism by philosophical arguments: contrary to Taine's esthetics, he maintained that, all schools being worthwhile in the view of Hartmann's concept of the unconscious, the best criterion of the beautiful is novelty; and impressionism consecrated that novelty in going from drawing to the magic of colors "like fingers in one's eyes." See the monograph of Médéric Dufour, *Une Philosophie de l'impressionisme. Etude sur l'esthétique de Jules Laforgue* (Vanier-Messein, 1904), and the article by G. Mesirca, "Laforgue e l'Impressionismo," *Rassegna d'Italia* 11-12 (1941): 25–34.

11. An interesting letter to Rivière from Fournier (April 23, 1906) analyzes his reactions with regard to Laforgue and the reasons that one may have for liking him, not without formulating some reservations on his verbal facility and on his monotonous repetitions on the famous misunderstanding between the sexes. Rivière resists (May 6, 1906). His judgments are more those of a young man who does not trust his senses or the spontaneity of his taste, but who insists upon understanding and analyzing. It is true that in the same letter (but this is a youthful indiscretion, and this perspective was long held by the French) Rivière suggests that Mallarmé, Rimbaud, and Verlaine are only precursors: "Their glory is in having made possible Régnier, Jammes, . . .who are the great ones," to whom he added Claudel.

12. At the moment when he rebelled against Taine's esthetic based on determinism—but also on ethics—Laforgue wrote to Charles Ephrussi about a person encountered in Prussia: "M. M. . . . must be, along with me, the only man in Berlin who adores *decadence* in everything."

Chapter 8

1. It is to a Swede, Ragnar von Holten, that we owe the best book on this painter. Its title is *Gustave Moreau, Symbolist* (in French, *L'Art fantastique de G. Moreau* [Paris: Pauvert, 1961]).

2. Letter to Emile Schuffenecker, August 14, 1888: *Lettres de Gauguin* (Paris: Grasset, 1946), p. 321.

3. Maurice Denis, *Théories* (Paris: Rouart et Watelin, 1913) and *Nouvelles Théories* (Paris: Rouart et Watelin, 1920).

4. Charles Chassé reports Puvis's words in his book: *Le Mouvement symboliste dans l'art du XIXe siecle* (Paris: Floury, 1947).

5. Odilon Redon, *Lettres* (Paris: Van Oest, 1923); from a letter to Gabriel Frizeau, an admirer of Claudel and a friend of St.-John Perse and Rivière, dated October 12, 1911. We know Redon's ideas by way of his notes entitled A *soi-même*, which are his journal kept from his twenty-seventh year until his death. The best work on Redon, beautifully illustrated, is that of Klaus Berger, *Redon, Fantasy and Color* (New York: McGraw-Hill, 1958).

6. On these points and on the history of Wagnerianism in France, Léon Guichard's work is the most precise and the most restrained: *La Musique et les lettres en France au*

temps du wagnérisme (Paris: Presses Universitaires de France, 1963). It is preferable to the hasty dissertation of Grange Woolley, *Wagner et le symbolisme français* (Paris: Presses Universitaires de France, 1931), and to the two volumes by Kurt Jaeckel, *Wagner in der französischen Literatur* (Breslau: Priebatsch, 1931–32).

7. J.-H. Bornecque, "Rêves et réalités du symbolisme," *Revue des sciences humaines* 77 (January-March 1955): 20.

8. Albert Bazaillas, *Musique et inconscience* (Paris: Alcan, 1908). In 1847 Wagner had been warned by one of his young correspondents, Eduard Hanslick, against that tendency: "Guard against giving too little esteem to the value of reflection. The unconsciously produced work of art belongs to periods separated from ours by immense intervals. The work of art from a period of high civilization can only be produced by a fully conscious artist." It is true that Wagner did not fear contradicting himself, or evolving, in the course of his various ideological enthusiasms.

9. Mallarmé, *Oeuvres* (Paris: Gallimard, 1942), pp. 307–09.

10. Other than the book by Léon Guichard, mentioned above, the best studies on the subject of Mallarmé and music are those of Suzanne Bernard, *Mallarmé et la musique* (Paris: Nizet, 1959); Charles Chassé, "Ce que Mallarmé pensait de la danse," *Les Lettres nouvelles* 4 (July-August 1956): 118–30; Aimé Patri, "Mallarmé et la musique du silence," *Revue musicale* 210 (January 1952): 101–11. An American critic who is particularly expert on the relationships between literature and music, Calvin Brown, has set down some penetrating reflections on Guichard's book in *Comparative Literature* 14 (Autumn 1965): 376–77, and on the one by Suzanne Bernard in the same journal (Summer 1961): 274–76.

11. On Debussy, his life, his music, and his relations with Parisian literary circles, Edward Lockspeiser has published two excellent volumes: *Debussy, His Life and Mind*, 2 vols. (London: Cassell, 1962 and 1965).

12. It is rarely clear ideas that tempt estheticians the most and that spread the most easily from one country to another. One easily picks up in the works of many commentators, and sometimes in those of the most distinguished of them, such generalizations on the synthesis of the arts—in the Englishman Herbert Read, for example, in *The Form of Things Unknown* (London: Faber, 1960), and in the great American poet Hart Crane, who makes reference to the French symbolist movement to affirm relationships between the arts in a 1925 essay, *General Aims and Theories*. T. S. Eliot, more prudent than some others, suspects that this community among writers and artists of a same period resides in their unconscious minds: "The Function of Criticism," in *Selected Essays* (New York: Harcourt, Brace, 1932).

13. *Oeuvres*, II (Paris: Editions de la Pléiade, 1960), p. 476.

14. *Oeuvres*, II, p. 1276.

15. Letter to Robert Bernard on February 15, 1944, in *Paul Valéry vivant* (Marseilles: Cahiers du sud, 1946).

16. *Oeuvres*, II, p. 705.

17. The poet (and novelist and naval officer) who has written the best-informed and most precise article on this subject is Victor Ségalen, "Les Synesthésies et l'époque symboliste," *Mercure de France* 148 (April 1902): 57–90. A good dissertation, already old, has treated the subject: Marie-Antoinette Chaix, *La Correspondance des arts dans la poésie contemporaine* (Paris: Alcan, 1919).

18. Henri Morier, *Le Rythme du vers libre symboliste*, 3 vols. (Geneva: Presses académiques, n.d.).

Chapter 9

1. Valéry spoke on several occasions—and always with affection and admiration—about Mallarmé. These texts are collected in the first volume of the Pléiade edition of his works (*Oeuvres* I and II). His letters (to Louÿs, to Gide) are equally valuable for showing his youthful fervor. With more distance, he traced a kind of balance sheet of symbolism with respect to the fiftieth anniversary of the movement (celebrated in 1936), in a remarkable essay from 1938, which was also included in that volume of the Pléiade edition (Paris: Gallimard, 1957), pp. 686–705. His foreword to the volume of verse by Lucien Fabre, *Connaissance de la déesse*, in 1920, is equally important (Pléiade, I, 1269–79).

2. For a young man who rebelled against the provinces and the too complacently displayed healthiness of the bourgeoisie, the term *decadent* had a heady aroma. "I am decadent," Valéry cried out in a letter to Louÿs on June 22, 1890. He took great delight in *A Rebours*. He even added: "I am above all Catholic, almost an idolater." But he was not to follow Huysmans in his conversion.

3. See Michel Décaudin, *La Crise des valeurs symbolistes: 1895–1914* (Toulouse: Privat, 1960); Marie-Louise Richi-Bidal, *Après le symbolisme: retour à l'humain* (Paris: Presses modernes, 1938). The latter work deals especially with unanimism.

4. Claude Martin, *Gide par lui-même* (Paris: Seuil, 1963), pp. 67–68. See also Catharine Savage, "Gide's Criticism of Symbolism," *Modern Language Review* 61 (October 1966): 601–09. Gide's lecture at Beirut, "Souvenirs littéraires et problèmes actuels," appeared in *L'Arche* 18-19 (September 1946): 3–19.

5. Unless one does it with a little humor, the better to bring out this or that aspect of this multifarious genius. He has long been characterized as baroque or gothic. Once earlier, we praised his "classicism" (*La Nouvelle Revue française* 20 [September 1932]: 432–41), and he was kind enough, with an amused smile, to call himself flattered. Much later, we emphasized in another article all that there was in him of the romantic and even what was Hugoesque. He was no longer of this world at that time. "Claudel, a Romantic in spite of Himself," *Proceedings of the American Philosophical Society* 114 (June 3, 1970): 179–86.

6. Letter to Gide, August 28, 1899, on the subject of *Paludes*.

7. There does not yet exist any precise study of Claudel and Verlaine, or even on Claudel and symbolism. John McCombie has written a book on Claudel's debt to Rimbaud (images, the *verset*, etc.): *The Prince and the Genie* (Amherst: The University of Massachusetts Press, 1972). There is also an article by A. E. A. Naughton on "Claudel and Mallarmé," *Romanic Review* 46 (December 1955): 258–74.

8. Paul Valéry, "Fragments du Narcisse," *Oeuvres* (Paris: Gallimard, 1957), vol. I, p. 190.

9. Ibid., pp. 228–29.

10. See the detailed study *La Wallonie* by Jackson Mathews (New York: King's Crown Press, 1947), and the book by Herman Braet, *L'Acceuil fait au symbolisme en Belgique, 1885–1900* (Brussels: Palais des Académies, 1967).

11. Guy Tost, "La Tentation symboliste chez d'Annunzio," *Revue des Sciences humaines* 77–80 (April-June 1955): 285–96; and "D'Annunzio et la France," in the collective volume, *L'Arte di G. d'Annunzio* (Milan: Mondadori, 1968), pp. 421–38.

12. Letter published in *La Revue d'Allemagne* (November-December 1928), and cited in the excellent work of Enid Lowrie Duthie, *L'Influence du symbolisme dans le renouveau poétique de l'Allemagne* (Paris: Champion, 1933). See also Freya Hobohn, *Die*

Bedeutung französischer Dichter im Werk und Weltbild Stefan George, no. 3 (Cologne: Romanische Arbeiten, 1931), and the fine dissertation of Claude David, *Stefan George* (Lyon and Paris, 1952), and finally, Manfred Osteiger, *Französische Symbolisten in der deutschen Literatur des Jahrhundertwende, 1869–1914* (Berne: Francke, 1971).

13. Hofmannsthal, like other German-language "symbolists," did not particularly value the symbol itself as a means of acceding to some absolute; far from it. In a "talk on Poetry," he states (with respect to Hölderlin) that the task of poetry is "to catch the thing itself" with more energy than the language of ordinary prose can do, and with more magic resonance than science has.

14. The most typical example in our century is that of André Breton. No one has ever preached revolt, destruction, the chaos of automatic writing, with so much seriousness and so impeccable and almost formal order. No one at all was further from the unbridled behavior of the decadents than he, and, moreover, from the symbolists who, he said, "were striving to stupefy the public with their more or less rhythmic but excessively overworked effects," but were not as much true poets as the naturalists (*Les Vases communicants* [Paris: Gallimard, 1933], pp. 106–07). Breton, besides, although he may have stated that "the great poets have been those with a keen auditory sense," and not visionaries (*La Clé des champs* [Paris: Sagittaire, 1953], p. 80), also was entirely insensitive to music.

15. Epilogue to *Per amica silentia lunae.*

16. *Poetry* 4 (April-September 1914): 26–27.

17. This is the thesis that inspired Edmund Wilson's *Axel's Castle* (New York: Scribners, 1931), a very well-known work that is, in our opinion, unduly favorable to French symbolism. Less dogmatically, Sir C. M. Bowra adopted an analogous perspective in a series of essays, *The Heritage of Symbolism* (London: Macmillan, 1943). On Yeats, see Northrop Frye, "Yeats and the Language of Symbolism," *University of Toronto Quarterly* 17 (October 1947): 1–17; and Marie-Hélène Pauly, "Yeats et les symbolistes français," *Revue de littérature comparée* 20 (January-March 1940): 13–33.

18. In *Criterion*, January 1930.

19. A solid and sound dissertation in French by a Canadian professor, Edward J. H. Greene, treats the subject in detail, with quite a few citations of little-known declarations by Eliot: *T. S. Eliot et la France* (Paris: Boivin, 1951). The very important work of Warren Ramsey, already mentioned above, studies Laforgue's posterity with Pound, Eliot, Crane, and others: *Jules Laforgue and the Ironic Inheritance* (New York: Oxford, 1953).

20. René Taupin, *L'Influence du symbolisme français sur la poésie américaine* (Paris: Champion, 1929).

21. Haskell Block, "The Impact of French Symbolism on Modern American Poetry," in Melvin J. Friedman and Frederick J. Hoffman, *The Shaken Realist* (Baton Rouge: Louisiana State University Press, 1970).

22. The differences between imagism and French symbolism have been accurately detailed by Warren Ramsey in "Uses of the Visible: American Imagism, French Symbolism," *Comparative Literature Studies* (Maryland) 4 (1967): 177–91. The double issue of this journal is entirely devoted to symbolism. The citation from Robinson Jeffers is taken from his preface to a volume of his *Collected Poetry* (New York: Random House, 1927).

BIBLIOGRAPHICAL SURVEY

Chapter 1

The oldest works on symbolism in general and on the French symbolist movement (such as that of André BARRE, 1911) are of little use today. Recollections about the period and the small groups of the time have little other than historical and anecdotal interest. The books of Gustave KAHN, *Symbolistes et décadents* (Paris: Vanier, 1902) and Albert MOCKEL, *Esthétique du symbolisme* (Bruxelles: Palais des Académies, 1962), in which he includes his *Propos de littérature* of 1894 and his articles on Mallarmé of 1899, are probably the most substantial.

Works of doctrinal polemics that attracted some attention during the confused struggles of the youthful symbolists, rich in declamations on the beautiful, the ideal, the religion of art, seem quite pompous today: Charles MORICE, *La Littérature de tout à l'heure* (Paris: Perrin, 1889) and *Du Sens religieux de la poésie* (Paris: Vanier, 1893) or Tancrède de VISAN, *L'Attitude du lyrisme contemporain* (Paris: Mercure de France, 1911). Edouard SCHURÉ, an advocate of Wagnerian opera and inclined toward a mysticism illuminated by a sound knowledge of the past, reads better today: *Histoire du drame musical* (Paris: Perrin, 1876), with a new edition in 1895. The dissertation of a specialist in German studies, deeply interested in musical poetry, also remains useful in certain of its aspects: Edmond DUMÉRIL, *Le Lied allemand et ses traductions poétiques en France* (Paris: Champion, 1933). The literary historian who has most scrupulously followed the developments of the symbolist movement year by year is an American, Kenneth Cornell, *The Symbolist Movement* (New Haven: Yale University Press, 1951) and *The Post-Symbolist Period* (New Haven: Yale University Press, 1958). *De Baudelaire au surréalisme* (Paris: Corti, 1933) an admirable work although it contains no central chapter on symbolism. Also admirable is the work of Guy MICHAUD, *Message poétique du symbolisme*, in four volumes (Paris: Nizet, 1947).

There exists no overall study on the notion and the word *symbol* among the romantics or prior to them, although various works on Hugo or Nerval have touched upon aspects of the subject. Very valuable indications are to be found at least in the essay by Pierre MOREAU, "Le Symbolisme de Baudelaire," included in *Ames et thèmes romantiques* (Paris: Corti, 1956) and still more in his small volume on *Les Destinées* of Vigny (Paris: Malfère, 1936) and Lloyd AUSTIN, *L'Univers poétique de Baudelaire* (Paris: Mercure de France, 1956). See also the large thesis of François GERMAIN, *L'Imagination de Vigny* (Paris: Corti, 1961) and Henri PEYRE, *Shelley et la France: lyrisme anglais et lyrisme français au XIXe siècle* (Université du Caire, 1935). Two recent works in English include very precise and penetrating studies of texts; that by James LAWLER, *The Language of Symbolism* (Princeton: Princeton University Press, 1969), and by Bernard WEINBERG, *The Limits of Symbolism* (Chicago: University of Chicago Press, 1966). Two shorter syntheses are those, also in English, of Joseph CHIARI, *Symbolism from Poe to Mallarmé* (London: Rockliff, 1957), and especially of Anna BALAKIAN, *The Symbolist Movement* (New York: Random House, 1967).

For foreign presentations or discussions of French symbolism, see Sir Maurice BOWRA, *The Heritage of Symbolism* (London: Macmillan, 1943); Louis CAZAMIAN,

Symbolisme et poésie: l'exemple anglais (Neuchâtel: La Baconnière, 1947); Arthur SY-MONS, *The Symbolist Movement in Literature* (London, 1899, and New York: Dutton, 1908); Edmund WILSON, *Axel's Castle* (New York: Scribner's, 1931). Also alluded to in our text are William York TINDALL, *The Literary Symbol* (New York: Columbia University Press, 1955), and E. M. W. TILLYARD, *Poetry Direct and Oblique* (London: Chatto & Windus, 1934).

On the symbolic elements in American prose with regard to transcendentalism, see the important work of Francis O. MATTHIESSEN, *American Renaissance: Art and Expression in the Age of Emerson and Whitman* (New York: Oxford University Press, 1942), and those of Charles FEIDELSON, *Symbolism and American Literature* (Chicago: University of Chicago Press, 1953), and of Harry LEVIN, *The Power of Blackness* (New York: Knopf, 1958). The first of these two books cites various texts from Emerson, Hawthorne, and Melville.

There exists an abundant literature—often confusing, however, because the texts themselves are confusing—on the symbolic, allegorical, hieroglyphic aspects of literature, art, and criticism in Germany during the period of Schlegel and Creuzer. On Goethe, see Curt MUELLER, *Die geschichtlichen Voraussetzungen des Symbolbegriffs in Goethes Kunstanschauung* (Leipzig: Mayer und Mueller, 1937), and Maurice MARACHE, *Le Symbole dans la pensée et l'oeuvre de Goethe* (Paris: Nizet, 1960). On Hölderlin, E. L. STAHL, *Hölderlin's Symbolism* (Oxford: Blackwell, 1943), and "Symbolist Theories in Germany," *The Modern Language Review* (June 1946): 306–17. On Schlegel, Liselotte DIECKMANN, "Friedrich Schlegel and Romantic Concepts of the Symbol," *The Germanic Review* (1959): 276–283.

Some precise observations (along with other very abstruse ones and, sometimes, attempts to systematize the esthetics and even the philosophical position of the French symbolists) are to be found in the ambitious studies of Emeric FISER, *Le Symbole littéraire* (Paris: Corti, 1943); A. C. LEHMANN, *The Symbolist Aesthetics in France* (Oxford: Blackwell, 1950); Svend JOHANSEN, *Le Symbolisme: étude sur les symbolistes français* (Copenhagen: Munksgaard, 1945).

Alongside the earlier anthologies of G. WALCH, *Anthologie des poètes français contemporains* (Paris: Delagrave, 1922) in three volumes (firmly rooted in the Parnassian movement), and VAN BEVER and LÉAUTAUD, *Poètes d'aujourd'hui, 1880–1900* (Paris: Mercure de France, 1900), a more recent work, provided with a long introduction, should be mentioned: Bernard DELVAILLE, *La Poésie symboliste* (Paris: Seghers, 1971).

The lamentable incomprehension of symbolism by journalists of the period has often been denounced; it is set forth objectively and in detail in the excellent volume by Jacques LETHÈVE, *Impressionistes et symbolistes devant la presse* (Paris: Armand Colin, 1959) in the collection "Kiosque."

Chapter 2

On correspondences, analogy, the symbol, and symbolism in Baudelaire, we refer the reader to the books of Jean POMMIER, *La Mystique de Baudelaire* (Paris: Les Belles Lettres, 1932), of Marc EIGELDINGER, *Le Platonisme de Baudelaire* (Neuchâtel: La Baconnière, 1951), and of Lloyd AUSTIN, *L'Univers poétique de Baudelaire: symbolisme et symbolique* (Paris: Mercure de France, 1956), as well as to Pierre MOREAU's essay, originally published in *Symposium* (May 1951) and included in *Ames et thèmes roman-tiques* (Paris: Corti, 1965). The most complete works on the poet, from the large disserta-tion by André FERRAN, *L'Esthétique de Baudelaire* (Paris: Hachette, 1933), to the book by Jean PRÉVOST have touched upon synesthesia, already treated in the more modest and earlier dissertation by Marie-Antoinette CHAIX, *La Correspondance des arts et la poésie contemporaine* (Paris: Alcan, 1919). Guy MICHAUD has of course a major chapter on Baudelaire in his *Message poétique du symbolisme* (Paris: Nizet, 1947), vol. I. See further the work by Margaret GILMAN, *Baudelaire the Critic* (New York: Columbia University Press, 1943), and the discerning study of the ambiguities of Baudelaire's poetry seen as a constant element of his poetics by Judd HUBERT, *L'Esthétique des "Fleurs du Mal"* (Geneva: Cailler, 1953).

We have decided not to include here, for fear of excessively extending the length of this work, forerunners or precursors of the symbolist movement who were hardly at all known by the symbolists and of whom one, at least, Nerval, has been the object—or the victim—of almost excessive critical attention since 1930. Others would be Lautréamont, Corbière (known by Verlaine and Laforgue), and of course Victor Hugo. But the visionary and esoteric side of Hugo was not really understood as such until thirty or forty years after his death and after the fray of 1885–95.

Chapter 3

The most useful works to consult concerning Rimbaud (other than those pages included in the volumes by Guy MICHAUD, Marcel RAYMOND, cited in the preceding chap-ters, or that of J.-P. RICHARD, *Poésie et profondeur* [Paris: Seuil, 1955]) seem to us to be: Yves BONNEFOY, *Rimbaud par lui-même* (Paris: Seuil, 1961); Wallace FOWLIE, *Rimbaud, a Critical Study* (Chicago: University of Chicago Press, 1955); Wilbur FROHOCK, *Rimbaud's Poetic Practice* (Cambridge: Harvard University Press, 1963); Jacques RIVIÈRE, *Rimbaud* (Paris: Kra, 1930); Marcel RUFF, *Rimbaud*, "Connais-sances des Lettres" (Paris: Hatier, 1968). On "Le Bateau ivre," see Charles CHADWICK, *Etudes sur Rimbaud* (Paris: Nizet, 1960), and Bernard WEINBERG, " 'Le Bateau ivre' or the Limits of Symbolism," *PMLA* 72 (March 1957): 165–193. On "Mémoire" see Ross CHAMBERS, *Essays in French Literature* (University of Western Australia) 15 (November 1969): 22–37, John LAPP, *Cahiers de l'Association des Etudes françaises* 23 (May 1971): 163–175. To be sure, all readers and commentators interested in Rimbaud should refer to the always valuable work of Yassu GAUCLÈRE and René ÉTIEMBLE, *Rimbaud* (Paris: Gallimard, 1950), and to the original and monumental *Mythe de Rim-baud* by ÉTIEMBLE (1952–54; reedited in 1961). *The Poetry of Rimbaud* by R. G. COHN, is perhaps the best study in any language (Princeton: Princeton University Press, 1973).

Chapter 4

There have appeared in quick succession, since around 1953, several general works on Verlaine of rare excellence: Antoine ADAM, *Verlaine, l'homme et l'oeuvre* (Paris: Hatier,

1953); Jacques-Henry BORNECQUE, *Verlaine par lui-même* (Paris: Seuil, 1966); Arthur FONTAINE, *Verlaine, homme de lettres* (Paris: Delagrave, 1937); Georges ZAYED, *La Formation littéraire de Verlaine* (Geneva: Droz, 1962; reprinted by Nizet in 1970; Eléonore ZIMMERMANN, *Magies de Verlaine* (Corti, 1967). Certain works particularly have sounded the depths of Verlainian psychology: Antoine ADAM, *Le Vrai Verlaine* (Geneva: Droz, 1936); Jacques BOREL, "L'envers de l'érotisme verlainien," *Critique* 157 (June 1960): 496–507; Octave NADAL, *Verlaine* (Paris: Mercure de France, 1961); Jean-Pierre RICHARD, "Fadeur de Verlaine," in *Poésie et profondeur* (Paris: Seuil, 1955), pp. 165–189; Marc SÉGUIN, *Ce Pauvre Bonheur: la dernière passion humaine de Verlaine* (Paris: Silvaire, 1958).

On the process of Verlaine's poetic creation and his art, in addition to the books mentioned above and *L'Etat présent des études sur Verlaine*, dated but still useful, by Claude CUÉNOT (Paris: Belles-Lettres, 1938), the following should be consulted: BORNECQUE, *Lumières sur "Les Fêtes Galantes,"* (Paris: Nizet 1959), and *Les Poèmes saturniens*, reedited by Nizet in 1967; Claude CUÉNOT, *Le Style de Verlaine* (Paris: C. D. U., 1963), reproduced by photo-lithography, and "Technique et esthétique du sonnet chez Verlaine," *Studi francesi*, 12 (September-December 1960): 456–471; P. MATHIEU, "Essai sur la métrique de Verlaine," *Revue d'Histoire littéraire de la France* 38 (October-December 1931): 561–92, and 39 (October-December 1932): 537–59; and the numerous very precise analyses in the work of Eléonore ZIMMERMANN. More particularly on Verlaine's "Art poétique," see BORNECQUE, "Poème et poétiques," *Dialogue* (Istanbul), 4 (1956): 13–30; Maurice GOT in *La Table ronde*, 159 (March 1961): 128–136; William L. SCHWARTZ, "Some Twentieth-Century Arts Poétiques," *PMLA* 47, no. 2 (June 1932): 593–606, and once again Eléonore ZIMMERMANN.

The question of the relations between Rimbaud and Verlaine, of the possible influence of the one on the other, has inspired an entire literature. Among recent works, other than that of Jules MOUQUET, already out of print, *Rimbaud raconté par Verlaine* (Paris: Mercure de France, 1934), and which brings together a number of texts, see also Charles CHADWICK, *Etudes sur Rimbaud* (Paris: Nizet, 1960); Antoine FONGARO, "Les Echos verlainiens chez Rimbaud," *Revue des Sciences humaines* 106 (April-June 1962), 263–72; Cecil A. HACKETT, "Verlaine's influence on Rimbaud," *Studies in Modern French Literature: Presented to P. M. Jones* (Manchester: Manchester University Press, 1961); and the work of G. ZAYED. Verlaine's relationships to England and English literature have been treated knowledgeably and in great detail by V. UNDERWOOD, *Verlaine et l'Angleterre* (Paris: Nizet, 1956). The entire rich and complex question of the literary ties, influences, etc. between Verlaine and Baudelaire needs to be taken up again since the hasty dissertation of Walter SCHWACHENBERG, *Verlaine und Baudelaire* (Arbeiten zur Romanischen Philologie, no. 33: Muenster, 1935). A better work is the one on Verlaine's lyricism in general by Marta VOGLER, *Die schoepferischen Werke der Verlaineschen Lyric* (Zürich, 1927).

On Verlainian impressionism, which is at the heart of the discerning work of Octave NADAL, see also Suzanne BERNARD, "Rimbaud, Proust et les impressionistes," *Revue des Sciences humaines* (new series) 78 (April-June 1955): 257–62; Michel DÉCAUDIN, "Poésie impressioniste et poésie symboliste," *Cahiers de l'Association internationale des études françaises* 12 (May 1960): 133–142; Ruth MOSER, *L'Impressionnisme français: peinture, littérature, musique* (Geneva: Droz, 1952); Karola ROST, *Der impressionistiche Stil Verlaines* (Muenster and Paris: Droz, 1935); "Symposium on Impressionism," *Year Book of Comparative and General Literature* 17 (Bloomington, Ind., 1968): 40–72.

Chapter 5

Several references to this or that commentary on individual poems of Mallarmé have been
given in the text, as well as references to four indispensable volumes of the poet's correspondence. A very large number of articles in specialized reviews or in festschrifts have
been devoted to Mallarmé. A whole bibliographical volume alone would be needed to
enumerate them, and a great proportion of these too ingenious articles are of limited
usefulness. Gardner DAVIES gives an overall summary in "Fifty Years of Mallarmé
Studies," *French Studies*, 1:1 (January 1947): 1–20, which ought to be brought up to date
for the thirty succeeding years. We cite here, not without some arbitrariness, only certain
of the essential studies.

Deborah AISH, *La Métaphore chez Mallarmé* (Geneva: Droz, 1938); Adèle AYDA,
"L'Influence d'Hugo sur Mallarmé," *Dialogue* 3 (Istanbul, July 1953): 140–64; Haskell
BLOCK, *Mallarmé and the Symbolist Drama* (Detroit: Wayne State University Press,
1963), and "Mallarmé the Alchemist," *Australian Journal of French Studies* 6 (1969):
163–78; Suzanne BERNARD, *Mallarmé et la musique* (Paris: Nizet, 1959); Maurice
BLANCHOT, several articles collected in his various critical works; Léon CELLIER,
Mallarmé et la Morte qui parle (Paris: Presses Universitaires de France, 1959); Charles
CHADWICK, *Mallarmé, sa pensée dans sa poésie* (Paris: Corti, 1962); Charles
CHASSÉ, *Lueurs sur Mallarmé* (Paris: Nouvelle Revue critique, 1947), and *Les Clefs de
Mallarmé* (Paris: Montaigne, 1954); A. P. CHISOLM, *Towards Hérodiade* (Melbourne:
Melbourne University Press, 1934), *L'Après-Midi d'un faune* (Manchester: Manchester
University Press, 1962), and "Le démon de l'analogie," *Essays in French Literature*,
University of Western Australia (November 1964); Robert G. COHN, *L'Oeuvre de
Mallarmé* ("Le Coup de dés") (Paris: Librairie des Lettres, 1951), and *Toward the Poems
of Mallarmé* (Berkeley: University of California Press, 1965); Gardner DAVIES, *Les
Tombeaux de Mallarmé* (Paris: Corti, 1950), and *Mallarmé et le drame solaire* (Paris:
Corti, 1953); Antoine FONGARO, "Mallarmé et Hugo," *Revue des Sciences humaines*
120 (October-December 1965): 515–28; Wallace FOWLIE, *Mallarmé* (Chicago: Univer-
sity of Chicago Press, 1953); Dr. GUTTMAN, *Introduction à la lecture des poètes* (Paris:
Nizet, 1969), Nouvelle Edition; David HAYMAN, *Joyce et Mallarmé*, 2 vols. (Paris:
Lettres Modernes, 1956); Charles MAURON, *Mallarmé l'obscur* (Paris: Denoël, 1950),
and *Psychanalyse de Mallarmé* (Neuchâtel: La Baconnière, 1950), and *Mallarmé par
lui-même* (Paris: Seuil, 1964); Guy MICHAUD, ¯*Mallarmé* (Paris: Hatier, 1958),
Nouvelle Edition; Henri MONDOR, *Vie de Mallarmé*, 2 vols. (Paris: Gallimard, 1941),
and *Histoire d'un faune* (Paris: Gallimard, 1948); Emilie NOULET, *L'Oeuvre poétique
de Mallarmé* (Geneva: Droz, 1940), *Dix poèmes de Mallarmé* (Geneva: Droz, 1948), and
Vingt poèmes de Mallarmé (Geneva: Droz, 1967); Georges POULET, *La Distance in-
térieure* (Paris: Plon, 1952); Jean-Pierre RICHARD, *L'Univers imaginaire de Mallarmé*
(Paris: Seuil, 1961), and *Pour un tombeau d'Anatole* (Paris: Seuil, 1961); Frederick
SAINT-AUBYN, *Mallarmé* (New York: Twayne, 1969); Jacques SCHERER, *L'Expres-
sion littéraire chez Mallarmé* (Geneva: Droz, 1947), and *Le Livre de Mallarmé* (Paris:
Gallimard, 1957); Albert THIBAUDET, *La Poésie de Stéphane Mallarmé* (Paris: Gal-
limard, 1926), Nouvelle Edition; Edith SEWELL, "Mallarmé and Infinity," *Life and
Letters* (February 1960), 105–14; Theophil SPOERRI, "Mallarmé's 'Après-Midi d'un

faune,'" *Trivium* (Zürich), 4, 3: 224–32; Kurt WAIS, *Mallarmé, Dichtung, Weisheit, Haltung* (Munich: Beck, 1952).

Chapter 6

It is not our intention to list here the titles already mentioned in the course of the second chapter (on the symbol and symbolism in general), and even less to mention the numerous books of more or less anecdotal and personal memoires on the movement by those who took part in it: Fontainas, Ghil, Mockel, Raynaud, Retté, etc. There is not much use in drawing up a list of the very large number of writings by symbolist poets or prose writers. For those essential titles referring to the relations between symbolism and Bergsonism, we refer the reader to the pages above. For the rest, we will be content with indicating the most recent learned and critical books on a few of the most important symbolists among those whom one can consider as minor poets: on Jammes, Arthur BERTSCHI, *Jammes* (Neuchâtel: La Baconnière, 1938), Rose M. DYSON, *Les Sensations et la sensibilité chez Jammes* (Geneva: Droz, 1954), Monique PARENT, *Rythme et versification dans la poésie de Jammes* (Paris: Belles-Lettres, 1957); on Kahn, J. IRESON, *L'Oeuvre poétique de Gustave Kahn* (Paris: Nizet, 1962); on Maeterlinck, Maurice LECAT, *Le Maeterlinckianisme* (Bruxelles: Castaine, 1937–39), Marcel POSTIC, *Maeterlinck et le symbolisme* (Paris: Nizet, 1970); on Merrill, Marjorie (Henry) ILSLEY, *Honoré* (Paris: Champion, 1927); on Mockel, Paul CHAMPAGNE, *Essai sur Mockel* (Paris: Champion, 1922); on Moréas, John Davis BUTLER, *Moréas, A critique of his Poetry and Philosophy* (Amsterdam: Mouton, 1967), Robert JOUANNY, *Moréas, écrivain français* (Paris: Minard, 1969); on Régnier, Mario MAURIN, *Henri de Régnier, le labyrinthe et le double* (especially on Régnier the novelist), (Montreal: Presses de l'Université, 1972); on Retté, W. K. CORNELL, *Retté* (New Haven: Yale University Press, 1942); on Rodenbach, Anny BODSON-THOMAS, *L'Esthétique de Rodenbach* (Brussels: Académie Royale de Belgique, 1942); on Royère, Clovis PIÉRARD, *Le Musicisme de Jean Royère* (Paris: Blaizot, 1937); on Samain, Georges BONNEAU, *Samain, poète symboliste: essai d'esthétique* (dissertation, Paris, 1925); on Tailhade, P. KOLNEY (dissertation, Paris, 1922); on Verhaeren, Charles BAUDOIN, *Le Symbole chez Verhaeren, essai de psychanalyse de l'art* (Geneva: Mongenet, 1924), Edmond ESTÈVE, *Verhaeren* (Paris: Boivin, 1928), Percy Mansell JONES, *Verhaeren* (New Haven: Yale University Press, 1957), Albert MOCKEL, *Un poète d'énergie, Verhaeren* (Paris: Mercure, 1929), Enid STARKIE, *Les Sources du lyrisme dans la poésie de Verhaeren* (dissertation, Paris, 1927), Ronald SUSSEX, *L'Idée d'humanité chez Verhaeren* (Paris: Nizet, 1938); on Viélé-Griffin, Jean de COURSE, *Viélé-Griffin, son oeuvre, sa pensée, son art* (Paris: Champion, 1930), Reinhard KUHN, *Viélé-Griffin* (Geneva: Droz, 1956).

Relatively few works have appeared on the themes or the few myths used in symbolist poetry—Narcissus, for example. See, however, on Salome, Helen Grace ZAGONA, *The Legend of Salome and the Principle of Art for Art's Sake* (Geneva: Droz, 1960); on Orpheus, Eva KUSHNER, *Le Mythe d'Orphée dans la littérature française contemporaine* (Paris: Nizet, 1961), Walter STRAUSS, *The Orphic Theme in Modern Literature: Descent and Return* (Cambridge: Harvard University Press, 1971), and Gwendolyn BAYS, *The Orphic Vision: Seers from Novalis to Rimbaud* (Lincoln: University of Nebraska Press, 1964).

Chapter 7

All the works dealing with the symbolist movement have devoted a few pages to the group of decadents, the most complete and the most exact being once again that of Guy MICHAUD. The anecdotal and picturesque books by Noël RICHARD and by Alain MERCIER on the occultism of certain symbolists have been cited in notes. The most important texts by Eliphas LÉVI (who died in 1875, before the symbolist era), difficult to obtain, have been reprinted in an excellently presented selection by Frank BOWMAN (Paris: Presses Universitaires de France, 1969). Without going all the way back to the history of the concept of decadence in Alexandria, Rome, or in France in the eighteenth century, one can point out a few general works on the romantic and postromantic period: Mario PRAZ, La Carne, la morte e il diavolo nella letteratura romantica (Milan: La Cultura, 1930), reedited since and translated into several languages; Swart KOLNRAAD, The Sense of Decadence in Nineteenth-Century France (The Hague, 1964); William GAUNT, The Aesthetic Adventure (New York: Harcourt, Brace, 1954); A. E. CARTER, The Idea of Decadence in French Literature, 1830–1900 (Toronto: University of Toronto Press, 1958). More superficial books are those of George Ross RIDGE, The Hero in Decadent Literature (Athens: University of Georgia Press, 1961), and John MILNER, Symbolists and Decadents (London: Studio Vista, 1971). For English literature, the best work is that of Albert J. FARMER, Le Mouvement esthétique et décadent en Angleterre: 1873–1900 (Paris: Champion, 1931). A recent monograph on Huysmans concerns itself with the decadent aspect of his work: François LIVI, Huysmans, "A Rebours" et l'esprit décadent (Paris: Nizet, 1972).

Chapter 8

Among the essential works on the relationships between literary symbolism and artistic symbolism, we mention Louis HAUTECOEUR, Littérature et peinture en France du XVIIe au XXe siècle (Paris: Armand Colin, 1942), and Bernard DORIVAL, Les Etapes de la peinture française contemporaine, 3 vols. (Paris: Gallimard, 1943–46). René HUYGHE has some rich and thought-provoking pages in several of his books, notably La Peinture française: les contemporains (Paris: Tisné, 1939), and in his work L'Art et l'homme, vol. 3 (chapters by Michel FLORISSOONE). The small book by Charles CHASSÉ, Le Mouvement symboliste dans l'art du XIXe siècle (Paris: Floury, 1947), assembles several curious citations from Moreau, Puvis, Gauguin, as does the larger work of Jacque CHARPIER and Pierre SEGHERS, L'Art de la peinture (Paris: Seghers, 1957) for the French artists who follow. From London there is the work of Edward LUCIE-SMITH, Symbolist Art (London: Thames & Hudson, 1972), which touches upon symbolist artists from five or six European countries. A collective work, edited by Ulrich FINKE, French Nineteenth-Century Painting and Literature (Manchester: University of Manchester Press, 1972) contains an essay by Jean SEZNEC which deals with Redon and literature. Other important works (by DENIS, MORICE, BERGER, et al.) have been indicated in the notes. The work of Charles E. GAUSS, The Aesthetic Theories of French Artists (Baltimore: Johns Hopkins University Press, 1950), strives to bring together the practice of painters (from Courbet to Dali) with their theoretical ideas and the philosophical problems they may have set for themselves.

Numerous articles on free verse appeared in the symbolist reviews during the controversies surrounding this subject. The two books by Robert de SOUZA on popular poetry and on rhythm—which are very restrained on the subject of free verse—contain some discerning and valuable remarks: *La Poésie populaire et le lyrisme sentimental* (Paris: Mercure, 1889), and *Le Rythme poétique* (Paris: Perrin, 1892). Rémy de GOURMONT has a discussion on the mute "e" in a long article in the *Mercure de France* 149 (May 1902), 289–303. Mathurin DONDO has published a monograph on the subject in English, *Vers Libre: a Logical Development of French Verse* (Paris: Champion, 1922) which mentions various titles by Kahn, Retté, Viélé-Griffin. The large book by Svend JOHANSEN, *Le Symbolisme* (Copenhagen: Munksgaard, 1945) has chapters on synesthesia, the symbol, the image, and incantation among the symbolist poets as well as some precise analyses of texts.

An actual bibliography of symbolism could only be a collective work of very great length, and it has not entered into this author's intentions to attempt one. A very useful *Post-Symbolist Bibliography*, containing more than four thousand titles and emphasizing especially works published from 1950 to 1970, has been published by Henry KRAWITZ (Metuchen, N. J.: The Scarecrow Press, 1973). In the present volume, only those titles considered as essential have been indicated.

INDEX